Developing Sustainable Balance of Payments in Small Countries

Andre Haughton

Developing Sustainable Balance of Payments in Small Countries

Lessons from Macroeconomic Deadlock in Jamaica

palgrave
macmillan

Andre Haughton
University of the West Indies
Mona, Jamaica

ISBN 978-3-319-53030-7 ISBN 978-3-319-53031-4 (eBook)
DOI 10.1007/978-3-319-53031-4

Library of Congress Control Number: 2017936951

Printed on acid-free paper

This Palgrave Macmillan imprint is published by Springer Nature
The registered company is Springer International Publishing AG
The registered company address is: Gewerbestrasse 11, 6330 Cham, Switzerland

Dedicated to Princess Aura

Foreword

Jamaica is a relatively small island of approximately 4,000 square miles with a population of three million people. It is reasonably endowed with productive resources for external earnings: bauxite and alumina, tourism, some highly fancied agricultural crops and the support of a diaspora of as many Jamaicans abroad as those who live in Jamaica. But despite this pleasant scenario of the external account, the economy still experiences a deficiency of external funding. This leads to heavy borrowing to close the gap to meet high import levels, public debt servicing and other external costs. This is the signal indicating the vulnerability of the Jamaican economy, which has only averaged 0.7 percent growth annually over the past 50 years.

Understanding and closing this gap is what this book, Developing Sustainable Balance of Payments in Small Countries: Lessons from Macroeconomic Deadlock in Jamaica, is about. It examines all the main variables that affect the Balance of Payments of the Jamaican economy, especially the deviations produced by the exchange rate policies.

It is useful to note that the most significant impact on the economy has its roots in the political culture because of deep antagonism between the socialist liberal left and the capitalist liberal right political parties leading to a one step forward, one step backward pattern of stagnation when governments change.

It is also important to note that the liberal significance of both political parties contains a generous dose of populism, which has been responsible for high expenditure.

Since 1980, the socialist tendency has been largely dormant because of the demise of socialism virtually worldwide. As a result, this has created two partisan political groupings: a committed liberal capitalist party that has sustained its beliefs since its inception 72 years ago while the democratic socialists group has restructured itself to a repentant socialist reluctant capitalist political group. This has narrowed the political dichotomy, which augurs well for new growth.

Now that the political system has become more balanced greater attention can be given to aligning of the productive system, which is where the discussions of this book leads us.

The range of discussions focuses on economic growth and includes:

- The level of external debt and the Net International Reserves that would be adequate to avoid excess on one hand, and inadequacy on the other;
- Foreign Direct Investments, capital formation, national savings and real growth;
- Exchange rate and monetary policies and their effect on movement of the rate of exchange and its impact on economic growth;
- The import and export trade, and policies to narrow the gap for the improvement of balance of payments.

These, and other issues, are the key variables to be analyzed to create a sustainable Balance of Payment for growth. The author, Dr. Andre Haughton, has tackled the problem of gaps in analysis that do not adequately deal with questions requiring deeper quantitative assessment for proper empirical analysis. This will enable a more lucid understanding to overcome the mysteries of growth.

The Most Honourable Edward Seaga ON, PC, LL.D. (Hon), D.Litt. (Hon)
Director
Edward Seaga Reseach Institute

Preface

Many developing countries seek Balance of Payments (BOP) and stability support from the International Monetary Fund (IMF) and other multilateral institutions. In practice, this is due to these countries' inability to generate sufficient intrinsic foreign currency necessary to conduct transactions with other countries and strengthen their Net International Reserves (NIR). Over the last 40 years, Jamaica has entered into 14 successive arrangements with the IMF, which has provided not just foreign currency support through Special Drawing Rights (SDRs) and drawdowns, but has also provided guidelines along the way geared towards increasing the indebted nation's macroeconomic stability, which is necessary to enhance its economic growth potential.

Throughout this time, however, Jamaica has only managed to generate 0.7 percent growth in Gross Domestic Product (GDP) on average per annum. The country has endured chronic macroeconomic instability and has experienced low and sometimes negative total factor productivity growth from 1974 to present. The amount of goods and services sold to the rest of the world per annum has been declining. As a result, the nation has not been earning enough to increase its stock of capital beyond depreciation annually. This is essentially the desirable scenario if Jamaica is ever to move from being a developing country to a fully developed nation.

The high economic growth rates Jamaica experienced in the 1960s averaging more than 5 percent per annum were reduced by high public borrowing in the early 1970s. Today, Jamaica is among the top five indebted nations in the world with a total debt ratio of 128 percent of GDP. With a gradually depreciating currency, Jamaica's foreign currency debt servicing requirements continue to increase. Jamaica, once a positive example to other developing countries who needed a recipe for development, is now an example of what is not to be done if a country wants its economy to remain stable with low debt, high growth rates and positive development results.

This book analyzes Jamaica's ability to satisfy its short- and long-run foreign currency obligations in light of recurrent BOP support from the IMF and other international lending agencies. It analyzes Jamaica's long-standing relationship with these multilateral lending agencies, which should serve as a useful case study for other developing countries, government officials, economists, economics students and practitioners worldwide.

This book is novel in that it analyzes the sustainability of foreign currency flows between Jamaica and the rest of the world from 1962 to 2015 in light of the country's adverse economic growth, stability and development pursuits. It provides an understanding of the underlying factors that influence the level of foreign currency flows across time, and determines the conditions necessary for the stream of inflows to offset the stream of outflows sustainably through different avenues in the long run. The research analyzes the adequacy of the nation's NIR accumulation strategy and establishes an equilibrium point that might exist. It examines the goods market by analyzing the impact of real and nominal exchange rate movements on the nation's prices, imports, exports and output growth. The research investigates the loanable funds market and provides an understanding of the impact of interest rates on the availability of credit for domestic investment. The impact of Foreign Direct Investment (FDI) on economic growth is also analyzed. The research provides recommendations on how Jamaica and other countries that find themselves in this deadlock position should strategize to improve their economic conditions.

This research began as an investigation into Jamaica's approach to earning or generating foreign currency amidst hesitation by the IMF to sign a foreign currency loan agreement without conditionality in 2013. Having returned to Jamaica from the UK in 2011 after writing my PhD on *'Essays on Monetary Policy in the Caribbean Region'*, at the University of Essex, I observed handicaps in Jamaica's interest rate determination relative to other countries. I was inquisitive about the causes of and solutions to the nation's foreign currency debt problem and deficiencies in the nation's GDP growth and export strategies. In 2012, I began writing for the *Jamaica Gleaner* newspaper; simplifying and explaining issues affecting the local economy in a global context. Writing these weekly 'Briefings' heightened my inquiry, which enabled me to delve deeper to ascertain Jamaica's long-term economic strategy for national development since its independence from Britain in 1962. To my surprise, after independence there was no long-term strategy to place the country on a path towards sustainable development. Indeed, it was only recently (2009) that Jamaica laid out its Vision 2030 goals.

Over the last 40 years, Jamaica has encountered significant internal as well as external challenges in its attempt to concurrently achieve economic growth, economic stability and economic development. Failure of both fiscal and monetary policies in their attempt to balance the market mechanism has given the 'invisible hand' the freedom to determine economic outcome in some instances, and it has. The global market has sold more goods and services to Jamaica than Jamaica sold to it. This has resulted in insufficient accumulation of foreign currency needed to conduct international business creating foreign currency liquidity problems. Sufficiency of the nation's foreign currency earnings has been a cause for concern and is now more questionable since the latest signed Extended Fund Facility (EFF) agreement with the IMF, which expires in 2017. This programme disburses an agreed-upon quota of foreign currency on a quarterly basis from 2013 to 2017 on condition that Jamaica passes quarterly review tests.

Now let us assume that Jamaica satisfies all the conditions stipulated in the EFF by the IMF, which concludes in 2017; then what? Will the implementation of these conditionalities be sufficient to ensure long-run solvency? What strategies are being implemented to ensure that if the IMF decides not to enter a new loan agreement, Jamaica can generate enough foreign currency on its own to satisfy demand and foreign obligations? The issue of liquidity management has brought itself to the forefront. In order to get a deeper understanding of how to approach the situation, it is important to review the economic policies and exchange rate strategies that Jamaica has pursued leading up to the current situation. The country must create more ways to earn or generate foreign currency or must revert to more borrowings when the current EFF expires.

The approach of the government thus far has been to borrow to provide foreign currency in an economy where exchange rates are market determined. This has increased the country's stock of foreign debt. The usual approach to servicing this debt has been to borrow further, thereby accumulating more public debt. Servicing this foreign currency debt along with debt denominated in domestic currency consumes a significant portion of the country's annual budget. As a consequence, there is minimal fiscal space available to expand the capacity of the domestic economy. The adverse foreign currency position has also been associated with weak economic growth and decline in total factor productivity. One of the main limitations has been the sustainability of the country's foreign currency flows. In this case, an optimal pattern of international currency flow must be established where a debtor country such as Jamaica can become solvent, and therefore able to satisfy its foreign currency obligations cheaper on a more consistent basis over the long term. This will provide room to redirect policy to other avenues that can enhance overall growth and development of the country.

Chapter 1 frames the analysis in its particular context and goes on to explore the rationale for each exchange rate regime and their impact on the progression of the nation's economy. Since gaining independence from Britain in 1962, Jamaica has employed five main types of exchange rate strategies. Each was designed to achieve specific objectives of the government, taking the local and global economic environment into account. Jamaica's exchange rate regime moved from a currency board to a crawling peg to a dual exchange rate, then to an auction and allocation system and finally to a free-floating exchange rate system.

Chapter 2 explores Jamaica's borrowing relationship with multilateral institutions including the IMF, Inter-American Development Bank (IDB) and the PetroCaribe arrangement with Venezuela. A Debt Sustainability Analysis (DSA) shows that increases in imports and the Treasury bill rate reduce the sustainability of Jamaica's foreign currency debt while improved by growth in real GDP. Having a larger foreign currency debt stock reduces debt sustainability. Jamaica's debt servicing requirements increase by US $56 million on average per annum as a result of currency depreciation. Approximately 18 percent of the variation in foreign currency debt is explained by the country's imports. Emerging from this chapter is that foreign currency debt can decrease if interest rates fall, fewer goods are imported and the exchange rate becomes more predictable.

Chapter 3 analyzes the economic, financial and political factors that influence the long-run level of Jamaica's current account balance. The issue is explored along the lines of the popular intertemporal model using the Bounds Test approach proposed by Brissimis et al (2013). The results indicate that there is a long-run relationship between the current account-to-GDP ratio and changes in the Real Effective Exchange Rate (REER), political stability, openness, investment, external debt stock, corruption and foreign reserves. A depreciation of the REER and an increase in GDP growth contributes positively to the sustainability of Jamaica's current account balance. Jamaica can improve its current account position in the long run by improving political stability and corruption control.

Chapter 4 dissects the current account and examines the correlation between the Real Exchange Rate (RER) and each component. The results indicate that as the RER depreciates, the cost of food, food raw material, durable goods and other raw material imported to the island increases. The results show no relationship between the RER and construction imports and other machine imports. The analysis further displays no correlation between each item of export and the RER. The results insinuate that strategies to depreciate the currency must be supported by strategies to expand exports. This should include the transformation of goods from primary to secondary and tertiary production processes where they can fetch more revenue from higher prices.

Chapter 5 analyzes the impact of exchange rate depreciation on output growth on the island. The results indicate that 1 percent depreciation of the domestic currency in one year leads to a potential loss of 0.3 percent to GDP growth in the year that follows. Over the 33-year period, total potential losses to GDP growth amounted to little less than US $4.5 billion. The findings suggest that pursuing policies to stabilize the exchange rate can lead to favourable growth in GDP through a variety of channels.

Chapter 6 analyzes the sustainability of the BOP on aggregate by analysing the dynamic relationship between the current account and capital account balance necessary to sustain economic activity. The analysis further examines the variables that contribute to capital account dynamics. The results show that positive shocks to openness and domestic credit cause an increase in the optimal capital requirements needed to sustain economic activity over time. Corruption in Jamaica has a negative impact on the flow of foreign capital. Political stability and law and order have positive impacts on the level of capital flows. Meanwhile an increase in real interest rate, increase in crude oil prices and a depreciation of the local currency have negative impacts on capital flows.

Chapter 7 analyzes the adequacy of reserves and the optimal level of reserves in Jamaica. In calibrating the optimal level of reserve holdings, we use a model proposed by Jeanne and Rancière (2006) and corroborated by a simple model proposed by Heller (1966). According to the model, the targeted level of reserves is 8.9 percent of GDP averaging US $1.226 billion over the last five years. Foreign exchange flexibility, GDP volatility and population growth significantly impact the targeted level of reserve holdings. Structural changes including structural reforms in the economy and economic shocks impact reserve holdings. The analysis shows that the actual reserve holdings are expected to trend downwards in the future while the optimal reserve is expected to increase, both converging gradually over time.

Chapter 8 investigates the relationship between FDI flows, gross capital formation (gross investment), national savings and GDP growth. The findings suggest that there is a negative relationship between real GDP growth and FDI, contrary to the proposition of the existing literature. Less developed financial systems and high inefficiency in the domestic economy results in misallocation of foreign capital in some instances. Investment and savings are important drivers for real GDP growth in the country. Efforts to increase national savings can also help capital formation which is necessary for GDP growth.

Chapter 9 analyzes the speed of adjustment and the monetary transmission mechanism in Jamaica. The results indicate that although incomplete, the pass-through process has improved. Stability tests confirm that monetary policy instruments display two different variances from 1990 to present. The first episode of high interest rate and high volatility occurred from 1990 to 1997 during the initial stages of liberalization of the financial sector. The second episode of falling rates and mild volatility occurred from 1997 to 2010. A widening gap between the lending rate and the Treasury bill rate is signalling that commercial banks during this time might be increasing the level of pass-through at a huge mark-up to the disadvantage of local investors.

In conclusion, the Jamaican economy has found itself in a deadlock in trying to maintain macroeconomic stability as well as increasing economic growth and productivity necessary for sustained economic development. Declining labor productivity and slow infrastructural development coupled with government inefficiency and ulterior motives have prevented the country from entering a steady-state growth path towards development. Jamaica's aim to achieve stability, growth and development should be guided by clear plans of linking short-run stability and growth tactics to long-run developmental strategic objectives. Although it appears to be in a deadlock, Jamaica has made significant strides in the right direction under the supervision of the IMF, the World Bank, the IDB and other multilateral lenders since 2013.

Acknowledgments

I would like to thank the Edward Seaga Research Institute and Culture Heath Arts Science and Education (CHASE) for providing the resources and facilities to help make this research possible. I am particularly grateful to the Most Honorable Edward Seaga for initiating the ideas to commence the research project resulting in these useful lessons to guide Jamaica's exchange rate strategy, trade policy, growth, export, foreign debt servicing and Net International Reserves (NIR) accumulation strategy. His experience of the country's economic progression spans more than six decades, which has helped to broaden my understanding of the country's economic challenges in a dense analysis.

I am grateful to my research assistants: Michael Marshall, Celia Wallace, Kemar White, Junius Olivier, Treshauna Turner, Kurt Wilson and Wendel Ivey for their invaluable contribution to this project. Their industriousness and dedication to the project is truly appreciated.

I thank my colleagues: Odayne Haughton, Dashon Hendricks, Dr. Roger McLeod, Dr. Emma Iglesias and Professor Densil Williams for their useful comments and suggestions. I thank Professor Alfred Francis, Professor Claremont Kirton and Dr. Michael Witter for helping me to understand the difference between economic theory and real-life empirical application. I thank my colleagues for helping me to realize that there are conflicting schools of thought within the discipline and underproduction is not only a characteristic of the country's physical output but is also a characteristic of the country's economic thoughts, ideas and the implementation of such.

I would like to thank the *Jamaica Gleaner* for providing a useful platform upon which I can communicate economics to the public. I am deeply indebted to my editors Paul Thompson and Tamara Hastings for their hard work and dedication to make this rigorous research a simple read for everyone.

About This Book

This book analyses Jamaica's ability to satisfy its short and long run foreign currency obligations in light of receiving recurrent Balance of Payments support from the IMF and other international lending agencies. The goods market is examined through an analysis of the impact of real and nominal exchange rate movements on the nation's prices, imports, exports and output growth. It looks at the efficiency of the loanable funds market and the monetary transmission mechanism in Jamaica and provides an understanding of the impact of interest rates on the availability of credit for domestic investment. Policy recommendations suggest that Jamaica and other developing countries in this type of situation should strategize to achieve their local economic objectives within the constraints of the global geopolitical environment.

Contents

List of Abbreviations

ARDL	Autoregressive Distributed Lag
BCCR	Central Bank of Costa Rica
BOJ	Bank of Jamaica
BOP	Balance of Payments
CHASE	Culture Heath Arts Science and Education
CIDA	Canadian International Development Agency
CPI	Consumer Price Index
CSME	Caribbean Single Market and Economy
DSA	Debt Sustainability Analysis
DSCR	Debt Servicing Coverage Ratio
EME	Emerging Market Economies
EDC	Export Development Canada
EFF	Extended Fund Facility
FDI	Foreign Direct Investment
FINSAC	Financial Sector Adjustment Company
GDP	Gross Domestic Product
IBRD	International Bank for Reconstruction and Development
ICT	Information and Communication Technology
IDB	Inter-American Development Bank
IMF	International Monetary Fund
JAMPRO	Jamaica Investment Promotions
JDX	Jamaica Debt Exchange
JUTC	Jamaica Urban Transit Company
KMF	Keynesian Mundell-Fleming
NCB	National Commercial Bank
NDX	National Debt Exchange
NIR	Net International Reserves

NKI	Net Capital Inflow
NPV	Net Present Value
OECS	Organisation of Eastern Caribbean States
REER	Real Effective Exchange Rate
RER	Real Exchange Rate
SBIs	Bank Indonesia Certificates
TNC	Transnational Corporation
USAID	United States Agency for International Development
VAR	Vector Autoregression

List of Figures

List of Tables

CHAPTER 1

Foreign Currency Flows and the Jamaican Economy

1.1 *Prelude*: What is the 'Deadlock' Issue?

Jamaica and many other developing countries borrow continuously from the International Monetary Fund (IMF) and other multilateral institutions for balance of payment support. Improper foreign currency liquidity management strategies coupled with sluggish economic growth have prolonged many of these borrowing arrangements indefinitely. Jamaica's thirteenth arrangement with the IMF, the Extended Fund Facility (EFF), was expected to last from 2013 to 2017, but ended prematurely due to a change in local government administration. The existing arrangement was replaced by a new Stand-By Arrangement (SBA) that will last for three years. This type of ongoing relationship with the IMF and other multilateral institutions will continue after 2019 if Jamaica does not reassess its overall foreign currency liquidity management strategy.

The country's import percentage of Gross Domestic Product (GDP) is more than 54 percent, which has contributed to an increasing demand for foreign currency support from international lending institutions. Traditionally, the IMF and World Bank provide a stamp of approval for countries to attract capital in the international capital market. Especially for country rescue lending, but more recently Brazil, Russia, India and China (BRIC countries) have established an alternative to the IMF in the supply of international liquidity to developing countries.

A. Haughton, *Developing Sustainable Balance of Payments in Small Countries*, DOI 10.1007/978-3-319-53031-4_1

These loans, when borrowed, must be repaid with interest in the future and are exacerbated by gradually depreciating currencies in many developing countries. Some developing countries, including Jamaica, have relaxed their foreign currency control mechanisms by allowing a more market-determined exchange rate in an attempt to increase foreign currency revenue earnings that might arise from economies of scale. However, slow and expensive technological absorption rates in production processes have contributed to diseconomies of scale in several aspects. As a result, economic growth remains anemic; average GDP growth in Jamaica, for example, is less than 1 percent per annum for the last five decades.

A constantly depreciating currency, it appears, disadvantageously increases the cost of imported inputs and the cost of foreign debt servicing payments thereby reducing national savings, which impedes the economy's growth potential. In this scenario, Jamaica and many other developing countries that are in this position appear to be stuck in 'macroeconomic deadlock' between proper foreign currency liquidity management, exchange rate determination and GDP growth strategies needed for economic development.

1.2 Jamaica Foreign Currency Liquidity Management 1962–Present

Foreign currency flows to and from the island are recorded in the Balance of Payments (BOP) via its three components: the current account, the capital account and the reserves. Inflows of foreign currency arising from the sale of Jamaican goods and services abroad, transfer payments received, investment by Jamaicans in foreign economies and foreign investment in Jamaica must be used to offset the outflow of foreign currency arising from Jamaica's purchases of goods and services from abroad, transfer payments to foreign countries, payment of international debt and Jamaican investments abroad. Net International Reserves (NIR) offset any imbalances between the current account and capital accounts flows such that the Balance of Payments (BOP) is always balanced. Nevertheless, operating a current account deficit below the international benchmark year to year can become a major concern if sustained by borrowed reserves.

'Large movements of private capital from one country to another may affect the liquidity of the banks in these countries and credit conditions, to

an extent that it is significant for domestic monetary policy'. – Bank of England[1]

Strong reliance on foreign capital inflow can easily jeopardize the country's objectives if there is a sudden pause or reduction of inflows at a critical point where debt obligations are pending to be satisfied. The possibility of a reduction in inflows or increase in outflow of foreign currency from the island exists if emerging markets and developed countries were to increase their interest rates and broaden their bond offers. To the extent where these economies are more stable than Jamaica's, foreigners will hastily repatriate their capital resulting in huge foreign currency obligations that Jamaica might not be readily able to meet. This is so because Jamaica does not have proper long-term foreign currency liquidity management strategies.

An analysis of the movement of capital (foreign investment) is relevant, given that capital is necessary for investment, which increases economic activity to stimulate growth. It is also important to determine what level of foreign investment can be absorbed by the local economy without encountering liquidity management difficulties.

1.2.1 How has Jamaica Managed its Foreign Currency Liquidity?

The flow of international capital or investment to and from small island economies is mainly influenced by the viability of the domestic economy while constrained by the global geopolitical economic environment. Jamaica's local economy is heavily service based, which accounts for more than 70 percent of the country's GDP. Most of the country's foreign currency receipts are generated from tourism and remittances, which each account for about 30 percent of GDP. The sale of bauxite/alumina accounts for about 5 percent of GDP. The majority of foreign currency inflows to the island have come from foreign currency borrowings from bilateral and multilateral institutions. Other inflows range from the sale of foreign currency bonds and other instruments to the global financial market and from capital investment by foreigners in the domestic economy. A small amount of inflows arise from the sale of domestic manufactured goods to the global marketplace. Meanwhile, outflows of foreign currency from the island stem mainly from Jamaican investment abroad, foreign debt servicing repayment, and the purchase of oil, other commodities and services from abroad.

Since the country gained independence in 1962, the volume of foreign currency inflows has been greater than the volume of foreign currency outflows (see Fig. 1.1 for more details). Quarterly data from 1995 to 2013 shows that total foreign currency inflows arising from trade, commerce, investment and debt display a similar pattern of behaviour to that of total foreign currency outflows; increasing or decreasing at the same time, sometimes with a one- or two-year lag, (see Fig. 1.1). Between 1995 and 2001, Jamaica's total foreign currency inflow averaged approximately US $355 million with a corresponding outflow averaging little more than US $252 million per month over the same period of time. Between 2001 and 2005, foreign currency inflow averaged about US $540 million while the total volume of foreign currency outflow averaged about US $383 million per month up to November 2005.

Foreign debt obligations in December 2005 were financed by borrowings to the tune of US $753 million, $570 million of which was used to make debt servicing payments. In Jamaica's case, foreign currency borrowing is always done marginally higher than the exact amount needed to service debt obligations and the remainder is stored as a part of the NIR. After debt servicing in 2005, foreign currency inflows and outflows both reverted to little more than their pre-2005 average and maintained a steady pace, though they fluctuated seasonally. Between 2005 and 2008,

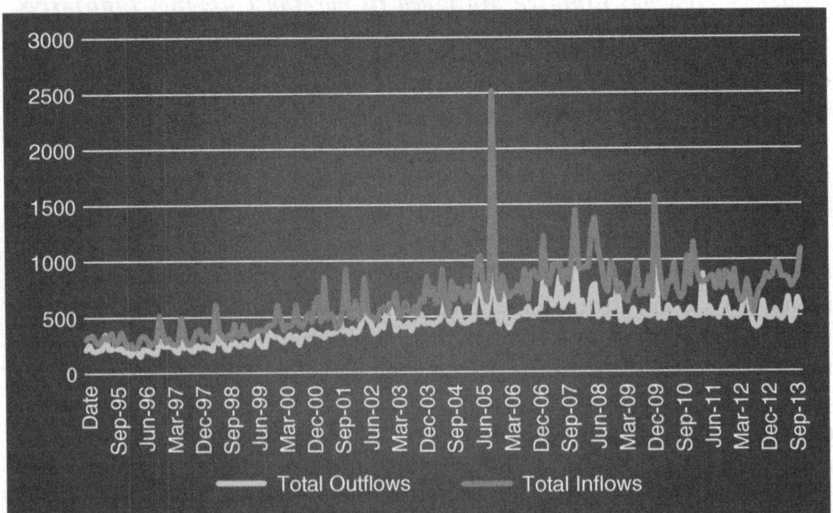

Fig. 1.1 Jamaica quarterly foreign currency inflow and outflow from 1995 to present: Bank of Jamaica

total foreign currency outflow averaged US $608 million while foreign currency inflow averaged US $906 million per month.

During the global financial crisis of 2008, foreign currency inflow increased again to the amount of US $1.3 billion and $1.4 billion in June and July 2008, respectively. This was used to service outflow requirements of US $750 million and $784 million in those two months. Foreign currency flows maintained its pre-financial crisis levels during 2009 before increasing significantly as a result of further borrowings to service foreign currency debt in January 2010. Foreign currency inflow amounted to US $1.56 billion and $1.01 billion in February and March 2010 and was used to service outflow of US $1.2 billion in February. By mid-2010 foreign currency flows reverted to their normal levels, and maintained a steady meandering pace up to 2015 when US $2 billion in foreign currency bonds were issued to service the PetroCaribe[2] debt owed to Venezuela and the remainder used to strengthen the NIR once more.

But important questions remain: what amount of the inflows are from income-earning sources, what amount arises from net transfers, what amount from borrowings, what amount from investment – direct or indirect – will be expelled from the country over time? The former must be able to sustain the latter in the long run. Holding all other factors equal, Jamaica's foreign currency earnings must be able to satisfy its short- and long-run foreign currency obligations. Otherwise the country's foreign currency dilemma will continue. Having received continuous balance of payment support from the IMF and other international lending agencies, questions arise if Jamaica's foreign currency flows are sustainable in the long run. Can Jamaica sustainably repay its foreign debt? What is the optimal level of reserves? What impact does foreign currency flows have on GDP growth? How effective is the monetary policy transmission mechanism? And most importantly, how should Jamaica strategize to increase economic stability to enhance its anemic economic growth, needed if the country wishes to develop? This book unravels these questions and provides policy recommendations as to the best way forward.

1.2.2 *How Did Jamaica Find Itself in This Position?*

Operating in a fragile global economic environment for the past two decades, the island offered higher interest rate bonds and other financial instruments to global investors than they would have received from emerging market economies and from more developed countries.[3]

These higher interest rates led to an increase in the sale of Jamaican foreign currency bonds and other foreign currency instruments in the global marketplace by helping to counterbalance the threat of debt defaults arising from Jamaica's continuous macroeconomic instability, low growth in national output and huge debt build-up. Inflows of foreign currency arising from these funds borrowed from the international market ought to have been invested to generate enough foreign currency to repay principal and higher interest rates in the future. Also, to provide a solid cushion of foreign currency for the island's NIR, which is necessary to increase the country's ability to sustain itself in the long run. Otherwise, the country will face greater burden when more foreign currency is required to service these debts than what was received from the investment in the first place.

The sustainability of these net borrowings of foreign currency has been a cause for concern since the early 1970s, after the first oil price shock, and remains relevant because Jamaica still seeks BOP support from international lending institutions including the IMF, World Bank and the Inter-American Development Bank (IDB). These loans continuously roll over due to Jamaica's inability to generate sufficient intrinsic international reserves on a consistent basis to repay principal and interest.

The issue has also become more relevant in light of a number of innate handicaps in the local economy, which antagonized access to the EFF SBA offered by the IMF[4] in 2013. The previous EFF program was suspended in 2010 due to failure of the government to meet the IMF's stipulated conditions.[5] After the programme was re-engaged in 2013, quarterly disbursements of foreign currency to support the NIR are only accessible if Jamaica passes quarterly economic review tests. The program ends in 2017. The reliance on foreign capital to support Jamaica's domestic investments and consumption levels has also increased the country's susceptibility to external shocks.

To prevent new borrowing after the EFF expires, Jamaica must establish an optimal pattern of international currency flows where it can become solvent – able to satisfy its foreign currency obligations consistently. A thorough understanding of the interrelationship between foreign currency inflow and outflows becomes important to drive macroeconomic policy to boost long-term growth and development. To appreciate this, a historical breakdown of the evolution of

Jamaica's exchange rate policy framework that has guided the flow of foreign currency over time is necessary.

1.3 Background: The Jamaican Exchange Rate Conundrum

In September 2016, the Jamaican dollar (JMD) exchange rate arrived at an all-time high of JMD \$128 to US \$1, coming from as low as approximately JMD \$6 to US \$1 at the beginning of 1990. Although the rate of depreciation per annum has not been severe enough to cause a currency crisis, the depreciating trend has been a national topic for discussion given its impact on prices, imports, consumption, production, output and exports and the nation's standard of living. It is more questionable given that over the said 25-year period from 1990 to present GDP growth has averaged just over 0.5 percent per annum.

Throughout the country's years of independence, Jamaica has employed five main types of exchange rate strategies. First, a currency board arrangement was established, which was later replaced by a crawling peg. The country then moved to a dual exchange rate, then to an auction and allocation system and finally to a free-floating exchange rate system. These were designed within the country's monetary policy framework as a balance to fiscal policy in the government's aim to achieve specific economic objectives. Each episode is explored in the sections that follow to provide an understanding of how Jamaica's foreign currency flows and exchange rate have evolved to suit local economic aspirations within the particular global economic environment.

1.3.1 The Crawling Peg and Dual Exchange Rate System

During the 1960s, foreign currency flows to the island were fairly stable. In 1961, the existing currency board system was strengthened by the establishment of the Bank of Jamaica (BOJ). The exchange rate was pegged at one Jamaican dollar to one British pound (GBP) (see Fig. 1.2). Annual inflation rate was low and industrial expansion, including a boom in the bauxite industry, encouraged production. In 1969 Jamaica decimalized its currency and now JMD \$2 could be

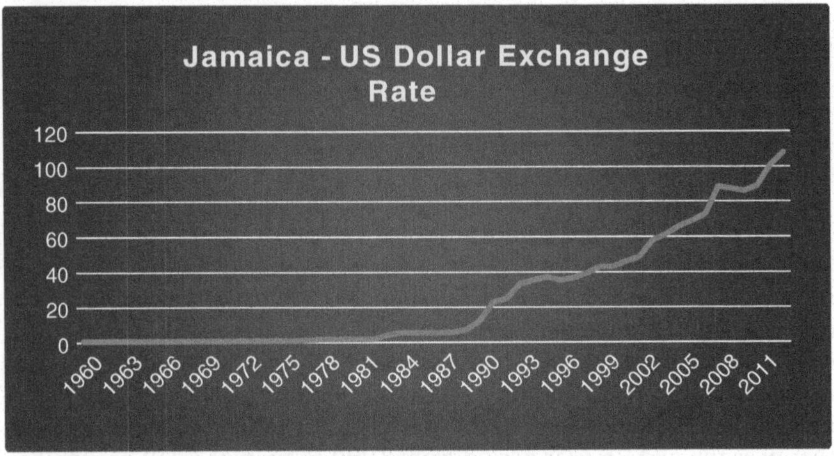

Fig. 1.2 Jamaica's nominal exchange rate: Bank of Jamaica

exchanged for GBP £1 or for US $2.40. The collapse of the Bretton Woods system increased uncertainty in the global foreign exchange market but the JMD remained firm; maintaining a high value whilst pegged to the British pound during this time.

As the domestic political economy became more nationalistic, Jamaica increased its imports relative to exports in 1972 and its current account deficit jumped to US $48 million or 3 percent of GDP. In 1973, the Jamaican exchange rate peg was switched from the British pound to the dollar; since the United States became Jamaica's major trading partner. At the time, the JMD valued more than the dollar; trading at JMD $0.909 to US $. The peg remained throughout the 1970s, maintaining the Jamaican dollar at a higher value than the US dollar. The stronger JMD was associated with an increase in the country's demand for foreign goods and services, which increased the demand for foreign currency. Consequently, Jamaica fulfilled its foreign currency demand with borrowed reserves. A new policy framework was imminent.

In 1973, the domestic inflation rate hiked to more than 30 percent, impacted negatively by the first global oil price shock (see point A on Fig. 1.3). After falling to about 10 percent in 1976, the inflation rate increased significantly to a little more than 25 percent by 1978 as a

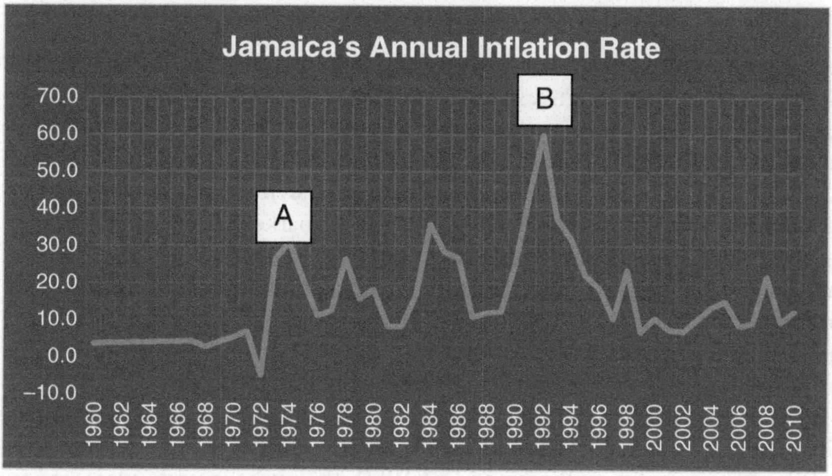

Fig. 1.3 Jamaica's annual inflation rate: Bank of Jamaica

result of the second oil price shock. If the country's demand for foreign currency remained the same, without exchange rate intervention, the country's foreign currency reserves would have been quickly depleted.

In an effort to combat the pressure on domestic holdings of foreign currency, Jamaica exercised a dual exchange rate system between 1977 and 1983. A basic rate of JMD $0.909 to US $1 was used for essential imports, government foreign spending and the bauxite sector while another rate of JMD $1.25 to US $1 was applied to all other transactions. Quantitative restriction on imports was the preferred method to constrain depletion of the borrowed reserves. From this strategy, the inflation rate fell gradually to about 8.3 percent by 1981. Also, Jamaica's current account deficit fell from 9 percent of GDP to less than 1 percent of GDP during the same period. The exchange rate depreciated further to about JMD $1.92 to US $1 in 1982 then to JMD $3.12 to US $1 by 1983 and then to JMD $5.15 to US $1 by 1984. These were the largest and most consecutive spells of currency depreciation the country encountered. Congruently, the inflation rate increased to 17 percent and 35.9 percent in 1983 and 1984, respectively. With such high inflation rates, the Bank of Jamaica had to intervene.

1.3.2 The Auction and Allocation Exchange Rate System

An auction and allocation exchange rate system was introduced between 1984 and 1990. Foreign exchange was sold on an auction basis, where amounts went to the highest bidder in most cases. A variety of different auction types were explored, which helped to increase the inflow of foreign currency to the banking sector. The auctions system served as an incentive to redirect foreign currency from the black market to the real banking sector. The Jamaican dollar exchange rate was maintained relatively stable via the practicing of strong, tight foreign currency distribution controls and import restrictions. In 1989, the importation of capital goods for rebuilding placed additional strain on the currency after the economy encountered a negative exogenous shock arising from Hurricane Gilbert in September 1988. This along with a rapid growth in commercial banks' credit offerings increased the demand for foreign currency resulting in further depreciation of the Jamaican dollar. By the end of 1989, the exchange rate increased to JMD $7.24 to US $1. Political uncertainty surrounding the local general elections also played a factor in the exchange rate depreciation.

The BOJ consequently restricted disbursement of foreign currency. Commercial banks were limited to a specific amount of foreign currency they could sell per week and a quota system was introduced for foreign travel and foreign purchases allowed to each person and business. The amount allotted was based on need, how much foreign currency was contributed to the system and how much foreign currency was available at the time. Some businessmen had holder accounts where they received the foreign currency, the rest was retained by the BOJ and the persons owed were paid in Jamaican dollars. Some of these businessmen were allowed to hold 50 percent of their foreign currency receipts in countries outside of the Caribbean Community (CARICOM). This system, along with demand management policies, was insufficient to keep the exchange rate stable and by 1990 the exchange rate reached JMD $12.22 to US $1. The reserves were depleted, sometimes negative and Jamaica had to borrow once more.

1.3.3 Free-Floating Exchange Rate

Under the guidance of the Washington Consensus recommended by the IMF, Jamaica liberalized its financial sector in 1992. Liberalization included: the decentralization of foreign currency disbursements via the introduction of Cambio[6] systems, and not so limited disbursements through commercial banks. Each person/business would have their foreign currency transferred to their account instead of being paid in Jamaican dollars by the BOJ. Liberalization of the market meant loosening existing exchange rate controls in a new system of market-driven exchange rate determination.

No exchange rate controls meant that foreign currency was supplied on demand. After a time, the reserves were insufficient to sustain a bottleneck build-up of demand for foreign currency. Reserves quickly depleted and the exchange rate depreciated further to appease demand, jumping to JMD $25.11 to US $1 in 1992. A rapid increase in prices ensued. The inflation rate reached 60 percent in 1992, and Jamaica had to borrow once more. Point **B** on Fig. 1.3 illustrates Jamaica's annual inflation rate. Huge foreign currency debt obligations, a constantly depreciating currency and excess demand for the US dollar prompted the government to urge local business owners to supply cheap foreign currency to help satisfy demand. Under the initiative, businessmen with a lot of foreign currency agreed with the government to sell US $1 million to the domestic exchange rate market daily at a rate of JMD $25 to US $1. The move was widely criticized as the effects of the initiative were short lived, and the exchange rate reached JMD $33.29 to US $1 by 1993. After liberalising its financial sector in the early 1990s, Jamaica did not put sufficient control mechanisms in place, and the exchange rate has continued to depreciate since. Jamaica has maintained this free-floating exchange rate system from 1992 to present. The JMD traded at $120 to US $1 at the end of October 2015.

Despite the depreciating currency under the floating exchange rate regime, Jamaica has failed to materialize real GDP growth on a consistent basis. Meanwhile, the country's foreign currency debt obligations have continued to increase. Although the aim of monetary policy is never to maneuver the value of a country's currency, other monetary policy actions have failed to properly balance fiscal policy given the government's aim of achieving economic stability, growth and development. The following chapter explores Jamaica's foreign currency debt situation using a debt sustainability analysis.

Notes

1. 'Inflow and outflow of Foreign Fund', www.bankofengland.co.uk/archive/Documents/historicpubs/qb/1962/qb62q293102.pdf.
2. Details on the PetroCaribe debt, the latest EFF with the IMF and other foreign currency debt obligations are discussed in Chapter 3.

3. Jamaica's interest rate policy is discussed in Chapter 9. Jamaica is normally a high interest rate regime, with an interest rate as a high as 35 percent in the early 1990s. It is only recently, with the latest IMF agreement, that interest rates began to fall consistently.
4. Jamaica's relationship with the IMF and other multilateral lending institutions is examined in Chapter 2.
5. See IMF Country Report on Jamaica 2013 for more details.
6. The Cambio is a retail outlet that buys and sells foreign currency.

CHAPTER 2

Foreign Currency Borrowing and Foreign Debt Sustainability

2.1 Foreign Currency Borrowing

The management of Jamaica's foreign currency holdings was tied to its mother country Great Britain prior to independence in 1962. During that period, no foreign currency borrowings occurred. As a result, Jamaica's foreign currency flows were sustainable. After independence, Jamaica became free to administer its own fiscal and monetary policy in a new paradigm. The establishment of the Bank of Jamaica (BOJ) required an international reserve cushion to begin with, so Jamaica borrowed its first loan from Britain. Throughout this time, there were no issues surrounding foreign currency debt since both countries used the same currency (the British pound), no exchange rate problems existed and interest rates were negligible. In the early 1970s, Jamaica decimalized its currency and relinquished the pound.

A sudden increase in foreign currency outflow requirements arising from the first negative oil price shock in 1974 increased Jamaica's demand for foreign currency, leading to a depletion of the Net International Reserves (NIR). This had to be financed by external borrowing thereby spurring the country's earliest phase of debt accumulation. At the same time, moneys earned from the exportation of bauxite were used for infrastructure development as well as to expand social security and safety net programmes. Jamaica signed its first loan agreement with the IMF in 1977.

A. Haughton, *Developing Sustainable Balance of Payments in Small Countries*, DOI 10.1007/978-3-319-53031-4_2

A second negative oil price shock occurred in 1978, increasing Jamaica's demand for foreign currency once more and depleting the reserves further. The IMF disbursed an additional US $74.8 million in loanable funds to Jamaica for NIR support in 1978. This triggered a corresponding increase in foreign currency and total debt (see point labelled **C** in Fig. 2.1). Economic policy during the 1980s forced a reversal in the debt-to-GDP trajectory, which reduced significantly (see point labelled **D** in Fig. 2.1).

Between 1980 and 1997, domestic debt climbed above foreign debt (see Fig. 2.1), peaking at approximately 150 percent of GDP in 1985 and 1991 when total debt was approximately 200 percent and 175 percent of GDP in those two years respectively. Total external debt displayed an increasing pattern over the 30-year period from 1983 to 2013 (see Fig. 2.2). It became a cause for concern after 1997 when it rose above domestic debt. Total external debt in 1983 was $1.6 billion and rose to more than $2.5 billion by 1993 (see Fig. 2.2). After the liberalization of the financial sector in 1992, several banks and insurance companies had huge debts denominated in foreign currency. The rapidly depreciating currency crippled their ability to satisfy these debt obligations, which led them to approach government for assistance. The government borrowed once more to create the Financial Sector Adjustment Company (FINSAC)[1] in 1997.

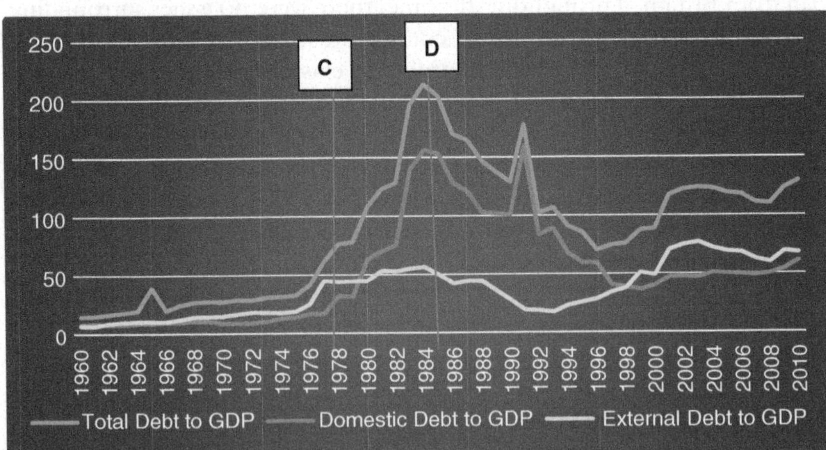

Fig. 2.1 Jamaica's debt to GDP ratio: Bank of Jamaica

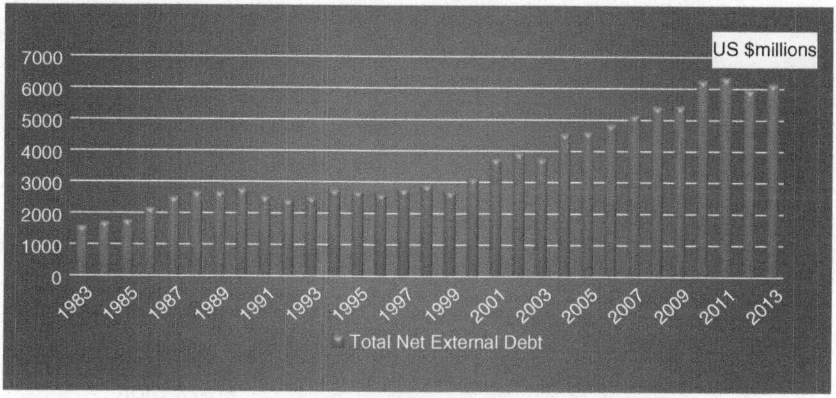

Fig. 2.2 Jamaica's Total net external debt: Bank of Jamaica

FINSAC acquired the assets of these companies who were'**too big to fail'** and settled their debts. **This move helped to appease the domestic financial crisis of 1997. But subsequently, the external debt continued along the same trajectory increasing to $3.8 billion by 2003.** Jamaica's debt servicing payments increased by more than 70 percent between 1999 and 2003 and increased to roughly 140 percent of GDP by 2014.

Figure 2.3 displays the average external debt held by each creditor group over the last 30 years. In the categories of external debt owed to multilateral institutions, other governments and others, 11 percent of the nation's external debt on average is owed to the Inter-American Development Bank (IDB), 9 percent of Jamaica's debt on average is owed to the International Bank for Reconstruction and Development (IBRD) of Canada and 3 percent is owed on average to other international institutions. Six percent of the external debt is owed to the international government institution, the United States Agency for International Development (USAID), while the Canadian International Development Agency (CIDA) and Export Development Canada (EDC) hold 1 percent on average. Bonds increased in popularity after 1996; they account for 47 percent of the debt on average. Other government institutions including the IMF and the World Bank hold 17 percent of the debt on average while commercial banks and other commercial entities hold 5 percent and 1 percent of the debt, respectively. Table 2.1 shows a more detailed breakdown of Jamaica's external debt holdings over the last three

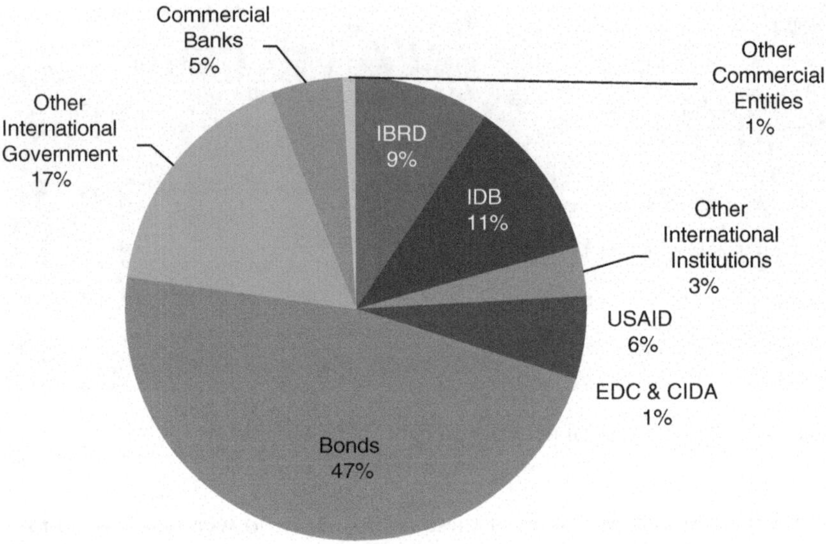

Fig. 2.3 Average percentage of external debt owed to creditors from 1983 – 2013: Bank of Jamaica

decades from 1983 to 2013. The ascendant trajectory of Jamaica's foreign currency debt is a cause for concern up to that point and the country sought further assistance from the IMF through an Extended Fund Facility (EFF) in 2013 and the Stand-By Arrangement (SBA) in 2016.

Total debt servicing payments account for more than 45 percent of Jamaica's budgeted tax receipts per annum. This, when added to public sector salaries and wages and recurrent expenditures, leaves less than 15 percent of the annual budget for infrastructural improvement and capital expansion. Lack of proper infrastructure reduces the country's ability to adopt new technology and reduces its ability to increase productivity and production. For a country's debt burden to fall, its economy must be growing at a faster pace than its interest rate payment obligations. If interest rates are higher than the growth rate of GDP, then a country's debt situation will worsen. This questions the sustainability of the nation's foreign currency debt over time. Other literatures have analyzed the country's domestic debt,[2]

Table 2.1 Jamaica's external debt in US millions

	External debt									
	International institutions				*International-government*					
	IBRD	*IDE*	*Other*	*USAID*	*EDC & CIDA*	*Other*	*Bonds*	*Commercial banks*	*Other commercial banks*	*Total net external Debt*
1983	306.4	104.3	106.6	361.7	61.4	207.6		317.3	144.4	1,609.7
1984	356	113.3	100.5	428.4	38.2	170.7		336.6	192.2	1,735.9
1985	375	116.4	104.6	459.4	35.5	191.8		336.5	181.3	1,800.5
1986	387.6	233.4	72.7	390.1	73.1	631.4		389.6	9.2	2,187.1
1987	390.6	282.6	84.3	409.9	73.07	857.5		388.1	10.4	2,533.8
1988	434.3	488.4	86.3	404.9	94.42	793.2		374.3	4.3	2,703.0
1989	460.8	450.5	84.9	404.1	99.4	834.7		362	3.8	2,711.3
1990	452.6	451.6	100.6	411.2	99.9	960.4		329.4	3.3	2,811.7
1991	430.2	311.4	106.1	419.6	100.2	911		288.1	2.6	2,570.9
1992	416.8	309.9	83.9	418.8	21.6	926.6		276.1	2.2	2,456.4
1993	448.3	284	76.8	338.6	22.1	1,084.80		265.7	24.9	2,545.2
1994	402.3	433.6	83.7	333.3	16.5	1,189.80		304.1	20.8	2,784.1
1995	345	430.2	78.2	375.6	16.3	1,174.50		283.2	16.1	2,719.1
1996	299.9	423.7	80.6	348.9	16.7	1,172.50	48	247.1	11.2	2,648.1
1997	392	391.4	82.6	397	13	1,027.10	250	234.3	6.2	2,793.1
1998	355.5	371	82.4	338.7	12.2	1,062.60	550	162.1	5.3	2,939.8
1999	349.7	352.6	89.5	265.7	34.1	1,006.3	450.0	147.2	21.0	2,716.1
2000	410.7	417.7	103.8	258.1	29.3	885.3	862.8	132.8	42.0	3,142.5
2001	458.0	393.4	105.6	201.1	28.5	793.8	1,655.7	97.7	43.5	3,777.3

(*continued*)

Table 2.1 (continued)

	External debt									
	International institutions				*International-government*					
	IBRD	*IDB*	*Other*	*USAID*	*EDC & CIDA*	*Other*	*Bonds*	*Commercial banks*	*Other commercial banks*	*Total net external Debt*
2002	487.9	468.5	123.1	177.6	29.1	768.6	1,812.6	45.0	61.3	3,973.7
2003	454.1	450.5	134.9	165.2	26.3	756.8	1,692.4	50.1	68.0	3,798.3
2004	428.6	576.2	182.8	151.4	22.7	738.9	2,397.1	35.1	53.5	4,586.3
2005	404.6	580.2	169.1	134.6	17.1	622.7	2,601.4	69.1	37.0	4,635.8
2006	372.0	530.7	185.2	116.8	13.7	568.1	2,934.0	121.7	36.6	4,878.8
2007	348.8	489.8	193.7	100.1	8.2	576.4	3,279.1	131.3	46.2	5,173.6
2008	309.2	559.8	231.5	69.5	0.3	600.2	3,489.5	146.6	35.0	5,441.6
2009	378.9	651.7	291.1	72.8	0.0	602.2	3,227.2	199.6	40.4	5,463.9
2010	571.5	1,229.0	327.9	45.0	0.0	618.9	3,194.6	270.8	29.4	6,287.1
2011	660.0	1,282.1	358.2	28.9	0.0	613.3	3,179.4	232.5	22.2	6,376.6
2012	661.6	1,236.4	357.2	17.4	0.0	556.8	2,922.8	219.0	14.7	5,985.9
2013	643.3	1,227.0	456.2	10.5	0.0	539.5	3,070.7	216.4	13.6	6,177.2

Source: Bank of Jamaica

and as a result, this chapter will focus on the sustainability of the nation's foreign currency debt.

2.1.1 *The PetroCaribe Arrangement*

Jamaica entered the PetroCaribe arrangement with Venezuela on 29 July 2005. Between 2006 and 2011, Jamaica's total oil bill under the agreement amounted to more than JMD $164 billion; 18 countries in total are a part of the agreement. The PetroCaribe development fund is an agreement between Venezuela and Caribbean countries, including Jamaica, that provides loan financing to the Ministry of Finance and Planning and other public bodies to finance development projects. **The arrangement is extensive and enables Jamaica to purchase oil on preferential conditions. Since the beginning of the arrangement, Jamaica buys oil at market value but pays only a percentage of the cost initially; the remainder is paid for over a 25-year period at 1 percent rate of interest.** This is granted in the form of loans that are accommodating and are furnished at low interest rates – between 1 percent and 3 percent per annum.

The agreement allows Jamaica to purchase at most 185,000 barrels of oil per day. Countries that are part of the agreement are mandated to pay 40 percent of their oil import bill within 90 days of purchase, and the remainder paid for over the next 25 years, providing that oil prices do not exceed US $100 per barrel. If oil prices reach US $150 per barrel, then the country is mandated only to 30 percent of the value in 90 days and the remainder paid on the same terms and conditions as before.

Funds from the PetroCaribe agreement were used for several projects including the following:

- The expansion and upgrade of the country's road network
- Upgrading of the Norman Manley International Airport
- Expansion of Jamaica's port infrastructure
- The refinancing of domestic public sector debt (to prevent job losses and agency closures)
- To support the public transportation system including the Jamaica Urban Transit Company (JUTC)
- The Petrojam Refinery upgrade project (Venezuela purchased 49 percent of the shares in the Petrojam Refinery in 2008)

Discussions surrounding the sustainability of the PetroCaribe arrangement increased after the death of the former Venezuelan President Hugo Chavez in March 2013. It became more prevalent in 2014 after Venezuela encountered cash flow problems as a result of a huge fall in global oil prices. In July 2015, Jamaica issued bonds with two different maturity periods to raise funds to repurchase Jamaica's PetroCaribe debt owed to Venezuela. The bonds, which were expected to raise US $2 billion in total, were divided into two separate issues; one generated US $1.35 billion maturing in 2028 with a yield of 6.75 percent and the other generated US $650 million, which will mature in 2045 with a yield of 7.875 percent. Proceeds from the bonds issue were used to repurchase $3.2 billion worth of debt owed to Venezuela at a discounted price of $1.5 billion or $0.47 per dollar. The remaining US $0.5 billion was used to strengthen the NIR.

The decision to repurchase its own debt at a discounted value has resulted in a temporary reduction in Jamaica's foreign currency debt stock. However, the higher interest of 6.75 percent and 7.85 percent in debt servicing payments to be made to these bond holders compared to the 1 percent on the PetroCaribe debt per annum questioned the long-run sustainability of such foreign currency debt swap, although done at a lower interest rate than what Jamaica is normally accustomed to. US $32 million per year was used to service the PetroCaribe debt compared to US $100 million a year to service these new bonds. The IMF has estimated, using Net Present Value (NPV) analysis, that the PetroCaribe debt buyback deal in 2015 will save Jamaica US $300 million or 2 percent of GDP based on the current exchange rate trajectory, which has been commended as a good move if the country's foreign debt is to become sustainable. As of May 2015, Jamaica's total public debt stock was JJMD $2.04 trillion, of which US $8.51 billion is external debt. The new bond issues were oversubscribed to the sum of $4.5 billion; more creditors were willing to lend to Jamaica than originally anticipated due to an increase in Jamaica's credibility on the international financial markets.

The lack of indigenous foreign currency-generating sources mean that Jamaica has to continuously borrow to repay its foreign currency debt. Issuing bonds to repay debt is a tricky scenario because the government will have to raise funds to repay these bonds when they mature in 2028 and 2045, plus debt servicing payments on an annual basis. Figure 2.4 shows that total net foreign currency debt owed to international institutions spiked from approximately US $1.3 billion to more than US $2.0 billion after the

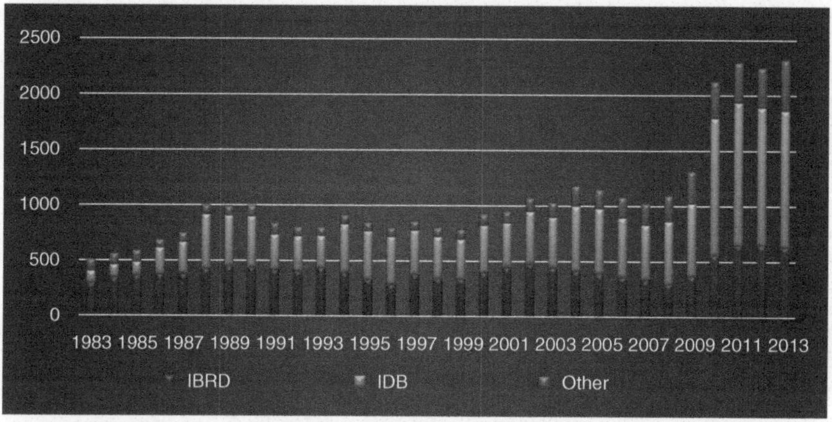

Fig. 2.4 Total net foreign currency debt in US $Millions owed to international institutions: Bank of Jamaica

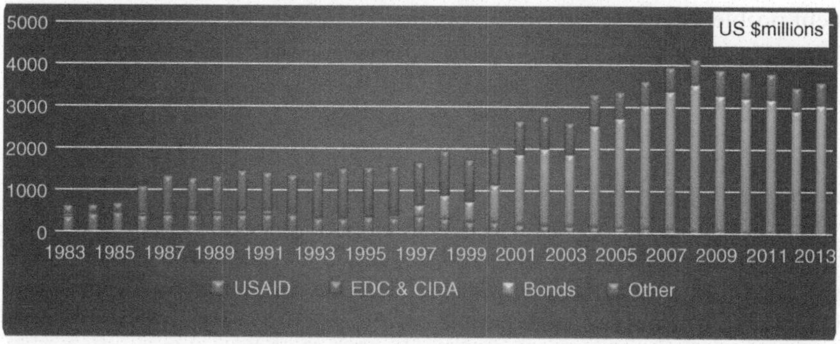

Fig. 2.5 Total Net foreign currency debt owed to international government: Bank of Jamaica

Global Financial Crisis of 2008. During the same time frame, net foreign currency debt owed to international government decreased gradually from US $4 billion to US $3 billion (see Fig. 2.5) and net foreign assets owed to private institutions decreased from approximately 300 million to approximately US $220 million (see Fig. 2.6). If Jamaica's economy does not grow at an increasing rate from now onwards, it is highly unlikely that the government will generate enough funds to service these bonds when they

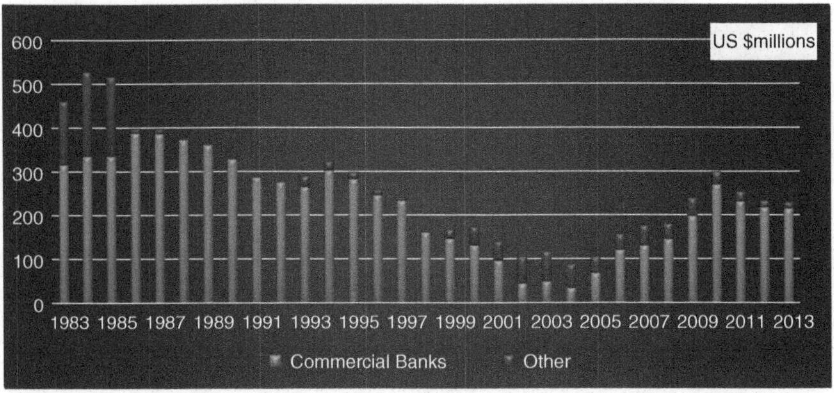

Fig. 2.6 Net foreign currency debt owed by private institutions: Bank of Jamaica

mature. As a result, they might have to issue more bonds to repay debt, trapping Jamaica in a borrowing cycle. The new bond issue buys the government time to think of a more sustainable strategy to combat Jamaica's high debt problem rather than issuing bonds to repay debt.

2.1.2 Debt Exchange and the Extended Fund Facility (EFF)

On 11 November 2016, the Executive Board of the IMF approved a three-year Stand-By Arrangement (SBA) for Jamaica to replace the EFF, which was expected to expire in March 2017. The SBA will make approximately US $1.64 billion available to Jamaica. This amounts to roughly 312 percent of Jamaica's quota in the IMF who see the support as necessary to help Jamaica continue its economic reform.

Fundamentally, the IMF continues to provide balance of payments and stability support for countries who have found themselves with foreign currency liquidity management problems through special drawing rights, drawdowns, SBAs and EFFs. They provide a stamp of approval that enables a country to seem viable to attract investment from the international capital market.

From 1977 to present, Jamaica has entered more than 13 different arrangements with the IMF (see Fig. 2.7). These include more than four decades of Structural Adjustment Policies and structural reform recommendations, for example, the Washington Consensus. Jamaica took a break from its relationship with the IMF after the engagement beginning 1992 expired.

JAMAICA'S BORROWING AGREEMENTS WITH THE IMF 1977-2014	
Standby Arrangement	11-Nov 2016
Extended Fund Facility	1-May 2013
Standby Arrangement	4-Feb 2010
Extended Fund Facility	11-Dec 1992
Standby Arrangement	28-Jun 1991
Standby Arrangement	23-Mar 1990
Standby Arrangement	19-Sep 1988
Standby Arrangement	2-Mar 1987
Standby Arrangement	17-Jul 1985
Standby Arrangement	22-Jun 1984
Extended Fund Facility	13-Apr 1981
Extended Fund Facility	11-Jun 1979
Extended Fund Facility	9-Jun 1978
Standby Arrangement	11-Aug 1977

Fig. 2.7 Start Dates of Jamaica's borrowing arrangement with the IMF

Jamaica, nevertheless, returned to resume its engagements when the country encountered foreign currency liquidity management problems in 2010.

The EFF agreement signed in 2013 came after a three-year delay when the original agreement in 2010 was cancelled due to the country's failure to meet certain conditions. Jamaica, desperately in need of foreign currency liquidity, had to carefully outline a strategic plan for debt reduction and economic growth through fiscal reform. Jamaica managed to convince the IMF that they had the will and capability to properly implement the recommendations that were necessary to increase macroeconomic stability and to enhance the country's ability to repay debts borrowed.

Along with technical support, Jamaica agreed to receive more than US $2 billion in loanable funds from the IMF, World Bank and IDB combined as stipulated by the most recent EFF agreement signed with IMF. These loanable funds are dispersed via quarterly drawdowns based on Jamaica's discipline and targets achieved.

An analysis of the sustainability of Jamaica's external debt obligations is critical to understand how the country can improve its foreign currency liquidity management strategy over the short to medium term.

With current debt-to-GDP ratio 128 percent of GDP coming down from 135 percent of GDP in 2013, and foreign currency debt more than 62 percent of GDP, Jamaica's debt remains among the top five highest in the world. The EFF SBA aims to reduce this total debt stock (foreign and domestic) as well as help stabilize the macroeconomy. The EFF[3] has three main objectives: (1) increase the flow of foreign currency necessary to cushion the NIR and restore Jamaica's balance of payments up to 2017 (the EFF provided the foreign currency needed to support Jamaica's high import bill); (2) increase international lenders confidence in the Jamaican economy so that Jamaica can attract a larger inflow of foreign currency.[4] (3) provide budgetary support, which will help to reduce the cost of external borrowings. Necessary conditions to receive drawdown funds from the EFF on a quarterly basis includes tax reform, pension reform and a more structured and sustainable public sector payment system. These are some of the main structural difficulties hampering the smooth flow of business operations and government efficiency limiting the amount of foreign currency the country can attract. The resulting increase in borrowings to support the country's imports will further increase debt service requirements and deplete government revenues, putting the country in a winding circular trap.

Along with the EFF, Jamaica successfully engaged its creditors in a couple of debt exchange programmes – the Jamaica Debt Exchange (JDX) in 2008 and the National Debt Exchange (NDX) in 2012 – to help reduce its debt burden. Under the JDX, interest rates fell by 5 percentage points on average, from 14.5 percent to about 9.5 percent. The reduction was welcomed initially but failed to significantly reduce Jamaica's foreign currency debt requirements, as it was still relatively high when compared to other highly indebted countries such as Greece and Japan who pay 6 percent and 3 percent, respectively. The argument for Jamaica's high interest rates in the initial stages was to compensate for the country's high macroeconomic instability and associated with double high inflation. The JDX wasn't enough to solve the problem and the government sought a second JDX four years later called the NDX.

The NDX entailed a lengthening of the maturity period of the debt instruments by three to five years on average and reducing the average interest rate by a further 1.7 percentage points from 9.5 percent to 7.8 percent per annum. Of the JMD $1.7 trillion in total debt the country owed at the beginning of 2013, approximately $1 trillion is domestic debt, owed predominantly to the major financial institutions including National Commercial Bank (NCB) and Scotiabank. The NDX targeted $840 billion in the debt exchange programme. Like the JDX of 2010, the new debt exchange proposed no reduction in the principal amounts borrowed, no 'hair cut'. Neither was there any proposal to reduce the foreign currency debt burden. The government created a committee to oversee and monitor the new proposals. In total, the new debt exchange is projected to save Jamaica $17 billion a year in interest expenses, but the net savings for the country will be a little less given that the government would have received 25 percent withholding tax on these interest payments annually.

For the medium term from 2013 to 2017, the government plans to reduce the public sector wage bill from 11 percent to 9 percent of GDP, scrap some waivers and concessions and increase the primary surplus target from 6.3 percent to a constant 7.5 percent of GDP for the next fiscal year. Overall, Jamaica qualifies to receive approximately US $1.3 billion of balance of payment support from the IMF. The government received $833 billion of this for the JDX and the remainder will be dispersed on a quarterly basis throughout the duration of the EFF, providing that Jamaica meets the conditionality stipulated. The JDX and NDX programmes provided a window from which the country could have reduced its debt burden tremendously, but the long-run success of both required some amount of debt write-offs instead of just debt payment extensions.

The JDX and the NDX targeted domestic debt and not the external debt stock denominated in foreign currency, which continues to increase as the exchange rate depreciates.[5] The Ministry of Finance found evidence to suggest that every 1 percent depreciation of the Jamaican dollar results in 0.5 percent increase in the foreign currency debt requirements. This puts further strain on the country's foreign currency requirements. High debt servicing requirements reduce national savings, which is essential for capital expansion. Capital expansion is critical for economic growth. The next section analyzes the sustainability of Jamaica's external debt within the current economic framework.

2.2 Jamaica's External Debt Sustainability Analysis (DSA)

Throughout the literature, evaluation of a country's external debt sustainability has relied on the Debt Sustainability Analysis (DSA) recommended by the IMF. It provides a basis upon which potential crises emanating from future debt default if foreign currency debt becomes unsustainable.

To begin the analysis, the DSA advises first assessing Jamaica's current debt structure the maturity period of the debt, whether the debt is fixed or floating, or whether it is indexed and by whom it is held. Most of Jamaica's external debt is multilaterally or bilaterally owned by the IMF, the IDB, the World Bank and Venezuela in the PetroCaribe agreement. This was discussed in the previous section. Upon assessment, the next step aims to identify any vulnerability and hindrances to the debt structure prior to the debt repayment period so that the necessary policy action can be taken to mitigate any difficulties in trying to satisfy payment. In the event that these vulnerabilities arise, the DSA recommends analysing alternative actions that can provide a better path for policy. This is addressed in the section that follows.

2.2.1 *Data and Methodology*

Proper debt analysis using the DSA involves the following four-step procedure:

1. Create a five-year forecast of the main variables that affect external debt repayments. These include GDP growth, interest rate, the exchange rate and inflation.
2. Analyze the debt-to-GDP ratio over a five-year period or greater. The model developed for the evolution of the debt is consistent across all countries, only making adjustments for country-specific factors, but the general framework is the same:

$$b_t - b_{t-1} = (r - g)b_t + \vartheta fx_t - \gamma imp_t + \alpha cpi_t \tag{1}$$

Here b_t represent external debt at time t, r is the real interest rate, g is the real GDP growth rate and imp_t represents imports, fx_t is the exchange rate. The model is estimated in the standard vector autoregression (VAR) structure. The results are provided in Section 2.3.

2.3 Results: External Debt Sustainability

Policy to reduce the rate of depreciation of the local currency is recommended considering that currency depreciation increases Jamaica's foreign currency debt obligations. Policies supporting fewer imports will also reduce the country's foreign debt burden. Jamaica's policy under the IMF promoted a depreciation of the currency to materialize fewer imports is counterintuitive if there are no close substitutes available locally and people don't adjust their consumption patterns in the long run. Import substitution is the best recommended approach. There is a positive upward trajectory between the nominal exchange rate and Jamaica's debt servicing requirements as illustrated by Figure 2.12 in the appendix.

2.3.1 Impulse Response Functions

The impulse response functions in the appendix show how the external debt responds to a 1 percent standard deviation shock to the respective policy variables over time. The standard impulse response functions last for 10 periods. In the figures that follow, the blue line is the actual response functions while the red lines represent +/− one standard deviation.

Figure 2.9 illustrates the response of the debt to a one standard deviation shock to inflation. A one standard deviation increase in inflation results in a minor decline in the external debt servicing. Subsequently, as the model adjusts the debt increases over the next two years. The effect disappears after about eight periods.

Figure 2.10 shows the impulse response function of the debt to a one standard deviation shock to real interest rates. A one standard deviation increase in the real interest rate results in an increase in the external debt in the first period. The debt subsequently falls the next three consecutive periods as the effect disappears gradually.

Figure 2.11 shows how the debt responds to a one standard deviation shock to the exchange rate. The external debt increases marginally in response to change in the exchange rate. An increase in the exchange rate causes the debt to increase in the first period. The effect disappears after the first five periods. Since liberating its financial sector in 1992, Jamaica has accrued approximately US $753 million of debt per annum. Of this, US $449 million represents principal and US $304 million in interest is owed on average each year to international lenders. Over the same time frame, the exchange rate depreciated at an average rate of 7 percent per annum, which increases the amount Jamaica must find to service each dollar of foreign debt accrued. Jamaica's debt servicing requirements increased by US $56 million on average per annum; US $33 million in principal payment and US $23 million in interest as a result of currency depreciation (see Table 2.2).

Not surprisingly, as domestic imports increase so does the external debt over the 40-year period of study. A one standard deviation increase in imports results in an instant increase in the external debt obligations. The effect falls in the second period, but increases again in the third period even more than it did in the first. This lagged effect insinuates that consumers borrow to consume and debt obligations become due after two periods (see Fig. 2.13).

Real GDP growth reduces the debt in the first two periods. Here again it appears that borrowings enhance growth marginally. However, repayments are due in the third period. The spike in the curve at year three indicates such (see Fig. 2.14).

2.3.2 *Variance Decomposition*

Most of the variation in the external debt is a result of the debt itself (see Fig. 2.8). High debt means high debt servicing over time. Debt is positively related to itself. In this case, as government borrows, interest and principal payments due reduce fiscal space in the budget, which the government must borrow to satisfy. This borrowing further increases debt servicing requirements. The effect, however, declines over time as some debts are serviced before others. After the first three periods, more than 60 percent of the variation in current debt is as a result of previous debt. The Consumer Price Index (CPI) accounts for 2 percent of the variation in the debt for the period and approximately 5 percent after (see Table 2.3). The real interest rate accounts for approximately 2 percent of the variation, while the exchange rate accounts for 0.5 percent. Imports account for the largest portion of the variation of the debt other than the debt itself. After the third period, imports account for more than 18 percent of the variation in foreign debt. These results are congruent with expectations; it is no secret that Jamaica borrow to supports its high import consumption bill. This pattern of behaviour has a real medium-term effect on debt repayments.

Table 2.2 The impact of currency depreciation on foreign debt servicing: Estimated from Bank of Jamaica's data

Year	*DbtActual*	*Principal*	*Interest*	*%dfx DbtActual*	*%dfx Principal*	*%dfx DebtInterest*	*%dfx*
1990	663.54	371.24	292.30	457.84	256.16	315.91	0.69
1991	620.57	364.67	255.90	546.10	320.91	480.57	0.88
1992	637.88	393.42	244.46	57.41	35.41	22.00	0.09
1993	542.12	340.55	201.57	178.90	112.38	66.52	0.33
1994	536.04	349.55	186.49	32.16	20.97	11.19	0.06
1995	592.56	400.39	192.17	29.63	20.02	9.61	0.05
1996	579.47	392.28	187.19	-28.97	-19.61	-9.36	-0.05
1997	523.07	344.77	178.30	15.69	10.34	5.35	0.03
1998	635.60	438.93	196.67	44.49	30.73	13.77	0.07
1999	603.45	418.05	185.40	60.35	41.81	18.54	0.10
2000	477.20	308.16	169.04	0.00	0.00	0.00	0.00
2001	591.42	319.63	271.79	41.40	22.37	19.03	0.07
2002	798.16	506.91	291.25	39.91	25.35	14.56	0.05
2003	812.76	500.42	312.34	154.42	95.08	59.34	0.19
2004	796.28	493.44	302.84	47.78	29.61	18.17	0.06
2005	901.24	543.03	358.21	63.09	38.01	25.07	0.07
2006	644.36	258.79	385.57	32.22	12.94	19.28	0.05
2007	911.35	483.40	427.95	45.57	24.17	21.40	0.05
2008	878.57	394.47	484.10	184.50	82.84	101.66	0.21
2009	590.95	387.70	203.25	-5.91	-3.88	-2.03	-0.01
2010	742.67	265.93	476.74	-7.43	-2.66	-4.77	-0.01
2011	1,162.30	677.91	484.39	11.62	6.78	4.84	0.01
2012	1,011.89	565.51	446.38	70.83	39.59	31.25	0.07
2013	991.35	584.88	406.47	138.79	81.88	56.91	0.14
2014	1,361.10	956.49	404.61	81.67	57.39	24.28	0.06
Average	753.12	448.90	304.23	56.00	33.11	22.90	0.07

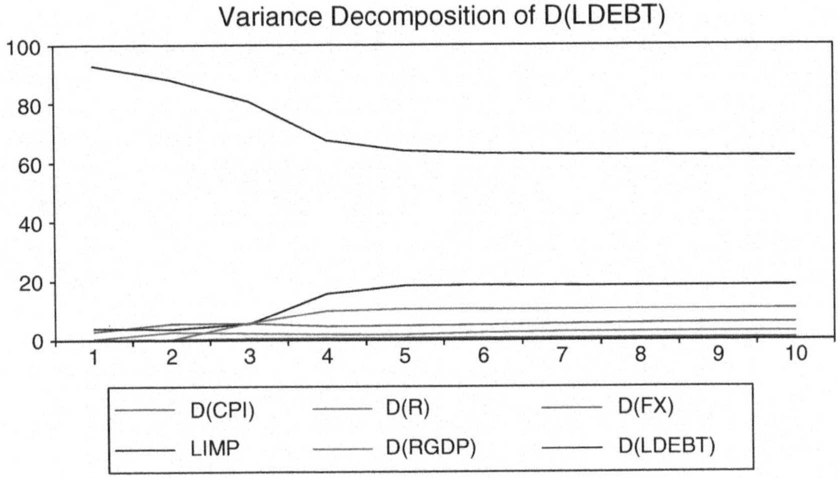

Fig. 2.8 Variance decomposition of shocks to external debt

2.3.3 *Existing Policy Analysis*

Jamaica borrowing to cushion its NIR and maintain the country's demand for imports is becoming more unsustainable. It appears the country's attempt to borrow its way out of problems is creating a cycle of perpetual borrowing. Figures 2.15 to 2.17 in the appendix illustrate Jamaica

Table 2.3 Variance decomposition of shocks to external debt

Variance decomposition of D(LDEBT):					
Period	*S.E.*	*D(CPI)*	*D(R)*	*D(FX)*	*LIMP*
1	0.243	2.742	0.187	0.000	3.906
2	0.286	5.429	2.538	0.055	3.584
3	0.312	5.509	2.132	0.307	5.349
4	0.348	4.553	1.743	0.385	15.688
5	0.362	4.726	1.684	0.393	18.421
6	0.368	4.898	2.294	0.491	18.598
7	0.371	5.247	2.600	0.514	18.415
8	0.373	5.529	2.650	0.510	18.318
9	0.375	5.652	2.648	0.510	18.384
10	0.376	5.694	2.639	0.508	18.449

foreign currency debt position with international institutions, international government and private institutions respectively. Jamaica first entered into an agreement with the IMF in 1973; the agreement lasted up until 1996. After this, bonds became the preferred option as a new source of borrowing and the cycle continued. Additional foreign currency requirements led to the signing of the EFF SBA with the IMF, resulting in an increase in foreign currency debt servicing requirements. Jamaica's inability to generate enough foreign currency to satisfy these obligations will lead to further foreign currency borrowing similar to the situation in Greece. This increase in borrowing will increase Jamaica's debt service requirements,and will further deplete government revenues, putting the country in a winding circular trap.

At the end of the EFF all borrowed sums have to be repaid to the IMF, and at this point if the NIR is depleted, the country might have to enter into a new IMF agreement, as it has been doing since the 1970s. The problem could be addressed if the country imports less of the goods that it can produce itself. This can only be achieved if the country increases capital investment necessary to increase productivity and boost efficiency.

2.4 Conclusion

The results indicate that Jamaica's foreign currency debt is unsustainable. An analysis of the debt impulse response functions indicates that manipulating certain variables can have an impact on the trajectory of the external debt. Exchange rate depreciation causes increases in Jamaica's foreign debt obligations each year. Jamaica's debt servicing requirements increase by US $56 million on average per annum; US $33 million in principal payment and US $23 million in interest as a result of currency depreciation. An increase in imports and the real interest rates also have an adverse effect on the nation's foreign currency debt obligations. As real GDP increases, the national debt falls over time. The results also indicate that as the debt stock increases, so does the country's debt servicing obligations. A one standard deviation shock to debt service requirements leads to further debt servicing requirements. Most of the variation in the debt is as a result of the debt itself. Eighteen percent of the variation in debt is a result of the imports. **The remainder can be explained by movements in imports, up to 2.6 percent, real interest rates and 0.5 percent the exchange rate.** Policy recommendations would suggest that keeping the exchange rate stable can reduce Jamaica foreign currency debt obligations. Policies supporting fewer imports will also reduce the country's foreign debt obligations. Jamaica's policy under the IMF promotes a depreciation of the currency to materialize fewer imports, but policies like these are counterintuitive on their own and should be supported by a strong push towards import substitution.

Appendix

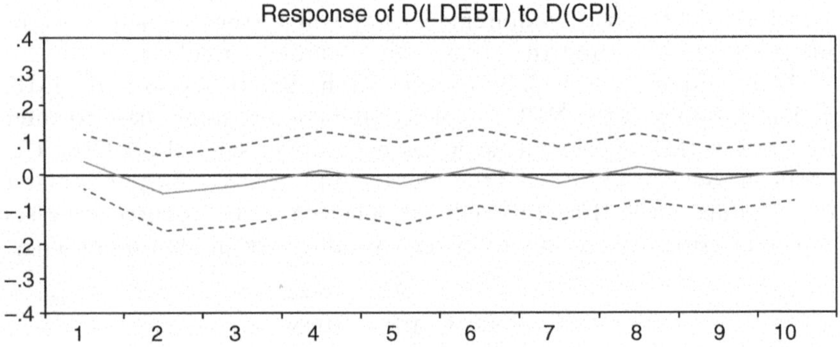

Fig. 2.9 Impulse response function of the foreign debt to CPI shocks

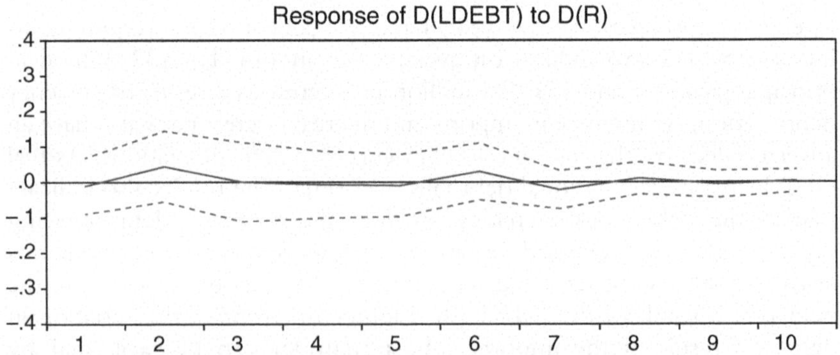

Fig. 2.10 Impulse response function of the foreign debt to real interest rate (R) shocks

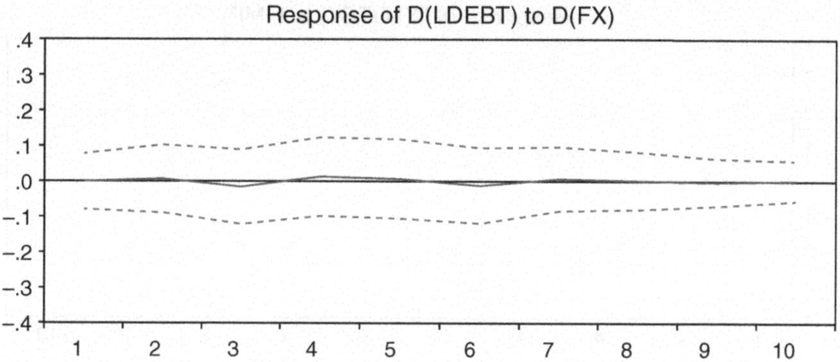

Fig. 2.11 Impulse response function of the foreign debt to exchange rate (FX) shocks

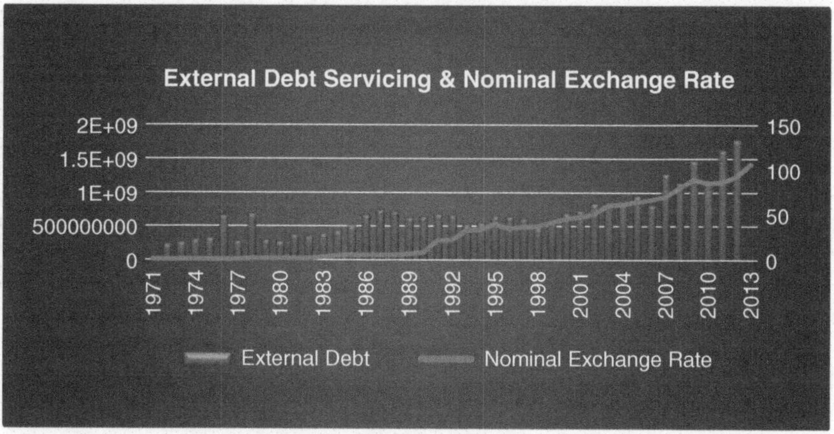

Fig. 2.12 Jamaica debt servicing and the nominal exchange rate: Bank of Jamaica

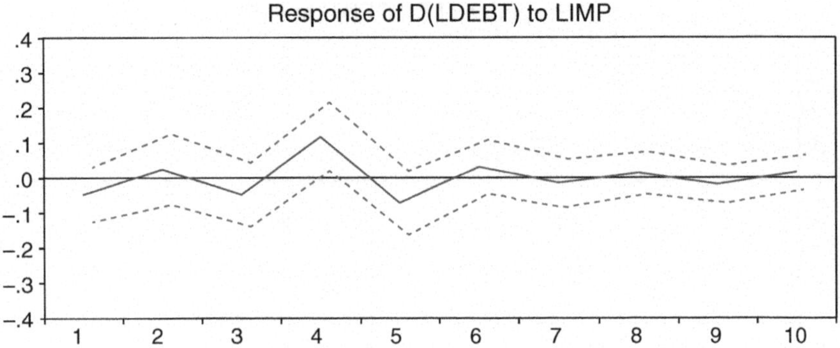

Fig. 2.13 Impulse response function of the foreign debt to shocks to imports

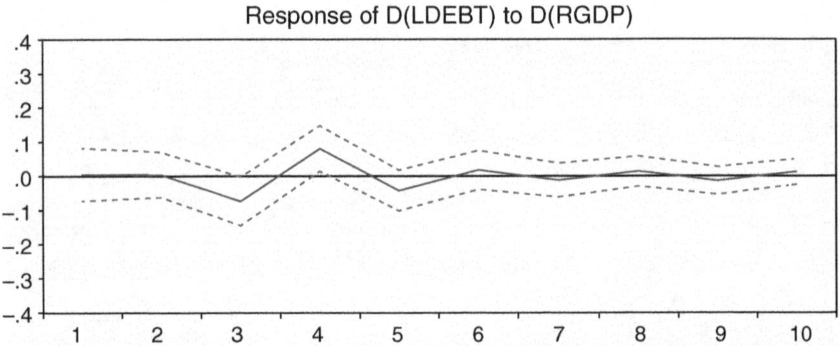

Fig. 2.14 Impulse response function of the foreign debt to shocks to real GDP

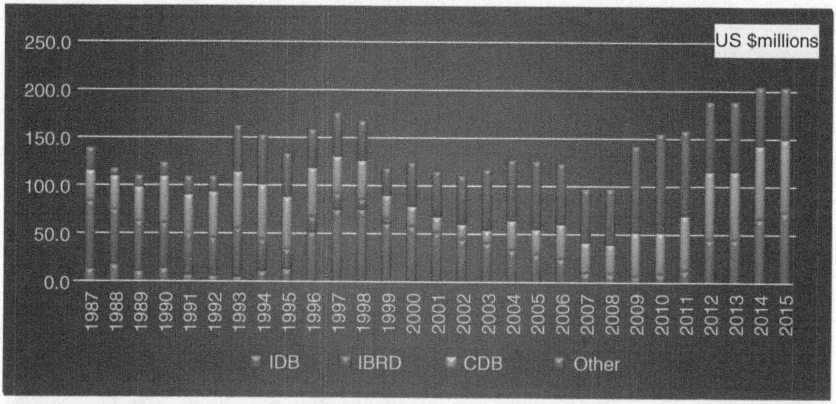

Fig. 2.15 Total Government foreign currency debt owed to international institutions

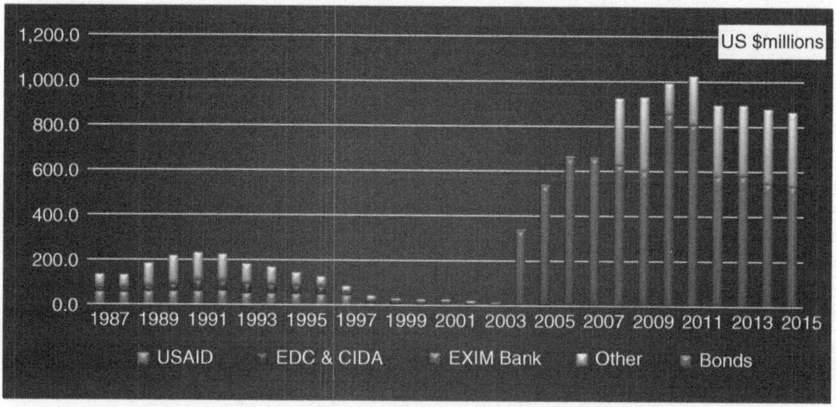

Fig. 2.16 Government foreign currency debt owed to international government

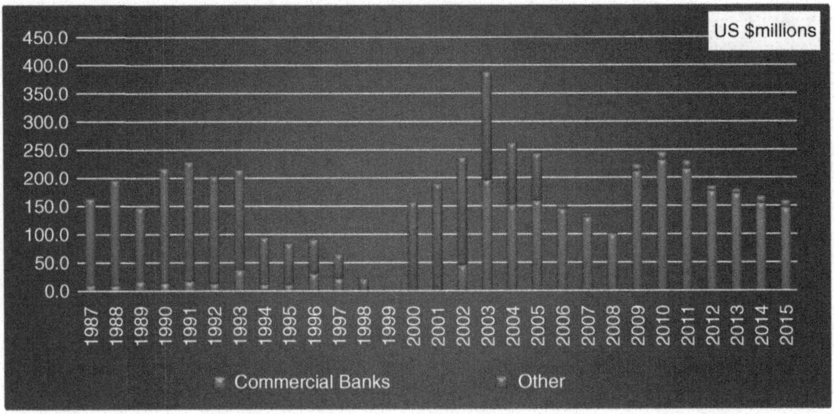

Fig. 2.17 Government foreign currency debt owed to private institutions

Notes

1. See The Financial Sector Adjustment Company (FINSAC) at www.Finsac.com.
2. See, for example, King and Tennant eds., Debt and Development in Small Islands Developing States (New York: Palgrave Macmillan, 2014).
3. For an extensive overview of the arrangement see the IMF country report 14/85, Jamaica.
4. On 1 July 2014, Jamaica secured USD $800 million in bond offers from the international lending market, a market that has been closed to Jamaica due to lack of confidence from international lenders caused by a failure of the government to pass the IMF test in 2010.
5. www.mof.gov.jm

CHAPTER 3

Determinants of Current Account Imbalances

3.1 The Current Account Balance

Jamaica's high foreign currency debt buildup and the country's inability to generate sufficient intrinsic foreign currency revenues to offset its foreign currency requirements is deeply rooted in the dynamics of the country's current account. Jamaica has consistently operated current account deficits. This condition was initiated from the time of the oil price shocks in the 1970s and has remained over the last 40 years. The balance has been negative for most of these years, indicating that Jamaica consistently imports more than it exports to the rest of the world due to its high foreign consumption patterns and strong reliability on foreign inputs for production processes. With low growth in GDP, the current account balance fluctuated between −14 percent and 3 percent of GDP prior to the global financial crisis of 2008. Jamaica has been unable to maintain a steady current account-to-GDP ratio. Its movement over time demonstrates a high level of volatility for the past 20 years (see Fig. 3.1).

Jamaica experienced its highest current account surplus in relation to GDP of 2.7 percent in the first quarter of 1997. Its lowest point, a deficit of –27.6 perecent of GDP recorded in the third quarter of 2008, in congruence with the global financial crisis of 2008. This was brewing from a year earlier as the country materialized a deficit of less than –23 percent of GDP in the fourth quarter of 2007. Subsequently, there was a drastic improvement

A. Haughton, *Developing Sustainable Balance of Payments in Small Countries*, DOI 10.1007/978-3-319-53031-4_3

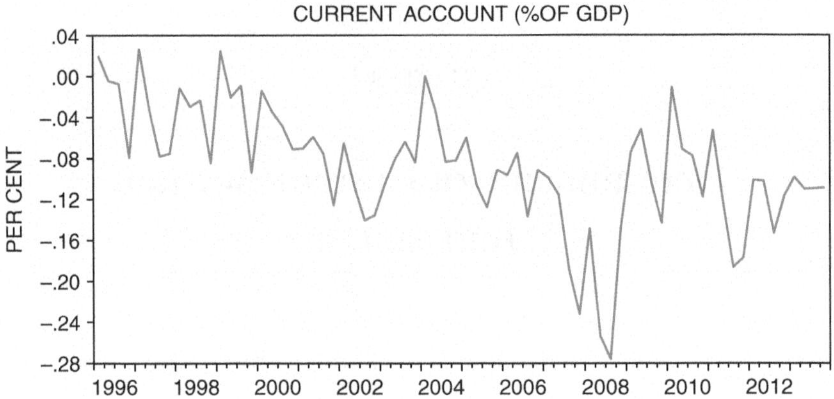

Fig. 3.1 Current account-to-GDP ratio

in the deficit, elevating to about –5 percent of GDP in the third quarter of 2009 only to fall again to about −13 percent of GDP in the fourth quarter. The current account-to-GDP ratio improved to almost zero in 2010, later falling once more to less than −15 percent of national output by the second quarter of 2011. Up to the beginning of 2014, the current account-to-GDP ratio was −13 percent of GDP, way below the international benchmark of 5 percent of GDP the country should have been maintaining.

Figure 3.2 illustrates Jamaica's current account balance from 1995 to 2013; it measures the extent to which the economy is a net borrower or net lender vis-à-vis the rest of the world over a particular period. The current account balance is the outcome of investment and saving decisions of optimizing agents. Against this background, the behaviour of the current account is an important indicator of the resource balance in the domestic economy and as such, is a critical variable in macroeconomic policy-making. Policies to address Jamaica's current account deficit have essentially involved exchange rate adjustments above the inflation differential of Jamaica in relation to its major trading partners. However, modelling of real exchange rate and of the current account determination has been, and remains, one of the most challenging topics of research in open-economy macroeconomics.

Jamaica's high propensity to consume foreign goods and services, with little to supply to the rest of the world, has resulted in continuous negative current account balances. Jamaica's high debt-to-GDP ratio has reduced the

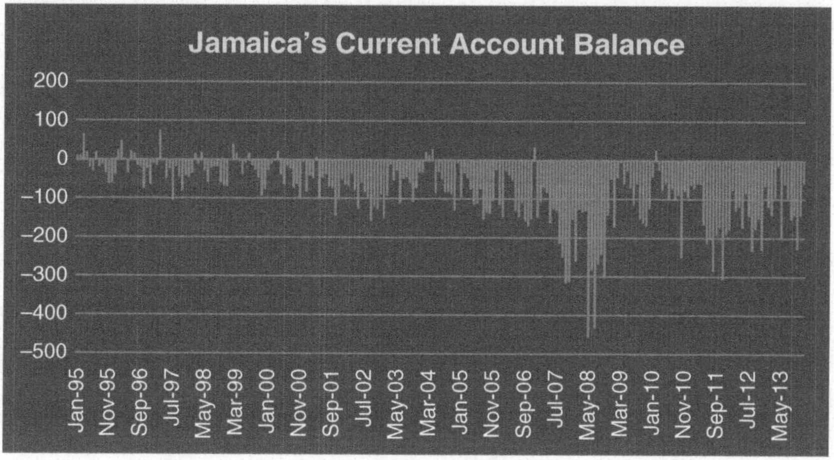

Fig. 3.2 Jamaica's current account balance from 1995Q1 to 2013Q4

country's ability to grow. Tax revenues are redirected from developmental projects to debt servicing and poor infrastructural development has led to poor growth in the country's output, as a result of a weak terms of trade (see Figures 3.3 to 3.7). The sustainability of Jamaica's current account has been a cause for concern, especially since the deficit is financed by medium-term foreign currency debt and/or depleting foreign currency reserves. Jamaica's ability to generate sufficient foreign currency inflow to satisfy long-run foreign currency obligations is questionable and must be analyzed thoroughly.

As part of the Extended Fund Facility (EFF), the International Monetary Fund (IMF) has advised that Jamaica's foreign currency flows can become more sustainable if the current account deficit improves to approximately 5 percent of national output or better. Motivated by economic theory, they assert that this can be achieved more quickly if the country relaxes its monetary policy interventions used to support the currency, which they suggest is overvalued. The first thing to recognize is that currency devaluation is usually done under a fixed exchange rate regime. Jamaica currently operates under a floating exchange rate system. Therefore, the exchange rate is determined by market demand, albeit with interventions by the Bank of Jamaica (BOJ) when the underlying market conditions change. A country's ability to maintain a strong value for its currency depends on the availability of foreign reserves. In the presence of high demand, the lack of adequate

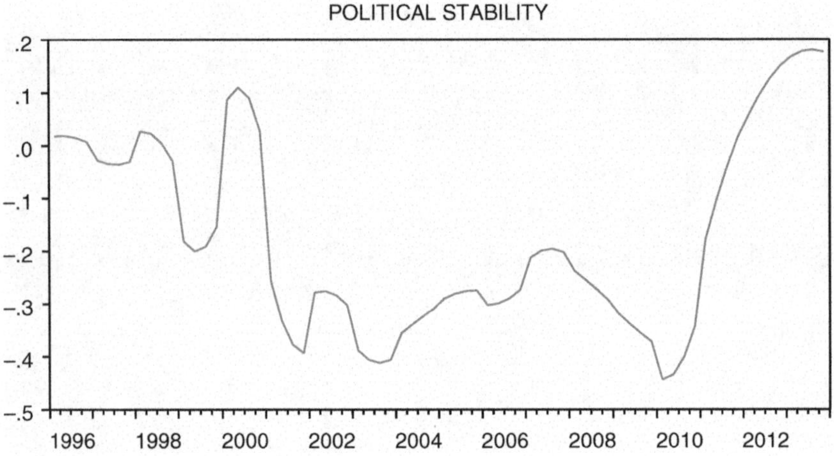

Fig. 3.3 Political stability

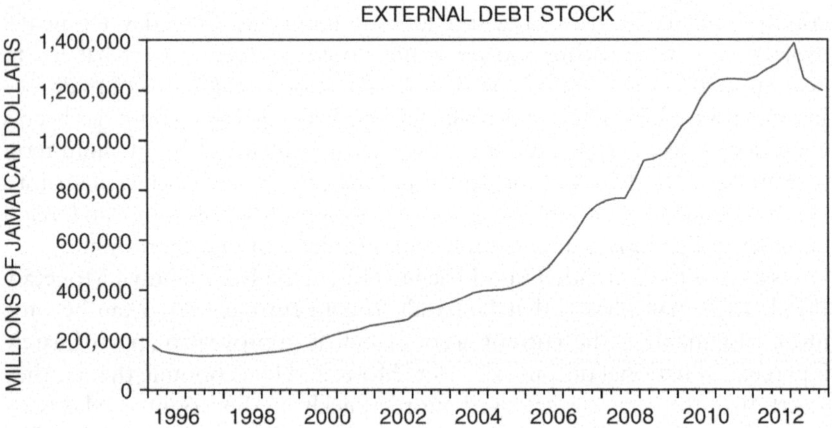

Fig. 3.4 External debt stock (millions of Jamaican dollars)

reserves pushes the exchange rate upwards leading to currency depreciations. If consumer preference for goods and services is flexible and demand is elastic, this should result in a change in consumption pattern where consumers choose cheaper Jamaican goods and services in lieu of the more

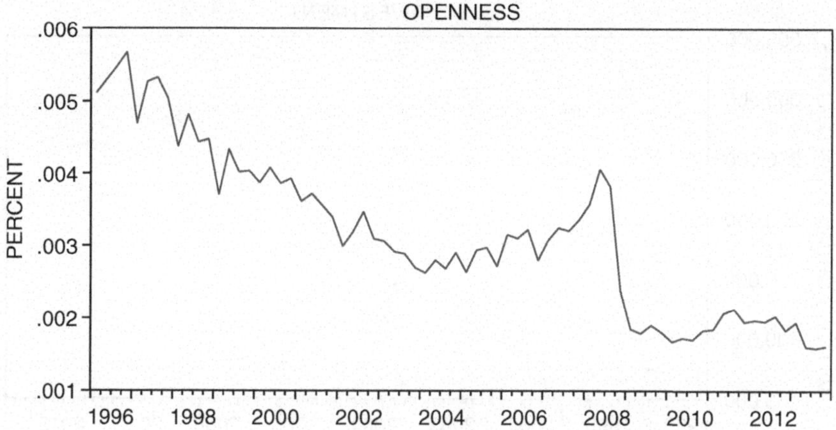

Fig. 3.5 Openness and Trade

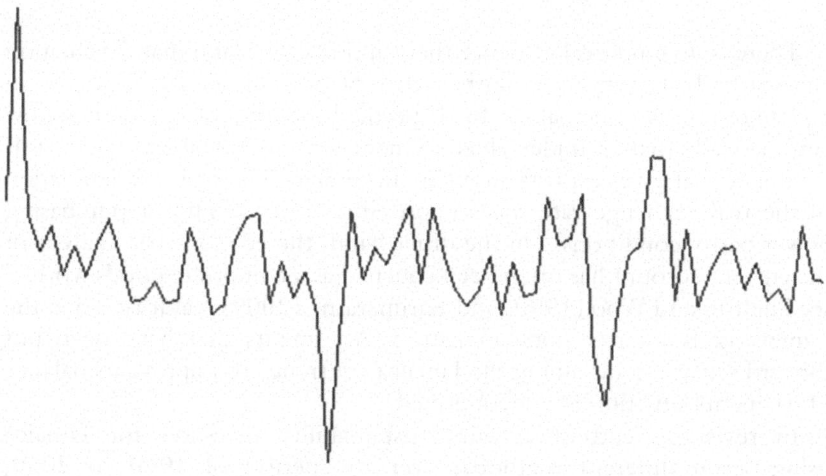

Fig. 3.6 Change in the Real Effective Exchange Rate (REER)

expensive foreign goods and services based on international price differentials. The depreciation should eradicate any disequilibrium between the supply of and the demand for foreign currency, such that the local dollar reaches its true exchange rate value.

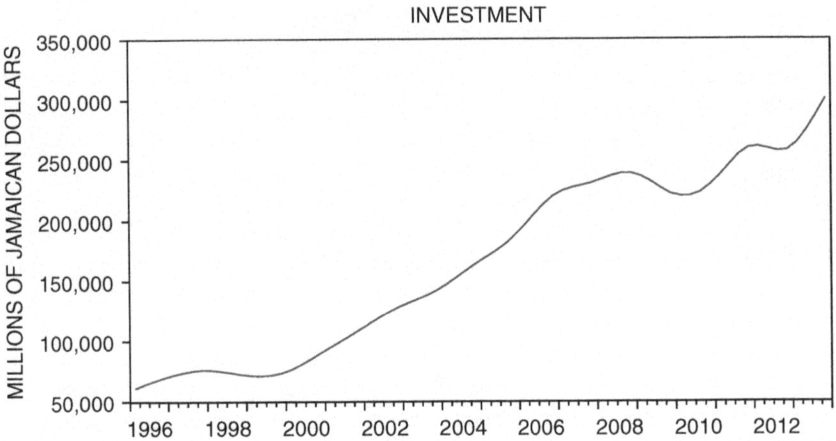

Fig. 3.7 Investment (millions of Jamaican dollars) bank of Jamaica

There is no empirical evidence that supports the claim that devaluation automatically restores a country's current account deficit. Even if an exchange rate is undervalued by a specified measure, it does not follow automatically that an undervalued exchange rate is a deliberate mercantilist policy that gives exports an unfair advantage. The typical examination of the real exchange rate relies upon either interest rate or purchasing power parity conditions. On the other hand, the econometric analysis of the current account has often been couched as a composite goods world – see Sheffrin and Woo (1990) and Karunaratne (2009) – at least when the framework is intertemporal in nature. Arguments that have been put forward regarding devaluing the Jamaican currency to improve its balance of payments situation are unconfirmed.

In revisiting current account sustainability measures for Jamaica using seven different methods, over the period of 1960 to 2009, Rochester (2009) found extensive evidence to suggest that Jamaica's current account deficit is not sustainable over time. Six of the seven models employed in this analysis indicated that the current account was not sustainable. Based on international standards, a current account-to-GDP ratio of 5 percent is acceptable for small island developing states such as Jamaica. Jamaica's new EFF agreement with the IMF is geared towards helping the country achieve this objective in the short to medium term. Jamaica's current account-to-GDP ratio was less than 9 percent at the beginning of 2014 and has been gradually falling since. If it maintains the same trajectory on a consistent basis, it might be able to become sustainable in the long run.

In light of Jamaica's unsustainable current account balance, it is important to understand whether there are any long-run drivers of current account movement over time. To this end, the aim of this chapter is to investigate and verify if there are any variables or group of variables that jointly influence the long-run movement of Jamaica's current account-to-GDP ratio. Given that the current account as it stands is unsustainable, the analysis explores the significant drivers of the current account focusing on the country's economic structure, macroeconomic policy and political economy. Some of these indicators are linked to the capital account as well as to the fundamentals underlying the current account.

This analysis employs a similar approach to that of Brissimis et al. (2013) who analyzed the determinants of current account imbalances in the European Union (EU) within the same intertemporal consumption smoothing approach using panel data for a group of 17 EU member states. The results indicate that all the determinants of saving and investment, including the level of development, demographics, macroeconomic and competitiveness, appear to be important long-run current account drivers.

3.1.1 Literature on Current Account Sustainability

Research on the sustainability of current account has been ongoing. Different researchers applying different techniques have yielded a variety of results (see Gould and Ruffin 1996; Fountas and Wu 1999; Wu, Chen and Lee 2001; and Mann (2002). Most have employed an intertemporal model of the current account to analyze the issue. More recently, Adedeji and Handa (2008) employed a set of macroeconomic indicators and the intertemporal model of the current account in an attempt to examine the excessiveness and sustainability of Nigeria's current account deficits over the period 1960–2003. Specific to the intertemporal model, Adedeji and Handa used the Present Value Model of the Current Account (PVMCA) to determine the optimal current account balance. The results from this model revealed that there were excessive current account deficits, relative to the estimated optimal current account balances. These excessive current account deficits were attributed to consumption tilting. Analysis of the macroeconomic indicators as an assessment tool of the Nigerian current account deficits revealed that they were excessive and unsustainable over the study period.

In an earlier but similar study, Adedeji (2001) used an identical approach to examine the size and sustainability of the Nigerian current account deficits over the period 1960–1997. The results showed that the Nigerian economy appeared to satisfy its intertemporal budget constraint during the period. However, there were some years during which current account deficits were identified. The results also support the view that current account deficits coupled with macroeconomic instability and structural weaknesses can lead to an external crisis.

To investigate the sustainability of the current account in the Czech Republic, Hungary and Slovenia, since their move towards market economy, Konya (2008) also utilized the intertemporal approach. Empirical analysis of the model showed that if real exports and real exchange rates are first difference stationary, then cointegration between the two is a necessary and sufficient condition for the economy to satisfy its intertemporal budget constraint. After performing various unit-root testing procedures and testing for cointegration, the study concluded that the Czech Republic and Slovenia operated within the confines of their intertemporal budget constraint. It also showed that their trade imbalances are sustainable.

Karunaratne (2010) highlights that after the Australian economy moved from a fixed to a floating exchange rate regime, the Keynesian Mundell Fleming (KMF) model was no longer useful in assessing the sustainability of Australia's current account deficits. The Intertemporal Optimization (ITO) paradigm was deemed more appropriate under the floating exchange. This intertemporal model was based on an extension of the permanent income hypothesis to the open economy. This hypothesis says that consumption expenditure depends on expected permanent income rather than on current disposable income. Within a floating exchange rate regime, the current account deficit is the residual outcome of rational optimization decisions of private agents. If, however, there was a fiscal balance, then the policy of targeting the reduction of the current account deficit based on the KMF paradigm was flawed. Results based on the application of the net present value criterion using vector autoregressions, unit-root and cointegration revealed that Australia's current account deficits were unsustainable during the fixed exchange period and over the whole study period (1960Q3–2007Q4), but not during the floating exchange rate period post–1983Q4. These results give credence to the need for a shift from the KMF to the ITO model when there is a switch from a fixed to a floating exchange rate regime.

The intertemporal model is used again in Baharumshah and Ismail (2012). They applied the F-test, the Bartlett test, and the Siegel–Tukey test to formally validate for equality of the variances of the optimal and actual consumption-smoothing current accounts. Results based on a vector autoregressive (VAR) model showed that the present value of the future net output closely reflects the evolution of the current account series with a small deviation between the actual and the estimated consumption-smoothing current account. The hypothesis of full-consumption smoothing could not be rejected given the data for the sample period, which further implies that there was a high degree of capital mobility. In addition, the variance ratio of the actual current account to the optimal current account is not statistically significant. Therefore, they concluded that there is no evidence to suggest inappropriate use of capital flows over the sample period.

3.2 Bounds Test for Cointegration

The current account sustainability analysis indicates that Jamaica's current account is unsustainable in the long run in line with the results of Rochester (2009). Subsequently the Bounds Test approach is used to examine the factors that might have a long-run impact on Jamaica's current account.

Variables employed are as follows:

- current account balance as a percentage of Gross Domestic Product (GDP)
- changes in the Real Effective Exchange Rate (C_REER)
- political stability (POL_STAB)
- openness and trade (OPEN)
- investment (INVEST)
- external debt stock (EXT_DEBT_STOCK)
- corruption control (CORR_CON)
- changes in foreign reserves (CHG_RES)

The augmented Dickey–Fuller unit root test is used to examine the stationarity properties of the variables used in the analysis. The results from the unit root tests confirm that the variables of interest are integrated of different orders over time (see Table 3.1). Therefore, the regular Engle and Granger

Table 3.1 Restrictions on linear coefficients

Test statistic	*Value*	*Df*	*Probability*
F-statistic	3.387679	(8, 61)	0.0028
Chi-square	27.10144	8	0.0007
Null Hypothesis: C(2)=C(3)=C(4)=C(5)=C(6)=C(7)=C(8)=C(9)=0			

(1987) and VAR-based tests of Johansen (1988) and Johansen and Juselius (1990) are mis-specified given these conditions. To correct this, we follow Lin (2012) by employing the Autoregressive Distributed Lag model (ARDL) Bounds Test approach proposed by Pesaran et al. (2001). This approach solves the problem, as it provides valid test results even if the variables are integrated of different orders. Using this Bounds Test procedure, the order of integration of the variables does not have to be the same; i.e., it accounts for the inclusion of both I(0) and I(1) in the same equation. Here, similar to Lin (2012), we employ the Bounds Test corresponding to the *Case v*, from Pesaran et al (2001), which accounts for an unrestricted intercept and an unrestricted trend in the model.

3.2.1 Model Specification

The ARDL model is specified in VAR terms as follows:

$$z_t = \alpha + \omega t + \sum_{i=1}^{p} \gamma_i z_{t-i} + \varepsilon_t, t = 1, 2 \ldots, T \tag{3.1}$$

where α represents a $(k+1)$ vector of intercepts/drifts and ω is a vector of $(k+1)$ trend coefficients. Given this, Pesaran et al. (2001) derived the following Vector Error Correction Model (VECM) corresponding to equation (3.1):

$$z_t = \alpha + \grave{u} t + \Pi z_{t-1} + \sum_{i=1}^{p} \theta_i \Delta z_{t-i} + \varepsilon_t, t = 1, 2 \ldots, T \tag{3.2}$$

Here the $(k+1) \times (k+1)$ matrices $\Pi = I_{k+1} + \sum_{i=1}^{p} \mu_j$ and $\theta_i = -\sum_{i=1}^{p} \mu_j i = 1, 2 \ldots, p-1$, as outlined by Lin (2012), contain the long-run multipliers and the short-run dynamic coefficients of the VECM, and z_t is the vector of dependent variables y_t and regressors x_t.

After regressing the ARDL model, the Bounds Test procedure requires conducting an F-test on the joint significance of lagged levels of the variables in the model. The null hypothesis is that the lagged levels of the variables are insignificant, i.e., $\Pi = 0$ against the alternative that they are jointly significant, i.e., $\Pi \neq 0$. Under the ARDL model, the F-statistic can no longer be compared to the critical values of the F-tables. Instead, the Bounds Test provides two asymptotic critical values for which to compare the calculated F-statistic. It provides a lower bound critical value assuming the variables are I(0) and an upper bound critical value assuming the variables are I(1). If the F-statistic is greater than the critical value for the upper bound, the null of no cointegrating relationship can be rejected. If the F-statistic falls between the upper and lower bound then the test is inconclusive, and if the F-statistic is lower than the critical value for the lower bound then the null of no cointegrating cannot be rejected.

3.3 Bounds Test Results

The results from the analysis of the long-run relationship between the variables using the Bounds Test for cointegration are provided in Table 3.2. The null hypothesis of no cointegration is rejected at the 10 percent, 5 percent and 1 percent level of significance, indicating there is a long-run relationship between the current account-to-GDP ratio and the dependent variables; percentage of Gross Domestic Product (GDP), changes in the real effective exchange rate (C_REER), political stability (POL_STAB), openness and trade (OPEN), investment (INVEST), external debt stock (EXT_DEBT_STOCK), corruption control (CORR_CON) and changes in foreign reserves (CHG_RES). A description of these variables and their impact on the current account-to-GDP ratio is provided in the section that follows.

3.3.1 Political Stability

Political stability is important for macroeconomic stability, which is necessary for growth. A country with high levels of political instability has reduced 'credibility of the current policy stance' (Adedeji and Handa, 2008). If the government is in favour of free capital mobility, then free capital movement

Table 3.2 Description of variables employed in current account analysis

Name of variable	*Description*	*Z(t)*	*p-value*	*5% critical value*	*Order of integration*
C_GDP	Change in GDP	4.289	0.000***	2.903	I(0)
C_REER	Change in REER	123.139	0.000***	2.903	I(0)
CHG_RES	Change in foreign exchange reserves	6.3913	8.931	2.903	I(1)
CORR_CON	Corruption control	2.6679	0.085	2.909	I(0)
INVEST	Investment	0.1509	0.9674	2.904	I(1)
EXT_DEBT_STOCK	External debt stock	0.1584	0.9676	2.910	I(1)
OPEN	Openness and trade	1.4912	0.5323	2.903	I(1)
POL_STAB	Political stability	1.607	0.4732	2.906	I(1)

is more likely to occur. The results indicate that there is a positive relationship between political stability and economic growth (see Fig. 3.3).

Jamaica experienced a relatively high level of political stability in varying patterns over the course of the study period. For the 17 years being examined, the People's National Party (PNP) governed the country for 13 years (1996–2007 and 2011–2013), with the only change of government being the period of (2007–2011) when the Jamaica Labour Party (JLP) was in power. However, despite this stability, Jamaica continued to experience political and economic turmoil. This inevitably led to reduced foreign investment and growth in the country.

3.3.2 Total External Debt

A large external debt makes it difficult to finance current account deficits, Fig. 3.4 displays total external debt stock in Jamaican currency. This also means that servicing the debt takes away from further investment in the country. With Jamaica being one of the most indebted countries in the world, sustaining the current account is made even more difficult. For Jamaica, total external debt is measured as debt owed to non-residents repayable in currency, goods or services. It is the sum of public, publicly guaranteed and private non-guaranteed long-term debt, use of IMF credit and short-term debt.[1]

3.3.3 Openness and Trade

The openness variable is measured as the ratio of net exports to GDP. The higher the ratio, the more open the economy, see Fig. 3.5 displaying Jamaica's level of openness from 1995 to 2013. A high degree of openness increases the vulnerability of the country to any external stimuli, often in the form of crises. This is often seen in countries with a thin export base as a result of the over-reliance on one-commodity exports. This vulnerability will increase, and the ability of the country to sustain deficits will weaken, if the country has a narrow export base and is particularly dependent on imported raw materials. It is reduced if the country's composition of trade is well diversified across commodities.

3.3.4 Real Effective Exchange Rate (REER)

The REER is a weighted average of a country's currency adjusted for inflation. Adedeji and Handa (2008) described a real appreciation of the exchange rate as being associated with a large current account deficit. The Jamaican experience is different as the two variables have run counter to theoretical predictions. The 1992 and 1994 appreciation in the REER occurred with current account surpluses. This counter argument lends support to Henry and Longmore's (2003) suggestion that policies in Jamaica that are directed at promoting current account sustainability through the real exchange rate changes may be ineffective. Figure 3.6 illustrates changes in Jamaica's REER from 1995 to 2013.

The evidence shows that an increase in the REER contributes positively to Jamaica's current account balance in the long run. As the REER appreciates in the long run, given the current political climate, Jamaica's current account position improves. This too is both economically and statistically significant indicated by P-value of 0.000, which is less than the 0.05 required for significance.

3.3.5 *Investment*

Increased investment domestically appears to have a positive impact on the long-run sustainability of Jamaica's current account as illustrated by the results. Investment in the Jamaican economy displays a gradually increasing trend from1995 to 2013 (see Fig. 3.7). The evidence shows that local investment boosts output/productivity, which can increase the country's exports, contributing positively to Jamaica's current account balance in the long run. Though not statistically significant, indicated by P-value of 0.000 greater than the 0.05 the rest are of economic importance.

The current account balance is the difference between national savings and domestic investment. Investment levels can have major implications for current account sustainability. High levels of investment imply higher future growth through the build-up of a larger productive capacity; they enhance solvency.

3.3.6 *Economic Growth*

As GDP grows, we expect that the country should be exporting more given that it is producing more. In this case, there is a positive relationship between GDP growth and Jamaica's current account balance. The relationship is both economically and statistically significant indicated by P-value of 0.000, which is less than the 0.05 required for significance.

The higher a country's GDP growth rate, the greater the current account imbalance it can sustain without increasing its external debt-to-GDP ratio. Also, a high GDP growth may reflect sustained capital accumulation rates driven by expectations of high profitability. If the growth rate exceeds (is less than) the real rate of interest on the external debt, then the addition to total GDP is greater (less) than that of external debt.

The annual growth rate for Jamaica during the study period was 2.4 percent. Jamaica experienced its highest growth for the study period in the fourth quarter of 2012 with a rate of 8 percent and the lowest growth of −3 percent in the second quarter of 2002. Changes in GDP from 1995 to 2013 is displayed in Fig. 3.8.

3.3.7 *Foreign Exchange Reserves*

Change in foreign exchange reserves is illustrated in Fig. 3.9. The results show no significant impact on the current account in the analysis.

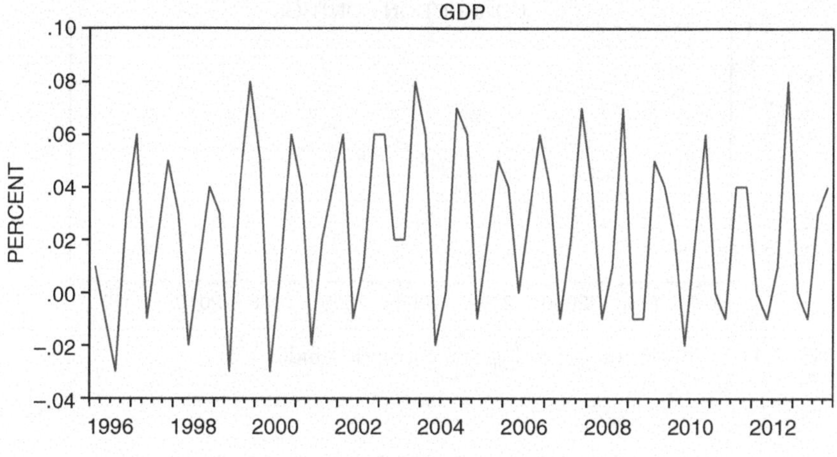

Fig. 3.8 Change in GDP from 1995 to 2013

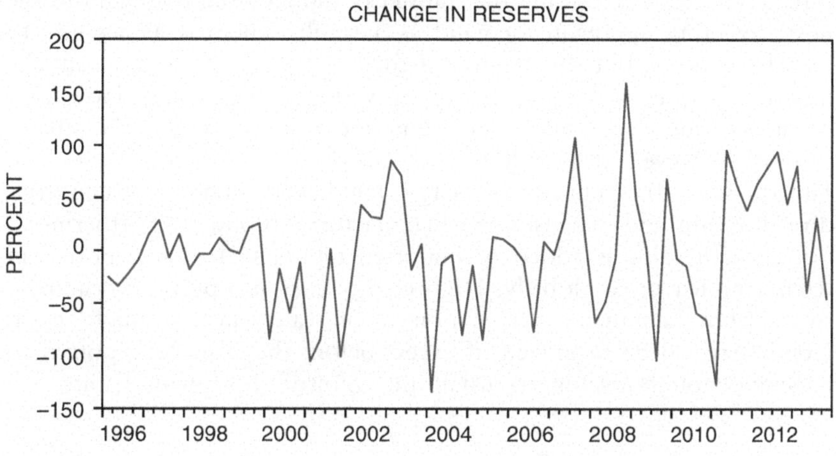

Fig. 3.9 Change in foreign exchange reserves: Bank of Jamaica

3.3.8 Corruption Control

Corruption is still prevalent in Jamaica and is sometimes seen as a solution to the high-level inefficiency that exists, corruption control in Jamaica based on the global corruption index is illustrated in Fig. 3.10. The

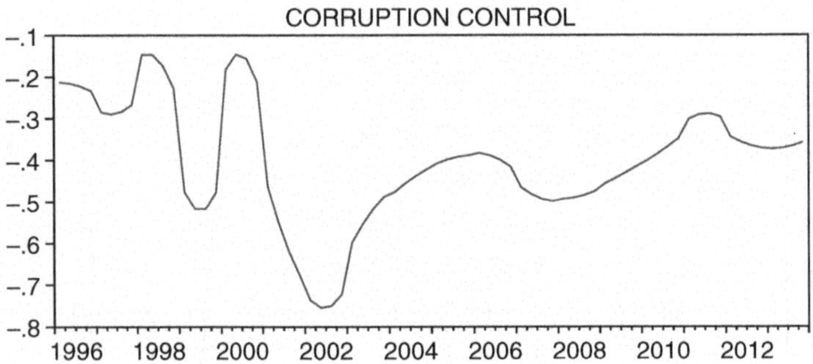

Fig. 3.10 Corruption control global corruption index

economy has been improving marginally on the books, but very little has improved in real life. Many are trapped in a low-income, high-expenditure cycle, which is limiting the transfer of money from one hand to the next, lowering aggregate demand as a result. There is an agenda to increase exports, but this is futile if there is no agenda to substantially increase output and productivity in various sectors and industries. Manufacturing is an important component in the country's mix of exports, however, it is still too expensive to manufacture goods in Jamaica due to the high cost of energy. This has constrained the country's diversification and expansion of manufactured products. Furthermore, not enough value is added to imported inputs such that exports can fetch a higher price globally. High energy cost also prevents manufacturers from capitalizing on economies of scale where it might exist. Goods have to be produced in excess before they can be exported to generate enough revenue to sustain the country's borrowing habits.

3.4 Conclusion

Having identified that Jamaica's current account balance is unsustainable over time (Rochester 2009), this analysis explores key drivers to the long-run sustainability of Jamaica's current account using similar approach to that of Brissimis et al (2013) who analyze the determinants of current account imbalances in the euro area. The Bounds Test for cointegration is employed using data from 1996 to present. The results indicate that there is a long-run relationship between the current account-to-GDP ratio and percentage of GDP, changes in the Real Effective Exchange Rate (C_REER), political stability (POL_STAB), openness and trade (OPEN), investment (INVEST), external debt stock (EXT_DEBT_STOCK), corruption control (CORR_CON) and changes in foreign reserves (CHG_RES).

A depreciation of the REER and an increase in GDP growth contributes positively to the sustainability of Jamaica's current account balance. By improving the political environment and increasing corruption control and political stability, Jamaica can improve its current account position in the long run.

Note

1. Short-term debt includes all debt having an original maturity of one year or less and interest in arrears on long-term debt. Data are in current US dollars.

CHAPTER 4

Current Account Subgroups and Real Exchange Rate Dynamics

4.1 Introduction

A policy geared towards increasing the amount of foreign currency a country earns from its exports is important for a country to increase its Debt Servicing Coverage Ratio (DSCR).[1] Jamaica often borrows foreign currency from the International Monetary Fund (IMF) and other international lending institutions.[2] As a complement to this borrowing arrangement, under the last Extended Fund Facility (EFF) granted to Jamaica by the IMF, it was recommended that the Jamaican dollar is overvalued and should depreciate to increase international competitiveness of the island's produce. The notion put forward is that depreciation will restore current account sustainability gradually. This, while being true in some regard based on economic theory, may turn out to be a problem if a devaluation strategy is incongruent with the country's aspirations to achieve sustained economic growth. In the previous chapter, we found that the current account on aggregate is unsustainable but can recover if certain macroeconomic and political and global conditions improve.

This chapter dissects Jamaica's current account balance into its various components; goods balance, service balance, income balance and current transfers, and analyzes the impact of the Real Exchange Rate (RER) changes on each of them. The Real Exchange Rate (RER) against the US Dollar is employed in the analysis as oppose the Real Effective Exchange Rate (REER) which is a weighted basket of all the major currencies due to the

A. Haughton, *Developing Sustainable Balance of Payments in Small Countries*, DOI 10.1007/978-3-319-53031-4_4

fact that most of Jamaica's international purchases are invoiced in US dollars, for example, oil. It goes one step further into understanding how Jamaica can increase the flow of foreign currency via the sale of goods or the provision of services to the global marketplace. This chapter is particularly interested in understanding how Real Exchange Rate (RER) depreciation impacts the major goods and services imported and exported from the island on an annual basis. Jamaica's export strategy is analyzed and recommendations are made on how the country can improve its current account balance beyond just exchange rate depreciation and/or devaluation.

It is generally agreed that economic activity can be impacted by changes in REER through altering the relative returns in the tradable and non-tradable sectors. The REER is a weighted average of the Jamaican dollar relative to an index or basket of other major currencies adjusted for inflation.[3] Using the *elasticities approach* to describe the effect of the REER on the current account components, an appreciation in the REER should result in lower export levels and higher import levels in each category, thus the goods balance, services balance, current transfers and income should fall. Alternatively, when the REER depreciates, these components should improve due to lower imports and higher exports.

Therefore, theoretically there should be a positive co-movement between each component of the current account and the real exchange rate. A similar relationship is observed using the RER. As such, RER is considered an appropriate proxy for the REER.[4] However, a number of studies have found no significant relationship between the REER and Jamaica's current account; see Henry and Longmore (2003) and Wilson and McLean (2014). Against this background, this study seeks to explore the influence of the RER on the various components of the current account. They are provided in order of their positive contribution to the overall current account balance. Current transfers and the services are in surplus, which helps to offset the negative income balance and goods balance, which contributes the most to Jamaica's current account deficit. Figures 4.1 to 4.4 illustrate the movement of each component of the current account plotted against RER changes.

The preliminary assessment suggests that adjustments in the RER have no significant or direct impact on the goods and income sub-accounts of the current account. However, movements in the RER appear to have some influence on the services sub-account. The goods deficit, influenced by a faster growth in imports relative to exports, has been the major driver of Jamaica's current account deficit over the period and is the least responsive to

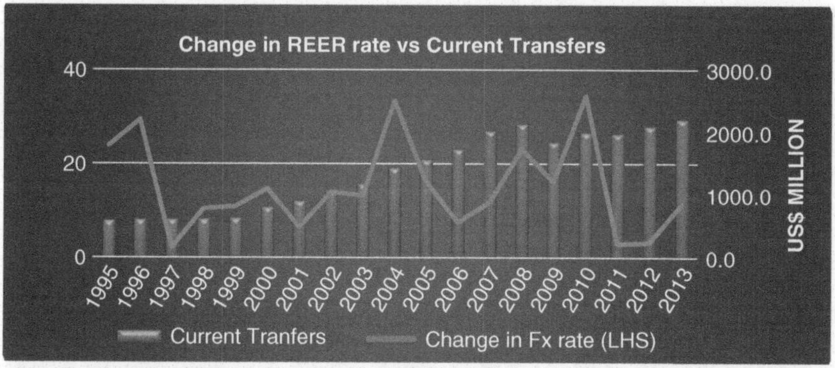

Fig. 4.1 Change in exchange rate vs current transfers: Bank of Jamaica

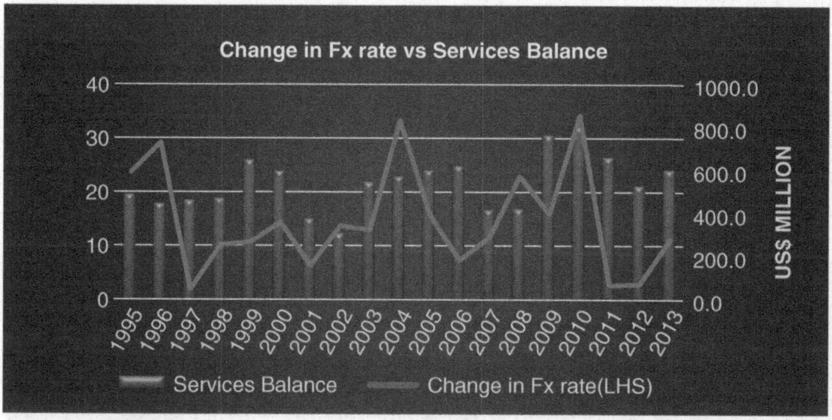

Fig. 4.2 Exchange rate and the services balance: Bank of Jamaica

fluctuations in the RER (see Figs. 4.4 to 4.6). In particular, Fig. 4.4 depicts the relationship between the RER and the goods balance, and shows that prior to 2008 there was a significant increase in the deficit on the goods sub-account, despite the trend depreciation in the RER since 1997. In fact, the deficit on the goods sub-account averaged 13.0 percent of GDP in fiscal year 1998/1999 and rose to 33.8 percent in fiscal year 2008/2009, while the depreciation in the RER ranged from 4.8 to 5.6 percent over the same period. This seemingly

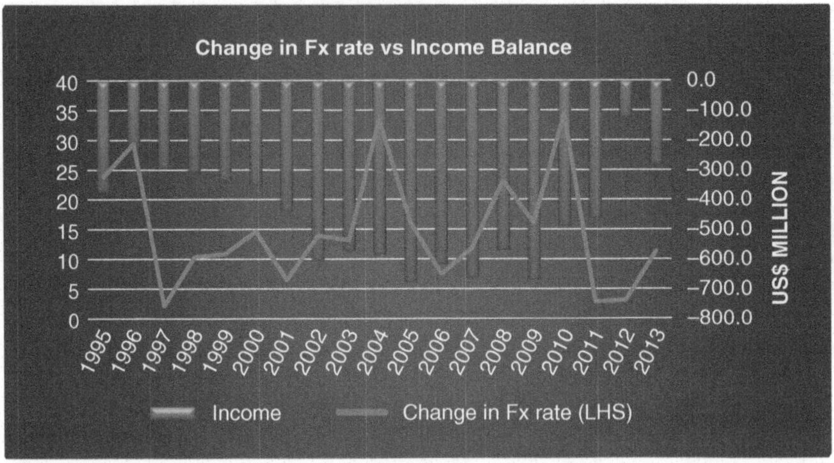

Fig. 4.3 Exchange rate and the income balance

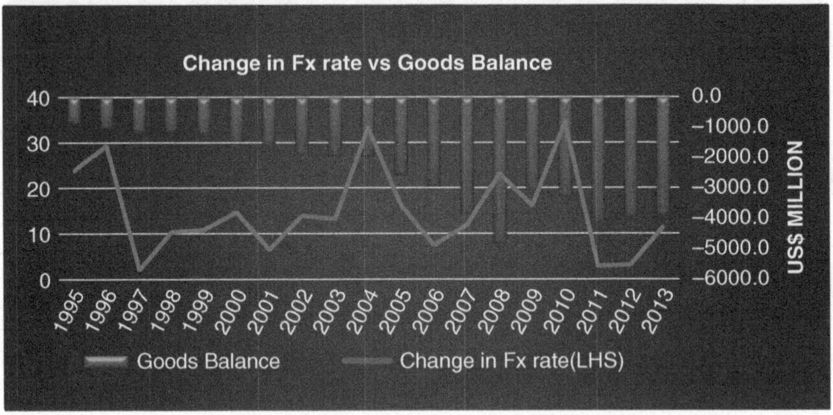

Fig. 4.4 Exchange rate and the goods balance

paradoxically movement between two variables is mostly explained by the composition of Jamaica's main imports and exports. Jamaica's main imports have been fuel and consumer goods while the main exports include products from the mining sector, and to a lesser extent, agricultural produce. Note: a

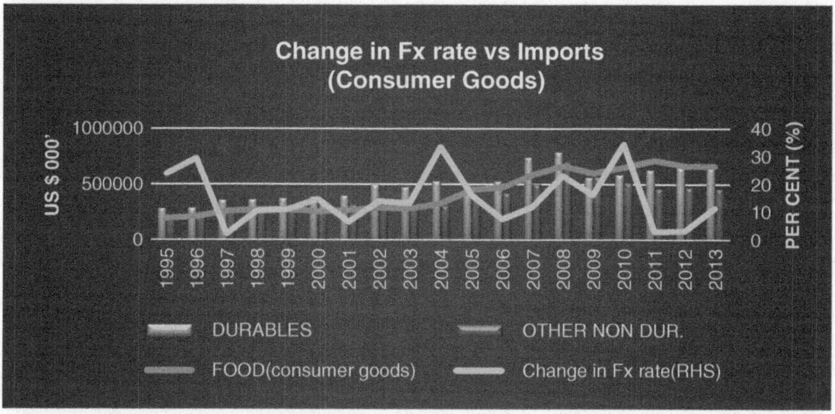

Fig. 4.5 Change in the exchange rate and the import of goods, Bank of Jamaica

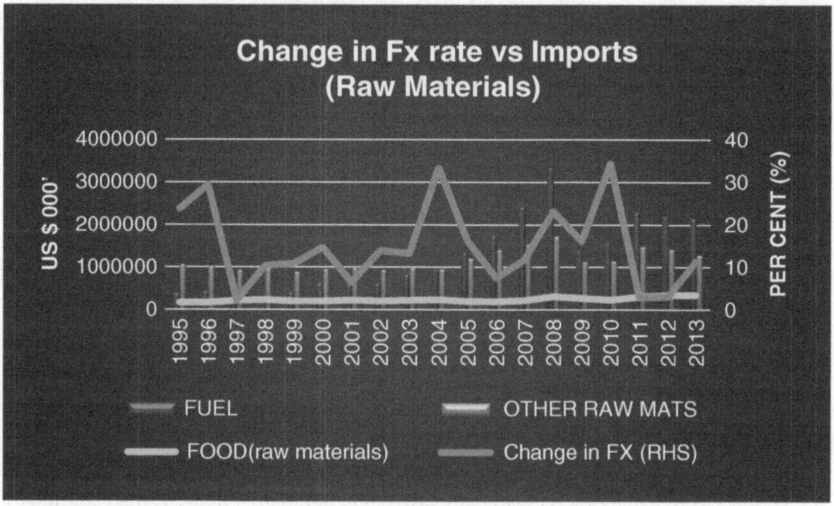

Fig. 4.6 Change in exchange rate and the imports of raw material

depreciation is illustrated by an increase in the RER. The opposite movement holds true for an appreciation in the RER.

The primary motivation for this chapter is to identify whether the argument for devaluation is valid for Jamaica. It explores the influence of the RER on selected components of the current account over the period 1995 to 2015, in particular, imports and the major components of exports, including tourism. It seeks to determine if the exchange rate depreciation is necessary and/or sufficient to foster current account sustainability and achieve economic growth at the same time. It also provides an alternative policy framework that can significantly increase the country's foreign currency earnings from exports and reduce the country's outflow of foreign currency for imports. The next section analyzes how Jamaica's net current transfers, services, net income balance and net goods balance change over time with the changes in the RER.

4.2 Analysis of the Current Account Components

Jamaica's current account is divided into four main categories: current transfers, services, income and the goods balance.

4.2.1 Current Transfers

Current transfers represent the flow of foreign currency from one country to the next with nothing to receive in return. These are unilateral allocations from one party to the next and do not include the transfer of any goods or services and therefore are not calculated as a part of Jamaica's GDP. Current transfers to and from Jamaica include remittances, foreign aids and grants, pensions and other official assistance. Current transfers to the Jamaican economy are consistently more than current transfers from the economy as evident by the positive net balance. These transfers are impacted by global economic conditions. From 1995 up to 2008, net current transfers to Jamaica demonstrate a consistent, increasing and positive contribution to the island's inflow of foreign currency and the country's current account balance. This steady increasing pattern appears to be independent of the variations of the RER. Though not counted as a part of GDP, current transfers over the years consistently contribute the most to Jamaica's current account balance averaging more than US $620 million from 1995 to 2002 and further increasing from US $1.2 billion in 2003 to US $2.15 billion in 2008 (see Fig. 4.1).

The global financial crisis of 2008 had a slight negative impact on the trajectory of net current transfers to the island, which fell to just over US $1.8 billion in 2009. Subsequently, current transfers display a steady increasing trend once more, gradually meandering to a high of US $2.2 billion in 2013, irrespective of fluctuations in the RER as illustrated by Fig. 4.2 from 1995 to 2013. Current transfers are ever increasing and although it is not a function of the RER, it poses no threat to the sustainability of Jamaica's current account. As it stands, exchange rate depreciation policy cannot impact the current account via the current transfers channel.

Note: A depreciation is illustrated by an increase in the RER. The opposite movement holds true for an appreciation in the RER. The next section examines the services balance, which represents the second highest contributor to the current account but the first highest contributor of foreign currency to the country's GDP.

4.2.2 The Services Balance

Jamaica is predominantly a service economy, accounting for up to 70 percent of the country's GDP. The island's major services come from the tourism industry, which is the number-one contributor to GDP foreign currency inflow – approximately 30 percent of GDP per annum. Other services include transportation, business services, royalties and licensing. The services balance has always been a positive contributor to Jamaica's foreign currency inflow. Figure 4.3 illustrates the movements of the services balance from 1995 to 2013. The model displays a similar pattern to the exchange movement with a one- or two-year lag difference, and in some instances, per annum. In Fig. 4.3, the green bars represent movement in foreign currency inflow from net services and the red line represents changes in the RER.

Changes in the RER plunged from 30 units in 1996 to a low of 2.1 units in 1997. The service balance did not respond, as it appears the value of the RER was a consequence of Jamaica's 1997 financial crisis, which was independent of the country's receipt and provision of services. The RER increased steadily between 1997 and 2000. While the net service balance improved, the RER increased from US $462 million in 1996 to US $655 million in 1999. Both the services balance and the RER fell in 2001, and while the RER improved in 2002, the services balance improved a year later in 2003, and maintained a steady increase up to 2006. The RER increased from 6.5 units in 2001 to 33.5 units in 2004, falling sharply again to 7.5 units in 2006. From 2006 to 2008 the RER increased while the service balance fell. After the global financial crisis of 2008 the services balance improved while the RER decreased initially, then improved by 2010. Both fell in 2011 and 2012, and improved thereafter. Based on the movement of both variables, a correlation analysis should show that as the RER increase (depreciates) the service balance increases, and vice versa. The service balance along with current transfers represent the bulk of Jamaica's foreign currency inflow. The other two components, income balance and the goods balance, are constantly negative, and from a current account point of view, represent the main contributors to foreign currency outflow from the island.

4.2.3 *The Income Balance*

Foreign currency flowing into the Jamaican economy would represent a credit to the income balance while a debit to the income account represents an outflow of foreign currency from the island. Income arises from the payment of salaries, portfolio investments including dividends, direct investment or any other type of investment in and out of the Jamaican economy. The net flow of income to and from the Jamaican economy is illustrated in Fig. 4.3. Notice the upside-down bell shape of the curve from 1996 onwards.

The income balance on the current account has always been negative with an average deficit of US $420 million over the last 25 years. Net current income between Jamaica and the rest of the world improved from a deficit of USD -$340 million to approximately USD -$225 million from 1995 to 1999, while the RER increased slightly during this time. From 1996 to 2002, the income balance deteriorated gradually from US $225 million in 1996 to US $605 million in 2002, despite the meandering fluctuation in the RER (see Fig. 4.3). The net income balance fell to its lowest points in 2005, 2007 and 2009 respectively, reaching a deficit of more than US $650 million. The most prosperous year appears to be 2012 as the deficit improved to approximately US $120 million. This was short-lived as the deficit worsened again in 2013 and has continued on that trajectory. All indications suggest that the income balance is independent of the RER and therefore cannot be affected by exchange rate depreciation policies. The next section examines the goods balance.

4.2.4 *The Goods Balance*

Along with the income balance, the net goods balance demonstrates a constant deficit over the last 25 years. Jamaica's net goods balance comprises consumer goods (durables and nondurables), raw materials including fuel, food and other raw materials, and capital goods, construction and other machinery. Figure 4.4 shows the goods balance relative to changes in the RER. The goods deficit, influenced by a faster growth in imports relative to exports, has been the major driver of Jamaica's current account deficit over the period and is the least responsive to fluctuations in the RER (see Figs. 4.4 to 4.7). In particular, Fig. 4.4 illustrates a constantly depleting good balance irrespective of whether the RER is appreciating or depreciating prior to 2008. Observe also that there was a significant increase in the deficit on the goods sub-account despite the trend depreciation in the RER since 1997. The current account goods balance fell to its lowest point during the global financial crisis of 2008.

The deficit on the goods sub-account averaged 13.0 percent of GDP in fiscal year 1998/1999 to 33.8 percent in fiscal year 2008/2009 while the depreciation in the RER ranged from 4.8 to 5.6 percent over the same period. More specifically, the deficit moved US -$829 million in 1995 to US -$4.8 billion in 2008 (see Fig. 4.5). After the global financial crisis of 2008, there seemed to be some correlation between the goods balance and the RER. Rapid appreciation of the RER from 34.5 percent in 2010 to 2.9 percent in 2011 was associated with a worsening of the current account deficit from US -$3.2 billion in 2010 to US $4.11 billion in 2011. The deficit has subsequently improved marginally to US -$3.9 billion by 2013, while the exchange rate depreciated to 11.4 percent by 2013.

Overall, the negative impact of the goods balance and the net income balance on the current account outweighs the positive arising from the services and current transfers. As a result, the Jamaican current account maintains a constant deficit and efforts are being made to reduce the deficit to 0.5 percent of GDP by 2016. Further analysis of the components of the goods imported to and exported from Jamaica is necessary to have a better understanding of how to engineer a sustainable current account deficit, which is important if the country is to improve productivity and achieve a sustainable foreign currency flow. The next section dissects the goods balance into its various components and analyzes the route of each and the impact of foreign currency depreciations on improving their net balances.

4.3 Analysis of Jamaica's Imports

For this study, the consumer goods imported and exported to and from Jamaica are food, other non-durables and durables. As stated earlier, an appreciation of the RER, recorded as a fall in the growth rate of the index, should result in increased importation of consumer goods if there are no close substitutes for these goods. Likewise, a depreciation of the RER, recorded as an increase in the growth rate of the index, should result in a fall in imports of consumer goods. Therefore, results from the correlation analysis should show a negative co-movement between the growth rate of the RER and these consumer goods. The appreciation of the RER makes imports cheaper, which means that as income increases, imports should increase, since imports are now cheaper than exports. The result of this is a widening of the current account balance.[5]

On average, there is a positive co-movement between the growth of the RER and imported consumer goods as shown in Fig. 4.5. This is not in line with a priori expectations using the elasticities approach. Rochester (2013) found that Jamaica has relied heavily on the importation of consumer goods since 1998. Based on economic theory, an increase in the RER represents a depreciation. When the RER depreciates a country should import less. However, Jamaica's heavy reliance on imports partially explains why the growth rate of the RER and the importation of consumer goods appear to be positively correlated.

Notably, Jamaica started to reduce imports of 'Other Non-Durables' in 2009 while the RER started to depreciate. While this is consistent with expectations, the reduction in the imports of non-durables could have also been influenced by the global financial crisis of 2008. Also of note is the levelling off of food imports, durables and non-durables, after the minimal increase in the RER from 2011–2012.

According to Wilson and McLean (2014), depreciation of a country's currency should improve its current account balance through increased exports and reduced imports. If consumers reduce their imports in the short run due to a price effect, the depreciation will eventually deteriorate the balance if consumers revert to consuming imports over exports as they did before, especially if the high-priced imports cannot be sustained.

The same relationship is expected between the change in the RER and raw material imports. However, Fig. 4.6 shows that this relationship only held for the variables in 2000 and 2003. This is not surprising, as Jamaica relies heavily on imported inputs for its production processes. A depreciation of the currency in this case means more foreign currency outflow.

4.3.1 Correlation Analysis of Imports

The correlation analysis between imports and the RER depicts that a weak positive relationship exists between food imports and the RER. A 0.136 correlation value indicates that the variables are weakly positively correlated. No linear relationship exists between the RER and durable imported goods variables. However, a correlation value of 0.033 indicates that the variables are weakly positively correlated.

The RER and food (raw material) correlation analysis shows that a weak positive relationship exists between both variables. A correlation value of 0.1 was calculated. This indicates that the variables are weakly correlated. The R-squared of 0.31 shows that 30 percent of the variation in raw materials is a result of changes in the REER. A correlation value of 0.031 states that the variables – other raw material imports and RER – are weakly positively correlated. The results confirm that as the RER increases (depreciates), **Jamaica imports more raw material food stuff.** Even when imports become more expensive, the reliance on such imports for domestic production process, in this case food, is imported based on the manufacturers' demand.

The correlation analysis for the variables RER and fuel imports shows that weak positive relationship exist between the variables. The correlation analysis produces a value of 0.04, which states that the variables are weakly positively correlated. No linear relationship exists between the variables constructions and RER shown by the scatter plot diagram. A value of 0.004 generated from the correlation analysis generates an inference that the variables are not correlated. The variables other machine imports and RER rate have no linear relationship. A small value of 0.007 was generated, which implies that the variables are not correlated.

4.4 Analysis of Traditional Exports

The volume of foreign currency earned from each item of export – bauxite, alumina, sugar, banana and coffee – vis-à-vis a change in the RER, display no clearly defined correlation (see Fig. 4.7). Contrary to its relationship with imports, exports will likely have a positive co-movement with the change in the RER. Therefore, a depreciation in the RER, recorded as an increase in the movement of the index, should result in more exports since exports are made cheaper than substitutes in foreign countries given the relative price differential.

Figure 4.7 shows the correlation between exports and changes in the RER. The results show that bauxite exports and REER have a weak positive relationship. A correlation value of 0.21 was generated, which also shows that variables are weakly positively correlated. The scatter diagram showing the relationship between alumina exports depicts that no relationship exists

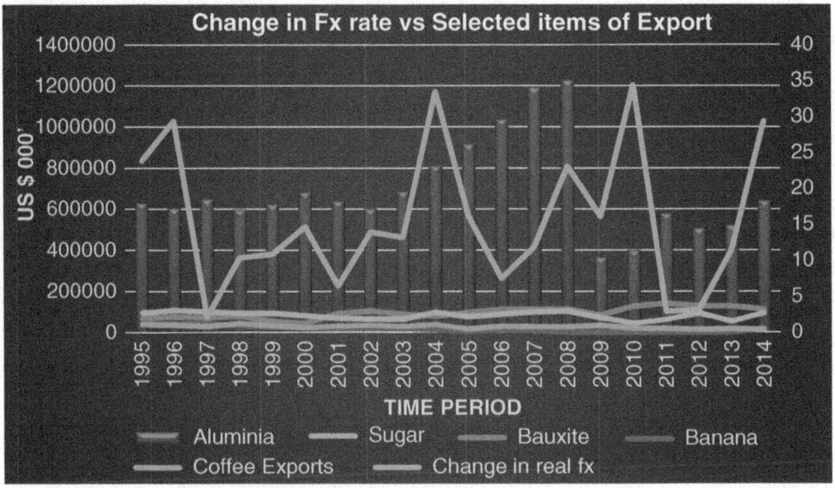

Fig. 4.7 Change in exchange rate and selected items of exports

between both variables. The correlation analysis generates a value of 0.001369, which has a value close to zero, which states that variables are not correlated. In 1974, Jamaica became the world's second largest producer of bauxite and alumina. Although much has changed since then and Jamaica's share of world bauxite output has fallen drastically since the 1970s, alumina is consistently the largest foreign exchange earner for the island. Over the last 25 years alumina has netted more than US $4 billion per annum. Even after the decline in bauxite and alumina production, and the closing down of bauxite companies in Jamaica after the global financial crisis of 2008, foreign currency revenues from bauxite and alumina remained above the revenues from the other farming exports.

Despite a fall in commodity prices, alumina remains the country's highest foreign currency revenue earner. The export of alumina has been relatively large when compared to the exports of bauxite, sugar and banana. Rochester (2013) also highlighted that Jamaica's main exports since 1998 have been from the mining sector. This is corroborated from the graph depicting the growth of the RER and selected exports. Jamaica's foreign currency revenue earned from the exportation of alumina increased steadily from 2002 to 2008. The upward trajectory lost inclination after the global financial crisis in 2008, alumina exports plummeted from more than US $1.2 billion 2008 to less than US $400 million in 2009. Revenue from alumina exports have remained below the pre-2002 figure and has not recovered since.

Traditionally, Jamaican sugar was mainly exported to Europe and the price of sugar was above international prices due to a preferential trade agreement. Thus, the movement in the export of sugar is independent of the RER because sugar was unaffected by the changes in the prices accounted for in the RER in Fig. 4.7. The scatter plot for sugar exports and REER shows that a very weak positive relationship exists between both variables. A value of 0.02 for the correlation analysis was generated, which depicts that the variables are very weakly correlated. The scatter plot shows that there is no significant relationship between banana exports and RER changes either. A correlation value of 0.03 shows that both variables are weakly positively correlated. Banana has recorded little to no exports, relative to previous periods, since 2008. This hiatus was caused by the disruption in the production of bananas after Hurricane Gustav in 2007. The production of coffee and its byproducts started to increase with the decline in banana production in the early 2000s. Bauxite, sugar, banana and coffee have earned Jamaica less than $200 million per annum each in foreign currency earnings from sales to the rest of the world over the last 25 years.

4.5 Jamaica's Economic Position: Import and Export Strategy

The Jamaican economy is trapped in a low-income, high-expenditure cycle, which is limiting the transfer of money from one hand to the next thereby lowering aggregate demand. An agenda to increase exports is in the pipeline, but cannot materialize and remains futile if there is no agenda to substantially expand output in the island. This increase can be achieved in two ways: (1) via an increase in the amount of labour and capital that enters the production process and (2) through an increase in the island's total factor productivity.

Figure 4.8 illustrates annual growth rate of total factor productivity per person employed in Jamaica. Notice that total factor productivity averaged roughly 4.8 percent per annum between 1962 and 1973, which coincided with high economic growth rates. Subsequently, the orientation changed and total factor productivity averaged -0.9 percent from 1974 to 2016. Jamaica has progressively lost productivity from over the last four decades,

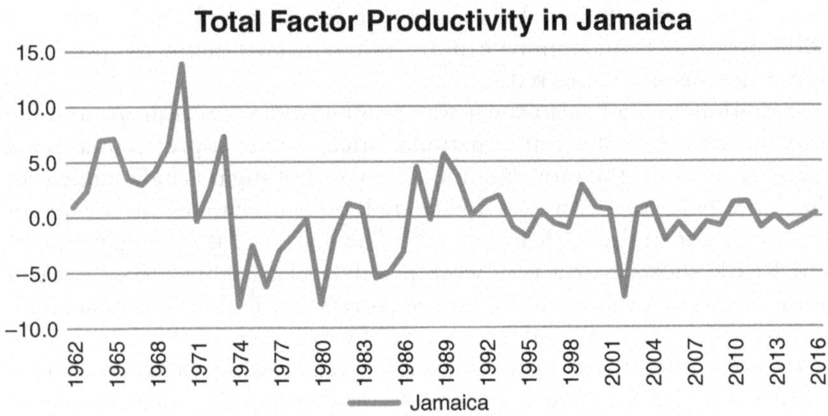

Fig. 4.8 Total Factor Productivity in Jamaica from 1953 to present: Source: The Conference Board, Total Economy data base

which seems to be a contributing factor to the nation's inability to benefit from economies of scale.

Services have been the champion of the country's exports. There are many services that Jamaica provides to the rest of the world including, tourism, travel, transportation and Information and Communication Technology (ICT). Jamaica's tourism is seasonal and the country predominantly relies heavily on the traditional sun, sand and sea tourism. Little is being done to take advantage of health, entertainment and sports tourism, which are other strong points of the island. Travel is complementary to tourism and also demonstrates seasonality; average foreign currency receipts from travel to the island has increased from US $100 million per quarter from 1995 to 2005 to an average of US $150 million per quarter between 2005 and 2015. Jamaica has considerably increased its provision of ICT over the past five years. Other than expanding the country's tourism attractors to include health, sports and entertainment more rigidly, the ICT sector appears to be another avenue through which, if explored to its fullest potential, can generate a considerable amount of foreign currency revenue for the island in the long run. Due to the nation's easy voice and other compatibilities, foreign firms are becoming more willing to subcontract ICT operations to local firms in Jamaica. This and other ICT service exports have been increasing. There are plans to channel resources for

Jamaica to increase its provision of logistics services to the rest of the world, which will increase business and commerce in the local economy.

From a goods point of view, the results indicate that Jamaica fetches the most of its foreign currency revenue from the exportation of alumina, which is a secondary product. Alumina generates significantly higher revenue than the exportation of bauxite in its primary stage of production. Notice that revenue generated from the farming products remain relatively the same even if the RER changes. Revenue from banana, sugar and coffee remains less than US $1.2 billion each year when compared to the revenues from alumina, which were more than US $2 billion in the worst years and more than US $4 billion in good times. The results would suggest that not much is being done to add enough value to Jamaica's agricultural outputs to enable exports to fetch more foreign currency globally. The export of primary products generates considerably less revenue than the export of goods with value added. The results suggest that Jamaica can increase its foreign currency revenues earned from the exportation of goods through vertical diversification of products. Policy recommendations here suggest that Jamaica should put more focus on transforming goods from the primary to the secondary stage and/or other stages of production to increase foreign currency revenue earned from goods exported.

Jamaica's traditional export strategy has always been on concessionary terms. Sugar, banana, bauxite and alumina all have their guaranteed preferred export markets once produced. If and when these concessions are removed, the country must find creative ways to penetrate markets on its own. The industries targeted by the national export strategy are: agroprocessing, agriculture, coffee, education, entertainment, fashion jewelry and accessories, ICT and mining. Plans to improve agroprocessing in Jamaica were geared towards increasing exports by more than 15 percent each year since 2008. However, the diagram shows that there have been no significant changes in the volume of foreign currency inflow from the sale of agricultural goods and their byproducts to the rest of the world. It might be the case that the quantity of exports has been increasing, but exchange rate depreciation has resulted in each item of export fetching a lower price in the market, thus total receipts don't change much.

Jamaica's agriculture export strategy outlined by Jamaica Investment Promotions (JAMPRO) is directed towards improving production efficiency and reducing the cost of production in the aquaculture sector. The export strategy for coffee is a little different. The aim is to broaden the spectrum of value added that can be derived from coffee; strategies to access new markets are also being developed such as improving access to overseas markets, introducing five new products each year, adopting at least 60 percent of international best practices for the exportation of agroprocessed goods and improving Jamaica's Agro-Processors Association to make it more vibrant.

Manufacturing is an important component in the country's mix of exports but it is expensive to manufacture goods in Jamaica due to the high cost of energy. Electricity currently cost US $0.40 per kilowatt hour on average compared to less than US $0.20 per kilowatt hour in the United States and less than US $0.10 per kilowatt hour in Trinidad and Tobago, the Caribbean's largest exporter of manufactured goods. The high cost of electricity has constrained the country's diversification and expansion of manufactured products. High energy costs also prevent manufacturers from capitalizing on economies of scale where it might exist. Something has to be produced in excess before it can be exported to generate enough revenue to sustain the country's borrowing habits.

Over the last two years, agricultural outputs have been severely impacted by drought conditions. The lower crop yields, which have come as a result of infrastructural issues, are also a handicap towards achieving a sustained increase in output. Jamaica should proceed to increase the provision of water and reduce the cost of electricity as a means of providing the right platform to increase the country's output. These circumstances have placed Jamaica in a very peculiar position, where the country cannot increase output without a massive infrastructural overhaul. This overhaul cannot occur unless the country clears its foreign debt obligations to free up fiscal room in the budget, and the country cannot clear it debts unless there is an increase in output. In this case, the country is in a deadlock and can only escape if it develops the fiscal flexibility to do so.

4.6 Conclusion

Jamaica's attempt to achieve current account sustainability hinges on the country achieving international competitiveness through the depreciation of the domestic currency. However, the success of such policies relies on whether each component of the current account is responsive to changes in the REER. This chapter dichotomizes the current account and examines the impact of changes to the RER on each component. The results show that current transfers to the Jamaican economy are consistently more than current transfers from the economy, as evident by the positive net balance. Over the last 25 years, net inflow of foreign currency as a result of current transfers, appears to be independent of the variations of the RER. Similar to net current transfers, the flow of foreign currency to the island from net services has always been positive. The data shows there is similar pattern of behaviour between the net services balance and the real exchange changes with about a one- or two-year lag difference in some instances per annum. On the flip side, the flow of foreign currency from net income has been consistently negative, where the flow of income displays a U-shaped behaviour from 1996 to 2015.

The net income balance is independent of the RER, therefore cannot be affected by exchange rate depreciation policies. Along with the income balance, the net goods balance demonstrates a constant deficit over the last 25 years. The goods deficit, influenced by a faster growth in imports relative to exports, has been the major driver of Jamaica's current account deficit over the period and is the least responsive to fluctuations in the RER prior to the global financial crisis of 2008. After the crisis, there seemed to be more correlation between the goods balance and changes in the RER, though the balance remained negative. Overall, the negative impact of the goods balance and the net income balance on the current account outweighs the positive arising from the services and current transfers. As a result, the Jamaican current account is constantly in deficit. Efforts to reduce the deficit to 0.5 percent of GDP by 2016 hinge on the depreciation of the currency, which is geared towards improving the inflow of foreign currency to the island.

Further analysis is done on each component of the goods balance to examine the effect of the RER on each. On average, there is a positive co-movement between the growth of the RER and imported consumer goods, which is not congruent with a priori expectations using the elasticities approach; heavy reliance partially explains why the growth rate of the RER and the imports of consumer goods appear to be positively correlated. The importation of "Other Non-Durables" reduced in 2009 while the RER started to depreciate. While this is consistent with expectations, lower imports of the reduction in the imports of non-durables could have also been influenced by the global financial crisis of 2008. There is also a weak positive relationship between food imports and RER, the RER and durable imported goods, RER and food (raw material), the RER and other raw material imports and the RER and fuel imports. These results, though not statistically significant, are still of economic consequence. The results indicate that as the REER increases (depreciates), Jamaica imports more food, more durable goods, more food raw materials and more other materials. Even when imports become more expensive, the reliance on such for domestic production process, in this case food, is import-based. No relationship exists between the RER and construction imports nor the RER and other machine imports.

An analysis of the country's main exports displayed that there exists little relationship between each item of export and the RER. The exportation of bauxite and its secondary product alumina fluctuated from year to year independent of the RER and generates the most foreign currency inflow of all Jamaica's exports. Foreign currency revenues, from the island's export of revenue agricultural products including banana, sugar and coffee maintain the same value irrespective of depreciations in the RER. In this case, even if the country is producing more per annum, having to sell each unit at a lower price each year means that the country earns less from its output. Coffee production for export has improved after the global financial crisis, while the production of banana has fallen.

The Jamaican economy is fragile and policies to depreciate the domestic currency to improve current account in the short run may lead to further worsening of the current account in the long run, if people do not change their consumption habits. Other than bauxite and its byproducts, Jamaica's main exports have been farming products, which have maintained a same flow of foreign currency to the island over the last 25 years. The results insinuate that strategies to depreciate the currency must be supported by strategies to expand exports. This export strategy relies heavily on the country's ability to transform goods from primary production to secondary production where it can fetch higher prices abroad and more revenue for the island.

Notes

1. Ability to cover foreign currency debt obligations, DSCR greater than one means a country is able to cover its foreign currency debt obligations sustainably. It's the difference between the net revenue and yearly debt obligations.
2. See Chapter 2.
3. The theory of the purchasing power parity (PPP) used in the calculation of the REER suggests that the domestic exchange rate adjusts for any relative price changes or any changes in the other major currencies, thus the REER should remain in equilibrium.
4. One representation of the REER is derived from using a composite weighting of the RER for a range of key trading partners (see Rochester 2013).
5. A widening of the deficit or narrowing of the surplus.

CHAPTER 5

Currency Depreciation and Economic Growth

5.1 Background and Literature

Jamaica's real GDP has grown at an average rate of 0.7 percent from 1970 to present. Recent efforts to improve the nation's economic growth rate has relied on recommendations of the Mundell–Fleming model, predisposing that currency depreciations increase the international competitiveness of domestic goods due to improvement in relative prices, which should result in GDP growth via more exports. However, empirical data has shown that Jamaica had its highest growth rates throughout the years where its exchange rate depreciated less proportionately to years when it depreciated more. Jamaica's exchange rate remained fairly stable throughout the 1970s and 1980s and average GDP growth was higher for those two decades compared to when the exchange rate was more flexible throughout the 1990s and 2000s. More severe currency depreciation ensued throughout the decades of the 1990s and 2000s and GDP growth stagnated.

More recently, the exchange rate depreciated by 7 percent, 14 percent, 6 percent and 5 percent in 2012, 2013, 2014 and 2015 respectively. Correspondingly, GDP growth remained low at 0.7 percent, 1.4 percent, 0.9 percent and 1 percent, respectively (see Fig. 5.1). According to the latest World Bank indicators, Jamaica's import content was more than 45 percent of GDP in 2015, this includes consumption goods and imported inputs to be used in production processes. As the nominal exchange rate depreciates, the cost of these imported inputs, for example, oil, tend to increase. this increases the cost of production in processes that rely on

A. Haughton, *Developing Sustainable Balance of Payments in Small Countries*, DOI 10.1007/978-3-319-53031-4_5

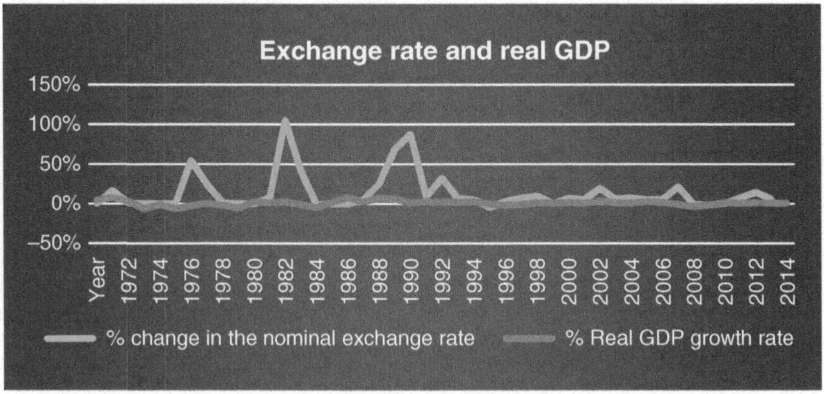

Fig. 5.1 % change in nominal exchange rate and % GDP growth rate

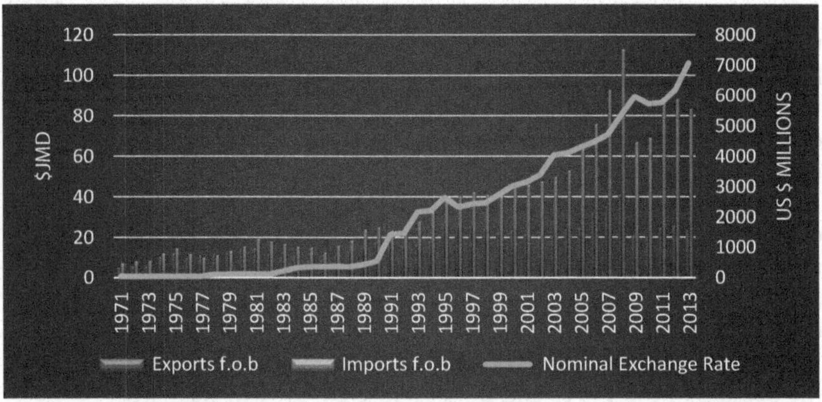

Fig. 5.2 Imports, Exports and the nominal exchange rate: Bank of Jamaica

these inputs. There is no real exchange rate issue here given that these imported inputs cannot be produced locally. Figure 5.2 shows that as the nominal exchange rate depreciated, the value of Jamaica's imports increases, indicated by the upward trend in both variables. As a result, the applicability of the predictions of the Mundell–Fleming model to the Jamaican situation is questionable given that the currency has been depreciating and GDP growth has not improved significantly.

Alejandro (1963) and Krugman and Taylor (1978) found evidence to suggest that there are channels through which currency devaluation may have contractionary effects on total output of a country, contrary to the predictions of the Mundell–Fleming model. Alejandro (1963) explains that devaluation has two effects: ***the initial*** effect and the ***reversal effect***. The ***initial effect*** supports the Mundell–Fleming prediction that currency depreciation improves a country's terms of trade and GDP through change in relative prices. This is determined by the price elasticity of demand and supply of imports and exports. A country can pursue devaluation policies if it has the capacity and the ability to expand production considerably to take advantage of economies of scale based on the initial effect. The ***reversal effect***, on the other hand, supports the claim that currency depreciation might reduce aggregate output if domestic demand is weak. In this case, profits are redistributed to the expansion of the tradable goods sector and reduce real wages. Since businesses have a higher propensity to save than workers, savings will increase. This discourages aggregate demand, hence total output falls.

If a country employs a large proportion of foreign inputs in its production processes, which must be paid for using foreign currency, then depreciation will increase a country's cost of production. Jamaica's importation of raw material is greater than all other imports by end use as illustrated by Figure 5.3. This results in no increase in output and no increase in exports; the export price will not improve. The exchange rate strategy needed to increase growth and export in countries with high import content might be different from those where the import content of GDP is lower. The import content of Jamaica's GDP is more 54.4 percent, which is relatively high when compared to most GDPs. For example, the import content of China's GDP is 18 percent, the United States' is 16 percent and Japan's is 19 percent.

Krugman and Taylor (1978) found evidence to corroborate the results of Alejandro (1963). They identify three channels through which currency depreciation can reduce consumer spending, worsen a country's terms of trade and lessen aggregate output.

1. If the country has an initial trade deficit, devaluation reduces the spending power of domestic citizens by reducing their real income through altering the price of traded goods. This will provide a net real transfer to foreigners, putting them at an advantage, which worsens the terms of trade further and leads to a fall in output in the short run.

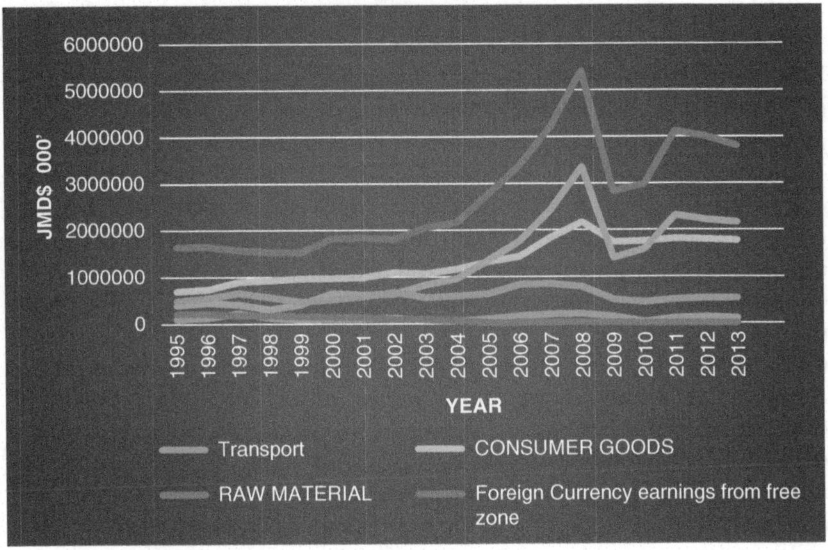

Fig. 5.3 Imports by end use: Bank of Jamaica

2. Through distributional channels, devaluation reduces the cost of home goods relative to traded goods leading to an unexpected increase in profits in the import and export sector. Krugman and Taylor (1978) outline that a redistribution of income from wages to profits might not necessarily lead to an increase in GDP. Firms normally have a higher propensity to save in most cases. In the Jamaican context, multilateral firms repatriate profits and less is available to boost investment in the domestic economy.
3. Through fiscal effects; taxes on imports and exports transfers' income from tradable goods sector to the government when the exchange rate depreciates. Here the private sector is paying more for imports than it earns from exports.

Van Wijnbergen (1986) found evidence from the supply side to suggest that currency depreciation can have a direct negative effect on output growth through three main avenues:

1. Domestic cost of intermediate goods. If a domestic firm uses a high percentage of imported inputs and the cost disadvantage arising from importing inputs is greater than the price benefits received from the export of the final goods, then domestic output might be negatively impacted by a depreciating currency.
2. Real wage indexation. Van Wijnbergen (1986) explains that real wage advantages foreigners receive via domestic currency depreciation can have contractionary effects on output.
3. Volume of real credit to firms. If devaluation is transferred to prices and real wages, this will reduce the country's monetary base and by extension the amount available to lend to the private sector.

Saibene and Sicouri (2012) analyze the effects of currency devaluation on economic growth in developing countries taking the role of foreign currency debt into consideration. They found that devaluation can have a negative effect on output in countries with a large proportion of debt denominated in foreign currency. The high proportion of Jamaica's debt being denominated in foreign currency has had significant negative balance sheet effects. Government spending has been constrained, low capital expansion has resulted, and banks may encounter problems if there is a currency mismatch between assets and liabilities. It has also been having a negative wealth effect on national investors.

The results of Krugman and Taylor (1978), Alejandro (1963) and Saibene and Sicouri (2012) are, however, counterintuitive to the expectations of the Mundell–Fleming model. The Mundell–Fleming model assumes that a country is capable of expanding output even when marginal costs are increasing, but this is not profit maximizing. Rational firms will choose not to do so, stopping production at that point where marginal cost is lowest in an attempt to maximize revenue.

The objective of this chapter is to analyze the impact of exchange depreciation on GDP growth in the Jamaican economy; the output Jamaica could potentially produce if the currency did not depreciate holding all other factors constant. Figure 5.1 shows changes in Jamaica's nominal exchange and GDP growth from 1971 to present. There were significant depreciations in the domestic currency in 1977, 1983, 1990 and 1991. What impact has this and other exchange rate fluctuations had on GDP real growth?

5.2 Data and Methodology

Annual data on real and nominal exchange rates, annual domestic investment (gross capital formation), exports, external debt-to-GDP ratio, Jamaica Consumer Price Index and world annual average GDP from 1971 to present are collected from the World Bank, the IMF International Financial Statistics (IFS) and the Edward Seaga Database Collection. The augmented Dickey–Fuller test and the Phillips–Perron unit root test are employed to verify the stationarity properties of the variables. Change in GDP is a stationary I(0) process, while the remaining variables are non-stationary I(1) processes.

Several model specifications were explored including the Instrumental Variable (IV) technique, GARCH-M(1,1), Ordinary Least Squares and Dynamic Ordinary Least Squares (DOLS).

The model specification is derived from the following equation:

$$\Delta gdp_t = \beta_0 + \beta_1 extdbt_t + \beta_2 \%\Delta fx_{t-1} + \beta_3 \Delta JACPI_t + \varepsilon_t \qquad (5.1)$$

Here, $\Delta rgdp_t$ is change in real GDP at time *t*, $extdbt_t$ is external debt-to-GDP ratio at time *t*, fx_{t-1} is the nominal exchange rate in time *t*-1, and $\Delta JACPI_t$ is Jamaica's Consumer Price Index at time *t*. The impact of exchange rate changes on GDP growth rate is isolated holding all other factors constant. Employing the changes in the previous year's exchange rate instead of current values is justified by Saibene and Sicouri (2012). Use of the nominal exchange rate is motivated by Fratzscher et al (2014) and many others who employ the nominal exchange rate to isolate its effect in the examination of its interaction with oil prices and other variables.

5.2.1 Assumptions

1. To fully understand the relationship between nominal exchange rate changes and GDP growth the model takes foreign currency debt and domestic inflation into consideration. The restriction is imposed that in any given year the exchange rate cannot impact GDP growth beyond the world average of 3.7 percent. In this case, no matter how the exchange rate depreciates/appreciates in a given year, its impact **on GDP changes *ceteris paribus* is constrained by global economic conditions.**

Average loss in GDP per annum is constrained by the world average GDP growth rate of 3.7 percent per annum, such that,

$$\beta_2 \times \%\Delta fx_t \leq 3.7 \, \forall t$$

This assumes that total loss of growth can never exceed the world average GDP growth rate in any given year.

The constraint is plausible given that the Jamaican economy is import and tourism dependent and susceptible to external shocks. These shocks arising from the global economic condition at each period in time along with domestic institutional weaknesses can limit the nation's potential growth.

2. The model takes into account Jamaica's capacity and productivity constraints by assuming that maximum potential GDP growth the country could achieve in a given year is within two standard deviations of the maximum growth threshold, irrespective of how much the currency depreciated the year before. The necessary adjustments are made to take into account Jamaica's annual average growth of 0.7 percent and the fact that GDP growth has never exceeded 7.9 percent per annum.

   With a capacity constraint, loss in potential GDP growth beyond the world average in any given year is due to factors other than exchange rate depreciations. The model takes into consideration years of extreme depreciation such as in the years 1989, 1990, 1991, 1993 and 2008. The results from the empirical analysis are given in the next section.

5.3 Results

The results for the potential impact of currency devaluation on GDP growth are indicated in Table 5.1. Potential losses to GDP growth in current years are shown as a function of exchange rate depreciation in the previous year. More specifically, the results indicate that for every 1 percent fall in the value of the local currency against the United States in time *t*-1, Jamaica loses 0.3 percent of potential real GDP growth on average in time t. This means that for every 1 percent of depreciation this year, GDP growth for next year falls by 0.3 percent and vice versa. This result accounts for the effect of outliers in years of extreme currency depreciation; potential growth effect each year is capped at the world GDP growth average rate of 3.7 percent per annum.

Before the liberalization of the financial sector in 1992, the nominal exchange rate was very low and changes were more volatile. However, periods of no change in the nominal exchange rate made potential impact of exchange rate depreciation less severe. Actual GDP experienced its highest growth rates of 7.8 percent and 8 percent in 1972 and 1987, respectively (see Table 5.1). In 1970, 1971, 1974, 1975, 1976, 1986, 1980, 1981, 1987 and 1999 the exchange rate was fairly stable making potential losses to GDP growth for each exact year that follows negligibly zero since the value of the currency did not change. Years given in Table 5.1 (1971, 1972, 1975, 1976, 1977, 1981, 1982, 1987 and 2000) represent years where the exchange rate was held relatively stable not depreciating in the previous year, as such, percentage change in the exchange rate is zero so no resulting effect on GDP growth in each exact year that follows.

Years given in Table 5.1 (1973, 1978, 1979, 1984, 1985, 1990, 1991, 1992 and 1994) are the years where potential losses to GDP growth as a result of exchange rate depreciation are more severe. Losses in potential GDP growth for these years exceed 3 percent per annum the following year. For these years, the exchange rate depreciated by more than 15 percent in the previous year (see Table 5.1).

In 1985, 1996, 2009 and 2010 the currency appreciated and actual GDP growth each year exactly after was negative. Years given in Table 5.1 (1986, 1997, 2010 and 2011) are the years where the exchange rate appreciated the previous year, illustrating that GDP growth would be worse if the currency did not appreciate these years (see Fig. 5.4). Figure 5.4 map the movement of actual real GDP growth rate and the potential effect of exchange rate depreciation. Post-liberalization is less volatile, but rapid consistent depreciation during this era made the potential loss to GDP growth more consistent.

Between 1971 and 1992 Jamaica's total potential loss was approximately 52 percent of GDP, see Figs. 5.4 and 5.5 graphically comparing the current to that of the potential GDP growth that could have been achieved. From 1993 to present, total loss was 53.4 percent, about 2.42 percent on average per annum. Considering this formulation, between 1990 and 2014, Jamaica potentially lost a total of 74 percent growth in GDP, or 2.42 percent on average, over the 25 year period. This represents a total potential loss of US $880.5 million between 1971 and 1992 after

Table 5.1 The effect of exchange rate changes on GDP growth before financial liberalization from 1971 to 1992

Year	*Nominal exchange rate*	*Percentage change in the nominal Exchange rate*	*Potential Exchange Rate GDP Growth*	*Actual GDP Growth*	*Potential GDP growth if exchange rate was Fixed*	*GDP (current US $)*	*GDP*nominal exchange rate (current US $)*
1971	0.77	0	0	4.4	4.4	1,679,379,386.90	–
1972	0.9	17	0	7.8	7.8	1,260,379,326.20	–
1973	0.91	1	3.1	2.8	5.9	1,570,002,486.20	48,670,077.07
1974	0.91	0	0.3	-5.9	-5.6	1,260,379,326.40	3,781,137.98
1975	0.91	0	0	-0.7	-0.7	1,260,379,326.30	–
1976	0.91	0	0	-6.3	-6.3	1,260,379,326.80	–
1977	1.41	55	0	-2.4	-2.4	1,260,379,326.20	–
1978	1.76	25	3.5	0.7	4.2	1,260,379,326.30	44,113,276.42
1979	1.78	1	3.4	-1.8	1.6	1,260,379,326.60	42,852,897.10
1980	1.78	0	0.3	-5.7	-5.4	2,679,379,386.60	8,038,138.16
1981	1.78	0	0	2.6	2.6	2,979,027,983.20	–
1982	1.92	8	0	1.2	1.2	3,293,496,330.40	–
1983	3.94	105	2.4	2.3	4.7	3,619,262,277.50	86,862,294.66
1984	5.58	42	3.6	-0.9	2.7	2,373,564,489.30	85,448,321.61
1985	5.5	-1	3.5	-4.6	-1.1	2,100,239,022.60	73,508,365.79
1986	5.51	0	-0.4	1.7	1.3	2,754,549,687.50	-11,018,198.75
1987	5.51	0	0.1	8	8	3,287,007,225.70	3,287,007.23
1988	5.77	5	0	2.2	2.2	3,828,342,820.30	–
1989	7.24	25	1.4	7	8.5	4,404,938,022.10	61,669,132.31
1990	12.22	69	3.6	6.3	9.9	4,592,208,208.10	165,319,495.49
1991	22.99	88	3.6	0.8	4.5	4,106,205,951.10	147,823,414.24
1992	25.11	9	3.4	2.8	6.2	3,535,452,384.60	120,205,381.08
Total						**55,625,710,946.90**	**880,560,740.39**

(continued)

Table 5.1 (continued)

Year	*Nominal exchange rate*	*Percentage change in the nominal Exchange rate*	*Potential Exchange Rate GDP Growth*	*Actual GDP Growth*	*Potential GDP growth if exchange rate was Fixed*	*GDP (current US $)*	*GDP*nominal exchange rate (current US $)*
1993	33.29	33	2.8	2.2	5	4,891,215,396.10	136,954,031.09
1994	35.35	6	3.7	1.9	5.6	4,938,132,518.60	182,710,903.19
1995	37.25	5	1.9	2.5	4.4	5,813,471,982.00	110,455,967.66
1996	35.51	-5	1.6	-0.2	1.4	6,527,302,708.70	104,436,843.34
1997	36.65	3	-1.4	-1.6	-3	7,472,532,256.80	-104,615,451.60
1998	39.2	7	1	-1.2	-0.2	8,742,153,396.60	87,421,533.97
1999	43.08	10	2.1	1	3.1	8,830,909,007.90	185,449,089.17
2000	43.08	0	3	0.8	3.7	9,008,629,730.20	270,258,891.91
2001	46.08	7	0	1.3	1.3	9,104,515,930.70	0.00
2002	48.54	5	2.1	0.7	2.8	9,718,989,515.90	204,098,779.83
2003	57.93	19	1.6	3.7	5.3	9,430,236,065.50	150,883,777.05
2004	61.34	6	3.2	1.3	4.5	10,173,234,920.30	325,543,517.45
2005	65.9	7	1.8	0.9	2.7	11,239,260,831.80	202,306,694.97
2006	69.1	5	2.2	2.9	5.1	11,927,661,729.80	262,408,558.06
2007	72.9	5	1.5	1.4	2.9	12,795,560,771.30	191,933,411.57
2008	88.5	21	1.6	-0.8	0.8	13,707,629,040.50	219,322,064.65
2009	87.4	-1	3.3	-3.4	-0.1	12,125,023,181.30	400,125,764.98
2010	86.1	-1	-0.4	-1.5	-1.8	13,230,844,040.00	-52,923,376.16
2011	86.6	1	-0.4	1.7	1.3	14,433,926,128.60	-57,735,704.51
2012	92.98	7	0.2	0.7	0.9	14,794,802,080.90	29,589,604.16
2013	106.38	14	2.2	1.3	3.5	14,362,262,584.90	315,969,776.87
2014	112.5	6	3.3	0.9	4.2	13,707,629,040.50	452,351,758.34
Total						**226,975,922,858.90**	**3,616,946,435.97**

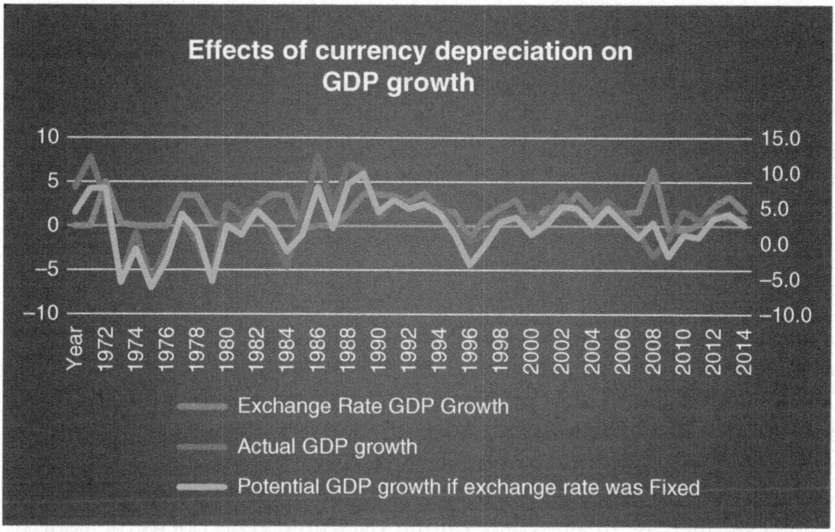

Fig. 5.4 The effect of currency depreciation on GDP growth from 1971 to 2014

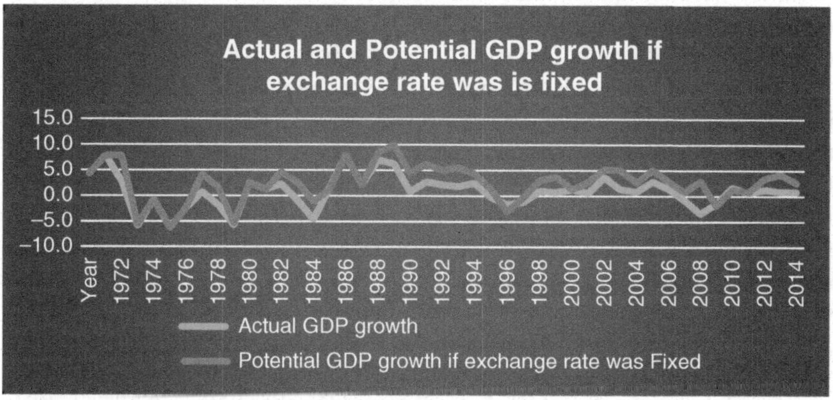

Fig. 5.5 Actual GDP growth and potential GDP growth rate if exchange rate was fixed from 1971 to 2014

which the losses appear to be even greater. Between 1993 and 2014, total potential loss to GDP growth amounted to more than US $3.6 million. If it is calculated from 1990 to present, total potential losses to GDP growth sum to little less than US $4 billion or JMD $480 billion over the 25-year period. These figures give rise to the need for steps to be taken regarding depreciation to counteract this dissipation of growth and its woeful impact on the economy.

5.4 Conclusion

Traditionally, the effect of currency devaluation/depreciation on economic growth in a country is examined within the predictions of the Mundell–Fleming model. In this model, GDP growth responds positively to currency depreciations through an increase in exports as a result of favourable domestic price advantage. However, constant exchange rate depreciations in Jamaica over the last two decades have not resulted in any significant increase in aggregate output over time. This opens the issue to investigations beyond Mundell–Fleming. Alejandro (1963), Krugman and Taylor (1978), Van Wijnbergen (1986) and Saibene and Sicouri (2012) found evidence to suggest that there might be channels through which currency devaluations may actually lead to losses in GDP growth. These include, through distributional channels, if the country uses high proportion of imported inputs or through fiscal effects.

Annual data on real and nominal exchange rates, annual domestic investment (gross capital formation), exports, external debt-to-GDP ratio, Jamaica Consumer Price Index and world annual average GDP from 1971 to present are collected from the World Bank, the IMF International Financial Statistics (IFS) and the Edward Seaga Database Collection. A variety of model specifications were explored and the results showed no significant relationship between the real exchange rate and GDP growth, so the effects of the nominal were explored taking domestic and foreign prices into consideration. Other adjustments to the model were made to take into account macroeconomic instability, exogenous shocks, global geopolitical environment and World GDP growth as well as Jamaica's actual GDP growth average.

The results indicate that nominal exchange rate changes in the year *t*-1 have an impact on GDP growth in year *t*. More specifically, a 1 percent depreciation of the domestic currency in one year leads to a potential loss of 0.3 percent to real GDP growth in the year that follows, constrained by a threshold of 3.7 percent. Over the last 25 years Jamaica has lost more than US $4 billion in GDP output due to currency depreciation. In 1971, 1972, 1975, 1976, 1977, 1981, 1982, 1987 and 2000, the exchange rate was held relatively stable, not depreciating in the previous year; as such, percentage change in the exchange rate is zero, so no resulting effect on GDP growth in each exact year that follows. However, in the years 1973, 1978, 1979, 1984, 1985, 1990, 1991, 1992 and 1994, potential losses to GDP growth as a result of exchange rate depreciation are more severe. Losses to potential GDP growth for these years exceed 3 percent per annum the following year, since the exchange rate depreciated by more than 15 percent in the previous year. In 1986, 1997, 2010 and 2011, the exchange rate appreciated instead of depreciated. Here, losses to GDP growth would be worse if the currency did not appreciate. Potential losses to GDP growth sum to little less than US $4 billion or JMD $480 billion over the 25-year period from 1990 to present.

The findings suggest that pursuing policies to stabilize the exchange rate can lead to favourable growth in gross domestic product through a variety of channels identified in this chapter. Importers of foreign inputs for production processes are more certain of the import prices they will pay. Constant depreciations, such as that which ensued after the liberalization of the financial sector in 1992, have resulted in potential losses in GDP growth in the country.

CHAPTER 6

Balance of Payments and Capital Account Sustainability

6.1 Introduction

Capital flow refers to the movement of money in and out of a country for the purpose of investment, trade or business production. The failure to manage capital flows can jeopardize both internal and external stability. According to Sarwono (2014) 'a surge of capital inflows can pose a range of policy challenges, including macroeconomic risks through excessive credit expansion, an overheating economy and an overhauled real exchange rate'. Sarwono also highlighted that exchange rate flexibility is important to managing capital flows. It can serve as a shock absorber that will lessen the cost of overheating and dampen the pressure on other asset prices. The Bank of Indonesia designed a capital flow management strategy that included a month-long holding period for Bank Indonesia Certificates (SBIs). This strengthens the loan-to-value ratio to manage excessive credit growth in certain sectors. This policy combination has been effective in sustaining capital inflows in Indonesia. We will analyze this situation in the context of the Jamaican economy.

Fischer (1997) informs of the role the International Monetary Fund (IMF) plays with capital liberalization. Free capital movements facilitate more efficient allocation of savings, helping to channel resources to their most productive uses, thereby increasing growth and welfare. The benefits from increased capital inflows to a developing state are the expansion in portfolio diversification. Fischer (1997) highlights the case in which

A. Haughton, *Developing Sustainable Balance of Payments in Small Countries*, DOI 10.1007/978-3-319-53031-4_6

capital inflows are too excessive thus causing them to be unsustainable for long periods. He also emphasized the difficulties in dealing with short-term capital inflows that are a direct result of high domestic interest rates, especially when the country's macroeconomic policy is one in which the exchange rate is not flexible. In cases like this, the best response is a tightening of fiscal policy or in other cases, increasing the flexibility of exchange rates. The main role of the IMF in countries, as Fischer (1997) puts it, is 'to promote the orderly liberalization of capital movements'. If the full liberalization of capital takes place, then the IMF will be able to develop its analysis and monitoring of the different types of capital controls that exist in order to find optimal methods of liberalization.

'Liberalization of capital outflows controls can allow Emerging Market Economies (EMEs) to reduce Net Capital Inflow (NKI) pressures…'. In order to examine the factors that motivate EMEs on change in capital outflow controls, Aizenman and Pasricha (2013) examined macroeconomic and fiscal factors of changes in capital account regulation for 22 EMEs between 2001 and 2010. They also estimate the revenue from external financial repression, i.e., the revenue obtained by preventing residents from freely investing abroad.[12] The major concerns that arise from rapid increases in NKI can be grouped into four main categories (see Aizenman and Pasricha 2013).

1. Concerns about overheating. NKIs to emerging markets are often procyclical, increasing when the economies are booming and retreating when the economies are slowing.[3] Surging capital inflows in periods of high economic growth can therefore lead to overheating concerns by further boosting growth, domestic credit expansion and inflationary pressures.
2. Concerns about foreign exchange valuation. NKI surges can lead to overvaluation of the exchange rate, thus hurting export competitiveness.
3. Concerns about financial stability. NKI surges can exacerbate asset price booms in real estate or financial markets and aggregate balance-sheet exposures, thus giving rise to financial stability concerns.
4. Concerns about macroeconomic volatility. The booms and busts in non-residents' inflow can be an independent source of macroeconomic volatility and can exacerbate existing cycles.

Aizenman and Pasricha (2013) defined external repression revenue as the additional cost that the government would have to bear to service its domestic debt in the absence of outflow controls. It is the difference between the effective interest rate on government's foreign borrowing less the rate paid by the government on domestic borrowing times the repression tax base. They found that the most significant associations of capital outflows liberalizations between 2001 and 2010 were as a result of concerns related to NKIs. It was also found the EMEs with high volatility in NKIs and higher balance-sheet exposures liberalized less. These concerns are also relevant to Jamaica and other small-island developing states that are experiencing current account and balance of payment problems (see Fig. 6.1).

Since the currency crisis in Korea in 1997, the nation has changed its exchange rate system from a market-oriented system to a free-floating system (Ahn 2008). Korea has also switched from monetary targeting to inflation targeting with call rate operating targeting. Korea has liberalized capital markets and as a result has seen increases in capital flows (inflows and outflows). Ahn (2008) points out that because of the currency crisis, Korea had deficits in the capital account from 1998 to 2001. As of 2002, Korea started experiencing capital account surpluses attributed to an increase

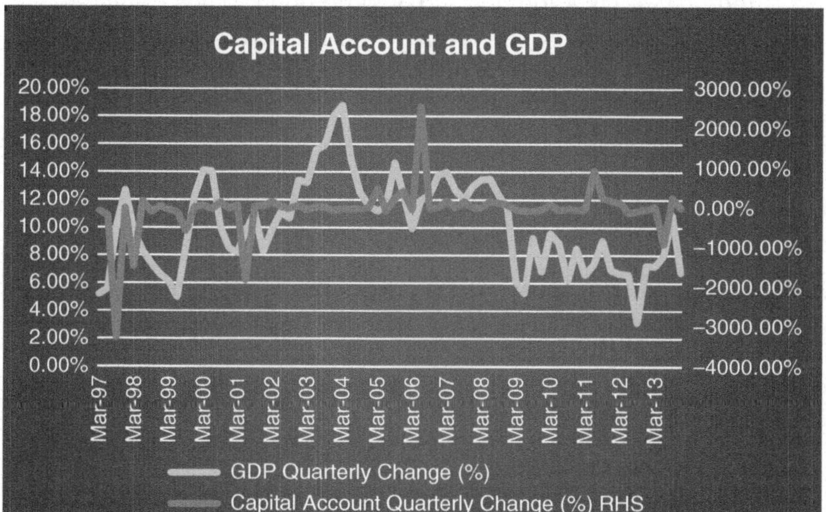

Fig. 6.1 Quarterly change in Capital Account and GDP in Jamaica

in foreign direct investment (FDI). Similar to Korea, Jamaica also experienced a Financial Crisis in 1997 and their economy transitioned through similar stages which provides good basis for research, changes in the change in Capital Account and GDP in Jamaica are illustrated in Figure 6.1.

The scale and frequency of capital flows in Korea have increased with the liberalization of the capital account. These increases have put appreciation pressures on the Won. The government therefore employed various methods to sustain these capital flows while still maintaining the foreign exchange market. Ahn (2008) identified these measures as follows:

1. Overseas direct investment. The limit on overseas direct investment in financial and insurance companies by residents was adjusted upwards from US $100 million per case to US $300 million. The limit was removed by March 2006.
2. Overseas portfolio investment. The range of foreign securities in which residents can invest was extended in March 2003, and all restrictions on them were abolished in March 2006. Overseas investment funds were exempted from capital gains taxation in June 2007.
3. Overseas real estate investment. The limit on the value of an individual's residential property overseas was raised in July 2005 and July 2006 (from US $300,000 to US $500,000 to US $1 million).

   Along these lines, this research will also analyze the sustainability of Jamaica's capital account flows over time. The next section discusses adequacy of reserves.

6.2 Balance of Payment Sustainability: Optimal Capital Account

Analyzing the balance of payment is essential to establish the optimal level of foreign currency inflow and outflow necessary to sustain economic activity in a country. Consider the following equation giving the Balance of Payments (BOP) as a function of the current account, capital account and net international reserves (NIR).

$$BOP_t = CU_t + CA_t + R_t + e_t \tag{6.1}$$

Where *BOP* is the balance of payments, *CU* is the current account balance, *CA* is the capital account balance, *R* is the NIR and *e* represents BOP errors. The composition of foreign currency inflow and outflow is shown here in equation (6.1). By lagging the data one period,

$$BOP_{t-1} = CU_{t-1} + CA_{t-1} + R_{t-1} + e_{t-1} \tag{6.2}$$

Subtracting equation (6.2) from equation (6.1)

$$BOP_t - BOP_{t-1} = CU_t - CU_{t-1} + CA_t - CA_{t-1} + R_t - R_{t-1} + e_t - e_{t-1} \tag{6.3}$$

Re-writing equation (6.3) in terms of differences where delta(Δ) represents change in a particular variable yields,

$$\Delta BOP_t = \Delta CU_t + \Delta CA_t + \Delta R_t + \Delta e_t \tag{6.4}$$

To examine the optimal foreign currency flows for the economy, it is important to examine BOP as a fraction of economic activity represented here by real GDP. Divide equation (6.4) by GDP such that:

$$\Delta \frac{BOP_t}{GDP_t} = \Delta \frac{CU_t}{GDP_t} + \Delta \frac{CA_t}{GDP_t} + \Delta \frac{R_t}{GDP_t} + \frac{e_t}{GDP_t} \tag{6.5}$$

At the optimal level of foreign currency flows, changes in balance of payment are just sufficient to offset changes in economic activity. The economy's maximizing level of foreign currency flows sufficient for economic activity occurs where $\Delta \frac{BOP}{GDP} = 0$, at this point BOP^*; positive capital account flows offsetting negative current account flows, is just enough to cover losses from the current account overtime.

$$\Delta \frac{CU}{GDP} + \Delta \frac{CA}{GDP} + \Delta \frac{R}{GDP} + \Delta \frac{e}{GDP} = 0 \tag{6.6}$$

Rearranging to make capital account to GDP ratio the subject of the formula then,

$$\Delta \frac{CA}{GDP} = -\Delta \frac{CU}{GDP} - \Delta \frac{R}{GDP} - \Delta \frac{e}{GDP} \tag{6.7}$$

Equation (6.7) can be examined to determine the optimal flow of foreign currency that can be absorbed by the Jamaican economy, if sustained by the capital account as is the case in Jamaica. Assuming reserve requirements is a function of foreign currency flows and foreign currency flows is a function of economic activity, errors to the BOP are e if demand for foreign currency flows are independent of reserve requirements and error, determined via economic activity and differences between the capital and current account then we can assume that changes is the reserves are normally distributed with a mean zero and a constant variance overtime

$$\Delta\frac{R}{GDP}+\Delta\frac{e}{GDP}=\varepsilon_t \tag{6.8}$$

Where the errors ε_t are independently and identically distributed, such that

$$\varepsilon_t \sim iid\left(0,\sigma^2\right) \tag{6.9}$$

To verify the optimal amount of foreign exchange that economy can absorb defined by the point $BOP^{*} where\ \Delta\frac{BOP}{GDP}=0$. Equation (6.7) can be expressed in regression form as follows;

$$CAP_t=\beta_0-\beta_1 CUA_t+\varepsilon_t \tag{6.10}$$

Where the capital account to GDP ratio $CAP_t=\frac{CA}{GDP}$ and the current account to GDP ratio $CUA_t=\frac{CU}{GDP}$

Equation 6.10 is regressed using uses dynamic least squares to estimate the long run coefficient, illustrating the relationship between the optimal capital account requirements for the present level of economic activity given the current account deficit. The sum of the ratio of the two is equally proportionate to economic activity, in this case the beta coefficient ($\hat{a}_1$) represent the relationship between both variables. If the absolute value of the $\hat{a}_1=1$ then changes in current account to GDP ratio is balanced by changes in the capital account ratio to maintain the optimal BOP/GDP ratio BOP* over time. Here foreign currency flows are fully absorbed by the economy's level of output and which will only adjust if the level of output (real GDP) changes significantly. The absolute value of the beta coefficient between the two must be equal to 1 indicating full pass through. If the sum of the ratio between both variables is greater than zero, such that actual $\frac{BOP_t}{GDP_t}>BOP^{*}$ and $\hat{a}_1>1$; foreign capital flows are more than enough to cover GDP but is not being fully absorbed by economic activity in this case foreign currency flows are larger in proportion to economic activity. On the flip side, if the sum of the ratio between the two is less than zero such that $\frac{BOP_t}{GDP_t} < BOP^*$ where $\hat{a}_1 < 1$; foreign capital flows are not sufficient to meet the demands of the economy. Foreign currency flows are not enough to cover GDP flows are fully absorbed by economic activity in this case foreign currency flows are small in proportion to economic activity and demand for foreign currency is way above the supply.

To estimate the model, we first ensure that the variables are stationary such that we do not have spurious regression. Results of the Augmented Dickey Fuller and Phillips Peron unit root tests indicated that the null of a unit root is rejected for both variables indicting stationarity in levels.

6.3 Results from the Dynamic Optimal Capital Account Model

The results from the dynamic optimal capital account model are provided in Table 6.1. The absolute value of $\hat{a}_1 = 0.961$, indicates that in the long run, more than 96 percent of the changes in the current account to economic activity ratio is offset by changes in the capital account to economic activity ratio. Notice the opposite symmetric movement between the current account and the capital account overtime as illustrated by Figure 6.2. Subsequently, the Wald test is employed to examine the null hypothesis that $\hat{a}_1 = 1$ versus the alternative that $\hat{a}_1 \neq 1$. The results are significant, the null hypothesis of $\hat{a}_1 = 1$ is rejected at the 1%, 5% and 10% level of significance. Here changes in current account to GDP ratio is balanced by changes in the capital account ratio to maintain the optimal BOP/GDP ratio BOP* over time. Here foreign currency flows overtime are sufficient and are fully absorbed by local economic activity. Figure 6.2 plots the trajectory of capital account and current account relative to economic activity in Jamaica. Notice the almost identical negative relationship. Current account deficits are offset by capital account surpluses independent of reserves and errors to the BOP.

Table 6.1 Capital requirement results *** indicates significance at the 1%, 5% and 10% level

Variable	*Coefficient*	*Standard error*	*t-statistic*	*p-value*
Current account	***-0.961	0.073	***-13.236	***0.000
Constant	-0.906	1.733	-0.523	0.604

R-squared 0.802

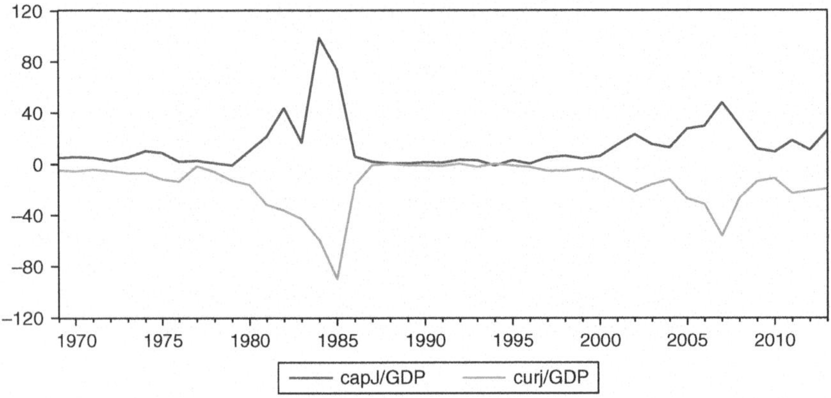

Fig. 6.2 Trajectory of capital account and current account relative to economic activity in Jamaica

6.4 Capital Account Drivers

Based on the results of the previous section, maintaining an optimal balance of payment path depends on the sustainability of the capital flows to the island. There are several factors that influence the sustainability capital flows that must be analyzed in the Jamaican situation.

We employ three sets of control variables: macroeconomic control variables, financial control variables and institutional control variables.

Macroeconomic control variables include real interest rate, exchange rate (ex) and economic openness (open). Chinn and Prasad (2003) and Aizenman and Noy (2009) posit that these variables can have an impact on the level of foreign currency flows. The direction and magnitude of the relationship have to be examined empirically.

Financial control variables include financial deepness, the ratio of private credit by banks and other deposit-taking institutions over GDP, financial development, the ratio of the value of total shares traded to average real market capitalization and financial account openness. According to Chinn and Ito (2006), financial openness and deepness strengthens the capacity of a country to absorb large inflows or outflows of foreign capital and it could increase the savings rate and affect foreign currency flows. Financial development may lead to an increase in the savings rate, which may have a positive effect on foreign currency flows. Institutional control variables include index of corruption, political stability and law and order. A high corruption index means the economy is less attractive to foreign capital investment. The more stable the political systems in a country, the more attractive the country is to foreign capital and likewise for law and order (see Yan and Yang 2012).

The financial accounts represent investment including foreign direct investment, portfolio investment and other investment and foreign currency liabilities, which represents a composition of liabilities of foreign direct investment, portfolio investment and other investment liabilities. The model employed is defined by equation (6.11) and summary statistics are provided in Tables 6.2 and 6.3:

$$\begin{aligned} CAP_t = {} & \Delta Crup_t + \Delta Dcred_t + Law_t + \Delta oil_t + PS_t + int_t \\ & + OP_t + \Delta reer_t + CAP_{t-1} + \mathring{a}_t \end{aligned} \tag{6.11}$$

The variables employed are defined as follows:

- corruption control ($Crup_t$)
- domestic credit to GDP ($Dcred_t$)
- law and order (Law_t)
- crude oil prices (oil_t)
- political stability (PS_t)
- real interest rate (int_t)
- real effective exchange rate ($reer_t$)
- openness (OP_t)
- lagged capital account-to-GDP ratio (CAP_{t-1})

Table 6.2 Summary statistics of capital account drivers

Summary statistics	*CAP/GDP*	*CURJ_GDP*	*DCRED/ GDP*	*LAWORDER*	*OIL*
Mean	14.037	−15.544	50.981	−1.053	49.176
Median	6.199	−11.283	51.106	0.000	41.400
Maximum	98.796	0.278	94.197	0.000	106.360
Minimum	−1.237	−89.895	25.890	−40.000	17.100
Std. Dev.	19.632	18.299	15.230	5.941	25.117
Skewness	2.622	−2.105	0.5400	−6.469	0.639
Kurtosis	10.505	8.009	3.507	42.911	2.219
Jarque-Bera	157.196	80.293	2.670	3300.580	4.209
Probability	0.000	0.000	0.263	0.000000	0.1218
Sum	631.666	−699.491	2294.184	−47.39000	2212.940
Sum Sq. Dev.	16959.27	14734.14	10206.03	1553.352	27758.71

Table 6.3 Summary statistics of capital account drivers cont'd

Summary statistics	*OPEN*	*POLSTAB*	*Corruption*	*REALINT*	*REER*
Mean	5.83E-07	-0.047	-0.151	1.401	43.415
Median	5.63E-07	0.000	0.000	1.526	0.000
Maximum	7.62E-07	0.400	0.000	6.460	144.100
Minimum	4.36E-07	-0.410	-0.740	-4.259	0.000
Std. Dev.	9.67E-08	0.155	0.206	2.402	51.865
Skewness	0.509048	-0.508	-1.0126	-0.192	0.384
Kurtosis	2.006921	4.181	2.749	2.307	1.273
Jarque-Bera	3.792608	4.560	7.811	1.177	6.694
Probability	0.150122	0.102	0.026	0.555	0.035
Sum	2.63E-05	-2.140	-6.800	63.075	1953.700
Sum Sq. Dev.	4.11E-13	1.059	1.934	253.875	118361.1

6.5 Results of the Capital Account Drivers

The results from the unit root tests are given in Table 6.4 and the results from estimating equation (6.11) are shown in Table 6.5. All variables in the model impact foreign currency flows congruent with a priori expectations. The level of corruption in Jamaica has a huge negative impact on the flow of foreign capital, which is of economic significance though not statistically significant, due to large standard deviation. As expected, political stability and law and order have positive impacts on the level of

Table 6.4 Unit root tests

Augmented Dickey Fuller			*Philips Perron*	
Variable	*Coefficient*	*p-value*	*Coefficient*	*p- value*
D(CORUPCTRL)	-1.293	0.623	-1.1212	0.6991
D(DOMCRED_GDP)	0.007	0.6795	-0.179	0.6159
LAWORDER	-6.548	**0.000	-6.548	**0.000
D(OIL)	-1.485	0.531	-1.480	0.534
POLSTAB	-2.240	**0.026	-2.354	**0.019
REALINT	-2.370	**0.0185	-2.348	**0.019
D(REER)	-0.619	0.444	-0.619	0.444
OPEN	-3.513	**0.0122	-3.372	**0.017
CAPJ_GDP	-3.510	**0.123	-2.554	**0.012

Table 6.4 shows the results of the Augmented Dickey fuller and Phillips Peron Unit root tests, Variables here are examined in levels, **means a rejection of the null of a unit root and variables are I(o) processes stationary in levels at the 5% s level, all other variables are I(1) becoming stationary after 1st differencing.

Table 6.5 Results

Variable	*Coefficient*	*Std. error*	*t-statistic*	*p-value*
D(CORUPCTRL)	-23.456	28.098	-0.834	0.409
DOMCRED_GDP	0.449	0.179	2.502	**0.017
LAWORDER	0.140	0.453	0.310	0.758
D(OIL)	-0.311	0.237	-1.313	0.198
D(POLSTAB)	13.329	24.721	0.539	0.593
REALINT	-0.043	1.074	-0.040	0.968
D(REER)	-0.019	0.098	-0.192	0.848
D(OPEN)	112.540	322.771	3.475	**0.001
CAPJ_GDP(-1)	0.451	0.132	3.404	**0.001

Durbin Watson 2.11, p-value from *F*-test 0.000**, 1969 to present, ** indicates significance at the, 5% level

capital flows. Meanwhile, an increase in real interest rate, increase in crude oil prices and a depreciation of the local currency have negative impacts on capital flows. The most significant drivers of the capital account are openness, domestic credit-to-GDP ratio and lagged values of the capital account-to-GDP ratio shown in red in Table 6.5. Next, the analysis is taken one step further to examine how shocks to the most significant variables impact the optimal capital account required to sustain economic activity.

6.5.1 Capital Account Vector Autoregressive (VAR) Analysis

To analyze the impact of shocks to openness and domestic credit to GDP on the capital account, the following VAR model is estimated to derive the necessary impulse response functions.

Let A_t be the vector of macroeconomic and financial variables with the following order[4]

$$A_t = [Open_t, DomCred_t, CAP_t] \tag{6.12}$$

Where $Open_t$ is the level of openness, $DomCred_t$ is the level of domestic credit to GDP ratio and CAP_t is the optimal capital account flows. We assume that the VAR is stable and therefore can be inverted and rewritten in the following moving average (MA) formation:

$$A_t = B(L)u_t, \tag{6.13}$$

where u_t is a(3×1) vector of reduced form residuals assumed to be identically independently distributed with mean zero and positive definite covariance matrixΨ.

$B(L) = \sum_{j=0}^{\infty} B_j L^j$ is a(3×3), convergent matrix polynomial in the lag operator L. Let e_t be the vector of underlying orthogonal structural shocks. Then u_t, can be written as a function of e_t, such that $u_t = Qe_t$, where Q is a lower diagonal (3×3) contemporaneous matrix. Substituting for u_t in equation (6.12) expresses it in terms of structural shocks as follows:

$$A_t = C(L)e_t, \tag{6.14}$$

Where $B(L)Q = C(L)$. Q can be identified if we assume that e_t is normalized with variance 1. The vector of structural shocks e_t is ordered same as A_t with openness causing increase in domestic credit which causes changes in the level of financial flows necessary to sustain domestic economic activity.

6.5.2 *Results*

Before examining the impact of shocks we first ensure that all three variables used are stationary. The results from the unit root tests are given in Table 6.4 and summarised in Table 6.6. This is a necessary condition for the moving average (MA) formation of the VAR to converge thus presenting our model in terms of shocks to the variables. The results are given in Fig. 6.3.

The VAR illustrates the impact of a one standard deviation shock to the level of openness and domestic credit to GDP on the optimal level of capital that the economy can absorb. As is expected, a one standard

Table 6.6 Result of Unit Root Test for reserve adequacy

Level	*First difference*	*Second difference*
Broad money	Gross international reserves	Percentage change in population
Trade openness	Foreign direct investments	
Foreign exchange flexibility	GDP volatility	
Debt service ratio		

Based on the results of the unit root test, the model is estimated in the following format:

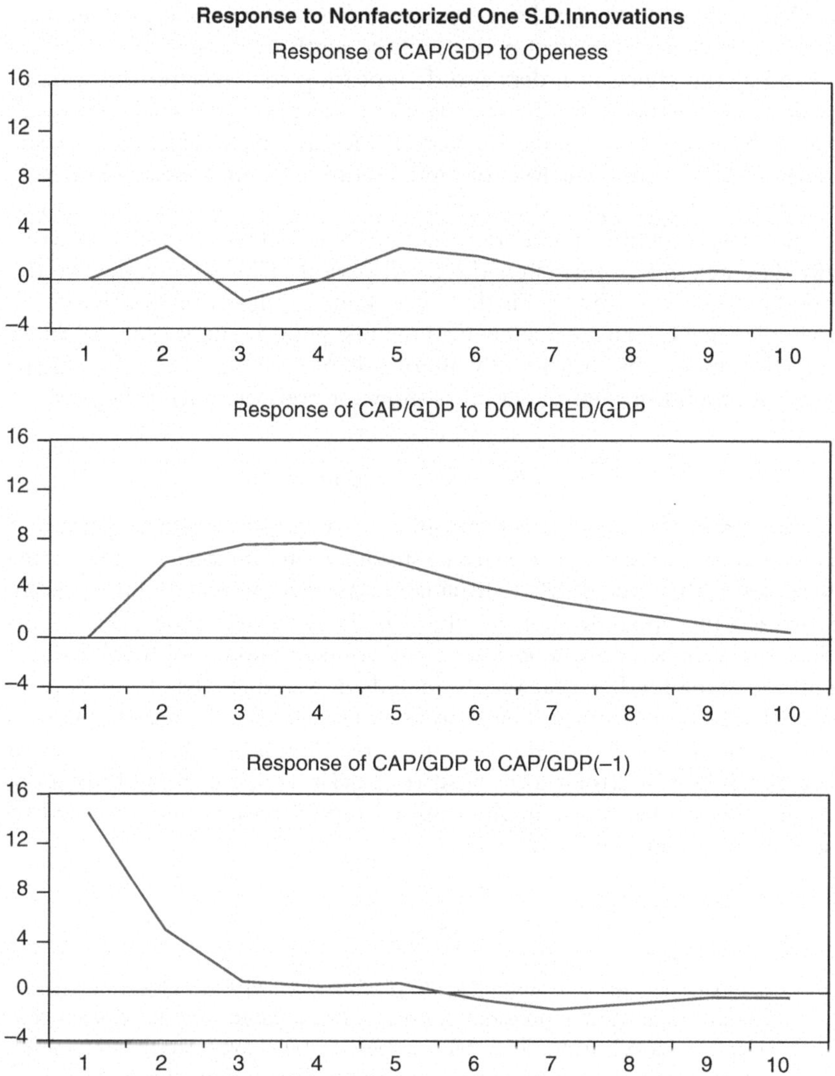

Fig. 6.3 Impulse response functions

deviation shock to the level of openness causes the optimal capital requirements to increase in the first period, subsequently decreasing in the second period as the effect meanders and disappearing to zero after the seventh period, as illustrated by the top panel in the graph shown in Fig. 6.3. Similarly, a one unit standard deviation increase in the level of domestic credit to GDP causes the level of capital required to increase at an increasing rate in the first period and increase at a decreasing rate in the third period, subsequently falling after the fourth period with the effect gradually disappearing to zero after the tenth period. This is illustrated by the middle panel in the graph. Finally, a one standard deviation positive shock to the level of capital requirements in the first period causes a gradual fall in capital requirements consistently afterwards per annum. The effect disappears at around the eighth period as shown in the last panel in Fig. 6.3.

6.6 Conclusion

By analyzing the dynamic relationship between the current account and capital account balance necessary to sustain economic activity, the results here show that the BOP is sustainable, as current account deficits are sustained by capital account surpluses in Jamaica over time. This means that the capital account is important to maintaining optimal foreign currency flow for Jamaica. We examined the variables that contribute to capital account dynamics. The analysis shows that the degree of openness and domestic credit to GDP are the most significant drivers of capital account inflow. Furthermore, positive shocks to openness and domestic credit causes an increase in the optimal capital requirements needed to sustain economic activity over time.

Notes

1. An extension of, Giovannini, A., & de Melo, M. (1993). Government revenue from financial repression. *American Economic Review, 83*, 4, 953–963.
2. This is measured as the difference between the (effective) external and domestic rate on government debt times the government's domestic debt.
3. Kaminsky G.L., Reinhart, C., & Végh, C.A. (2005). When it rains, it pours: Procyclical capital flows and macroeconomic policies. *NBER Macroeconomics Annual 2004,* Volume 19 (2005), MIT Press.
4. The ordering of the variables are important due to the effect of the Cholesky decomposition.

CHAPTER 7

Net International Reserve Adequacy and the Optimal Reserves

7.1 Background

The Net International Reserves (NIR) indicate to the rest of the world the ease or difficulty with which a country can satisfy its foreign currency obligations over a period of time, usually a month or a year. International investors, international lending institutions and international rating agencies are particularly interested in the level of a country's foreign currency reserves, the level of demand pressure on these reserves, as well as the forecast trajectory of the reserve progression in the future. This is in order to make informed decisions regarding the country's ability to service present and future foreign currency obligations. Fundamentally, Balance of Payments (BOP) sustainability depends on the adequacy of a country's reserves.

At the beginning of the 2015/2016 fiscal year, Jamaica's NIR stood at roughly US $2.4 billion from April to May. Foreign currency debt servicing obligations in June and July, arising from the repayment of Jamaica's debt from the PetroCaribe arrangement plus other debt servicing obligations, had a negative impact on the NIR such that it fell from US $2.4 billion to US $2.1 billion in June of the same year. Anticipating a larger foreign currency outflow, necessary to service debt – both interest and principal – Jamaica made a bond issue to the sum of US $2 billion in July 2015, $1.5 billion of which was used to dissolve the PetroCaribe arrangement, and $500 million to strengthen the reserves. At the end of July 2015, Jamaica's NIR was close to US $2.4 billion or 30 weeks of imports.[1]

A. Haughton, *Developing Sustainable Balance of Payments in Small Countries*, DOI 10.1007/978-3-319-53031-4_7

The sinuous trajectory of Jamaica's NIR has not only occurred since 2015 but has been a recurring feature since independence. This has been due to the country's reliance on borrowed funds to support the difference between what it earns and what it consumes from the rest of the world, in addition to constant borrowing to support its foreign currency debt obligations. An overview of Jamaica's NIR position over time – from Q1 1987 to Q4 2013 – is shown in Figs. 7.1 and 7.2. Notice that from the first quarter of 1987 to the last quarter of 1994, the highest amount of reserves that Jamaica accumulated in a given period was US $111.3 million. This occurred in the third quarter of 1989. Over the same period, the lowest the NIR has ever been is –$132.5 billion in the second quarter of 1992. The huge foreign currency outflow requirements arose from the rapid depreciation of Jamaica's foreign currency associated with the liberation of the country's financial sector in 1992. The reserve hovered steadily at around zero from 1992 up to 1994 as illustrated by Fig. 7.1.

From the first quarter of 1995 to the last quarter of 1999, Jamaica's NIR hovered within a narrower band when compared to previous years, reaching a high of US $103 million in 1999, only to fall to a low –$363.7 million in the last quarter of 2001 (see Fig. 7.2). Foreign currency borrowings in 2001 reignited the NIR, increasing it to a new all-time high of US $257.3 million in the first quarter of 2003. After 2003, Jamaica's NIR was predominantly less than zero, meandering up and down to service foreign currency flows as usual. In the third quarter of 2008, Jamaica's NIR jumped to a new high of US $448.5 million. In the aftermath of the 2008 global financial crisis, the NIR took a sharp negative turn in the first quarter of 2009. The NIR

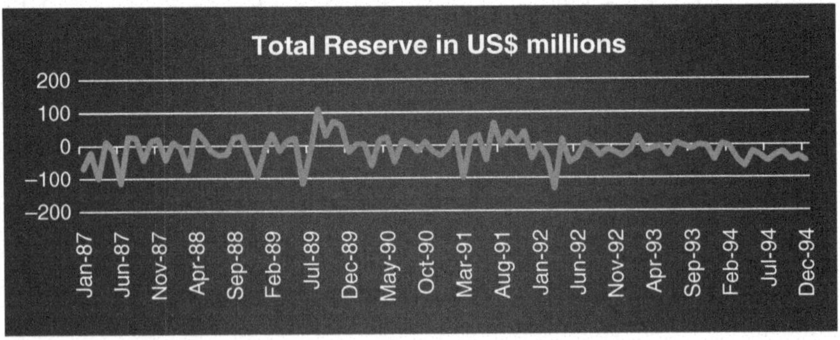

Fig. 7.1 Movement in reserves from 1987Q1 to 1994Q4

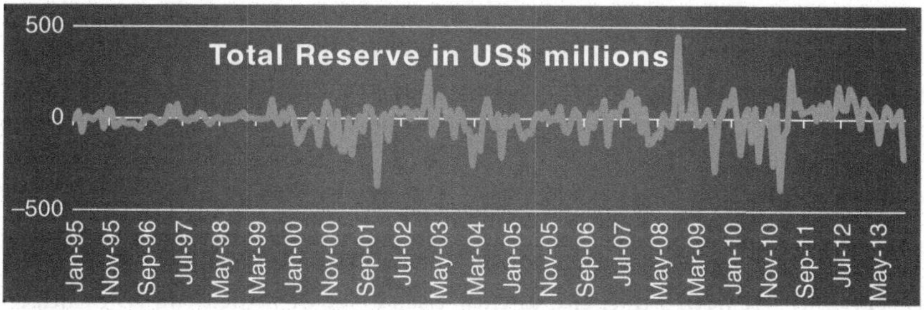

Fig. 7.2 Movement in reserves from 1995Q1 to 2013Q

remained relatively low up to 2013 due to Jamaica's inability to satisfy IMF conditionality necessary to arrive at an agreement to receive NIR support. This plus the country's high level of macroeconomic instability, resulted in a decline in the country's bond rating on the indices of most global bond agencies including Moody's, S&P and Fitch.

During this era, Jamaica's ability to service foreign currency outflow obligations including debt was questionable, as the country was unable to intrinsically generate enough reserves to support its foreign demand and strengthen its NIR at the same time. The country required international foreign currency support, massive restructuring of the country's approach to the management of the economy, specifically fiscal and monetary policy and their effectiveness. Before receiving further support, Jamaica has to prove to the International Monetary Fund (IMF) that it will be capable of repaying borrowed funds when they become due. Jamaica had to demonstrate to the IMF that they could improve tax collection and the efficiency of the tax collection system, make debt repayment a priority in the budget, reduce the country's demand for foreign and push towards fiscal consolidation among other conditionalities. This plan has been gradually worked on since 2013, and as such the IMF was lenient in lending the country more funds, not just for NIR support but also for fiscal support.

Since then, other international lending agencies and other international lending countries, businesses, and individuals have been more willing to lend to Jamaica, given that the country has the IMF's approval. But with all the foreign currency flowing in, and future requirements for foreign currency to flow out, the question remains: Is Jamaica's economy rigid enough to generate enough actual reserve to meet optimal reserves requirements in the future? The aim of this chapter is to analyze Jamaica's reserve position to see if the country will be able to sustain its foreign currency demand requirements in the long run.

7.2 Literature on NIR Adequacy and Optimality

Nechi (2010) adopts a two-pronged approach to estimating optimal reserves in Mexico. First, the author uses a set of indicators to evaluate the sufficiency of reserves based on macroeconomic variables such as external short-term debt, imports and money demand. The second approach estimates the optimal level of reserves using cost-benefit analysis. Nechi uniquely introduces the sustainability of the balance of payments as a constraint in the analysis of the direct trade-off between holding reserves to control the cost of crises and the (opportunity) cost of holding reserves. The optimal level of reserves minimizes the total cost.

In analyzing the sustainability of the BOP and the effects of reserve policy, Nechi specifies a model that regresses nominal reserves to GDP on a vector of observable variables that are exogenous to the economy to plot the reserve process. The constant of the econometric model thus captures the target level of reserves-GDP (the country's reserve policy). The first set of observables consists of internationally traded financial securities while the second set of variables relate to the oil industry. The results of Nechi's Ordinary Least Squares (OLS) regression indicate that the long-run target level of reserves to GDP is 4.64 percent.

Nechi then employs a framework he developed in 2009, which allows the stock of reserves to influence the likelihood of BOP crisis. The author uses this to determine the adequacy of reserve policy. He comments that if a current reserve policy is going to require a drastic shift or lead to a crisis unless bailed out, then the policy is inadequate. Nechi sets up a condition that must be satisfied for the current reserve policy to be adequate. This condition dictates that reserve policy is adequate if the stock of reserves plus the present discounted value of the trade balance less the net liability position of the economy is greater or equal to theta multiplied by GDP. Theta captures foreign investors' perception of the ability of the country to meets its external obligations. Where the aforementioned condition is violated, the country faces a BOP crisis. The author found that Mexico holds fewer reserves than is adequate.

Nechi goes further by developing a cost-benefit analysis to determine the optimal level of reserves in the presence of risk of a BOP crisis under the specifications of the reserve adequacy approach. The author identifies the benefit of holding reserves to be the ability to avoid a reduction in output in the case of a deficit in the balance of payments. The total cost of holding reserves is broken down into a social cost (the loss in output if crisis occurs) and an opportunity cost (the yield forgone from not investing reserves in assets). Optimal reserve policy, according to the theory, corresponds to the level of reserve-to-GDP ratio associated with the lowest total expected cost. The author introduces a perception of the probability of bailout into his model to examine whether the policymaker's perception of bailout in case of crisis influences the optimal level of reserves. Nechi uses data for the period Q1 1981 –Q4 2006 to estimate his model. Estimation results suggest that in the absence of bailout, the optimal level of reserves is 9 percent to GDP, significantly higher than Mexico's reserve policy of 4.64 percent. The results indicate that Mexico's current reserve policy is sub-optimal. When the possibility of bailout is introduced, estimation results suggest that the optimal reserve policy is 5 percent. The result is quite close to the reserve policy target of 4.64 percent. This suggests the Mexican policymaker's belief that the economy will be bailed out in the event of a crisis, giving him reason to account for bailouts in his optimization.

In analyzing the optimal level of reserves for low-income countries, Barnichon (2008) aims to quantify the optimal level of international reserves for small open economies with limited access to foreign capital and high susceptibility to natural disasters or terms of trade shocks by applying an analytical framework to the Caribbean and the Sahel region in sub-Saharan Africa. The model explores the intertemporal optimization problem of a small open economy that holds foreign reserves in order to regulate import fluctuations in response to large external disturbances. Balance of payment constraints result in a country only being able to buy imports if it receives enough foreign exchange inflow. Sudden disruptions in the inflow of foreign exchange caused by natural disasters or terms of trade shocks prevent a country from being able to import the level of foreign goods required, which translates to a welfare loss. With optimal international reserves, a country can minimize the negative impact of such shocks. The paper uses data on natural disasters and terms of trade shocks since 1960 to calibrate and numerically solve the model to estimate the optimal level of international reserves for the Caribbean and Sahel countries.

As it concerns natural disasters, the analysis covers hurricanes in the Caribbean and droughts in the Sahel region. In the Caribbean, the optimal level of reserves estimated should cover 1.42 months of imports, which is only slightly more than the expected duration of a hurricane-related disaster. The estimated optimal level of reserves in the Sahel region amounts to 1.93 months of imports. Droughts are more costly than hurricanes, as the duration usually brings the population close to subsistence levels for a long period of time. Reserves are used progressively to minimize the resulting decline in exports for the duration.

With regard to self-insurance against terms of trade shocks, the primary sector in Caribbean countries represents a smaller portion of GDP than the Sahel countries. Caribbean countries are therefore less susceptible to the prices of primary goods, with a 10 percent decline in terms of trade every 17 years, compared to the Sahel region's 15 percent decline every 10 years. By assuming that terms of trade shocks last only a year, and only accounting for changes in the exchange rate, the optimal level of reserves is estimated to be less than 0.01 months for Caribbean countries, and 2.43 months for a country in the Sahel.

When both natural disasters and terms of trade shocks are accounted for, the optimal reserves for the Caribbean is estimated at 1.52 months of imports for a Caribbean country, and 4.10 months of imports for a Sahel country. The results show that a country's level of optimal reserves can be sensitive to the country's specific needs. Therefore, rules which state that the optimal level of international reserves ought to be three months of imports are imprecise. Factors such as the size of shocks, the importance of the export sector and the level of risk aversion are essential to such estimation.

Jeanne and Ranciere (2006) developed a model of the optimal level of international reserves for a small open economy seeking insurance against sudden stops in capital flows. The authors derive a closed-form expression for optimal reserves. They derive the formula under the assumption of a binding borrowing constraint. Jeanne and Ranciere then develop a set of conditions necessary for this condition to be satisfied in equilibrium. The authors then extend their insurance model, introducing the idea of the opportunity cost of reserves, to calibrate a new model that seeks to explain holding of reserves in emerging countries. Jeanne and Ranciere find the optimal level of reserves, given by their benchmark calibration, to be 9.1 percent of GDP. This figure is equivalent to 91 percent of short-term external debt.

This figure is relatively close to reserve to GDP for years up to 2003 (11 percent on average). When compared to more recent levels of reserves to GDP, the figure is significantly lower than the level observed in recent periods. Specifically, the accumulation of reserves in emerging markets of Asia is far in excess of this optimal level. The authors concur with much of the existing literature that the build-up of reserves in these markets is an unintended consequence of policies that seek to maintain large current account surpluses. In the context of this view, the framework developed in the paper could help to assess the fraction of the public sector's foreign assets that should be held in reserves to ensure against the volatility of capital flows.

Rodriguez and Funk (2012) applied the model of optimal international reserves determination developed by Jeanne and Ranciere (2006, 2011) to the Costa Rican economy. The authors introduced the extensions first implemented by Goncalves (2007) to develop a model that takes into account that maintaining reserves diminished the probability of sudden stop in the future. Rodriguez and Funk use this model to estimate the optimal amount of reserves between 2005 and 2010. According to the results, the authors find that optimal reserves to GDP for Costa Rica should be between 13 percent and 18 percent. The paper considers the optimal reserves in the case of an abstraction for the period of financial crisis (2008–2009) and finds that the BCCR[2] should have maintained average reserves of 15.35 percent for the period. The results of their estimation, they argue, show little volatility over time when the period is excluded.

The authors extended their work by estimating optimal reserves for three different scenarios representing different severities of crises. Under a mild crisis, they found that the optimal level of reserves is 14.38 percent. For an average crisis, the authors found that the optimal level of reserves is 15.35 percent. For a severe crisis, the study finds that the optimal level of reserves is 16.06 percent. The authors observe that holding different levels of reserves for each of these three different levels of severity allows the central bank to decrease the volatility in the acquisition of reserves. They found that the bank should try to increase its holdings of international reserves in the medium term. They comment that the bank should implement measures to foster a decrease in the optimal level of reserves in the future. The next section estimates Jamaica's reserve demand.

7.3 Reserve Demand

7.3.1 *Model Specification*

Consider the following model illustrating the relation between gross international reserves and a group of independent variables as follows:

$$\begin{aligned} GIR_t = \acute{a}_t + \hat{a}_1 M2_t + \hat{a}_2 Open_t + \hat{a}_3 FDI_t + \hat{a}_4 GDPV_t \\ + \hat{a}_5 FX\_flex_t + \hat{a}_6 Debt\_service_t + \hat{a}_7 Pop_t + \mathring{a}_t \end{aligned} \tag{7.1}$$

Where:

- GIR_t represents the Gross International Reserves[3]
- $M2_t$ represents broad money
- $Open_t$ represents trade openness, which is the sum of export and imports as a percentage of Gross Domestic Product (GDP)
- FDI_t represents Foreign Direct Investments (FDI)
- $GDPV_t$ represents GDP volatility[4]
- FX_flex represents the foreign exchange flexibility[5]
- $Debt\_service_t$ represents the debt servicing ratio
- Pop_t represents the log of the domestic population
- α_t is a constant
- β_t are the estimated coefficients

7.3.2 *Unit Root Test*

The augmented Dickey–Fuller unit root test was used to assess the stationarity of the variables. The results are presented in Table 7.1:

$$\begin{aligned} \Delta GIR_t = \acute{a}_t + \hat{a}_1 M2_t + \hat{a}_2 Open_{t-1} + \hat{a}_3 \Delta FDI_t + \hat{a}_4 \Delta GDPV_{t-4} \\ + \hat{a}_5 Fxflex_t + \hat{a}_6 Debt\_serv_{t-4} + \hat{a}_7 \Delta_2 \Delta Pop_{t-3} + \mathring{a}_t \end{aligned} \tag{7.2}$$

the Dependent Variable here is Gross International Reserves. The appropriate lag lengths were determined using a Vector Autoregression (VAR) process and the Schwarz Bayesian information criterion (SBIC), which is proposed for quarterly data of any sample size.

Table 7.1 Results of reserve demand regression

Variable	*Coefficient*	*Std. Error*	*t-Statistic*	*Prob.*
Constant	0.088694	0.125494	0.706763	0.4826
Broad money	-0.019181	0.346955	-0.055285	0.9561
Trade openness	-0.387855	0.215965	-1.795916	**0.0779
Foreign direct investments	-1.003203	0.913968	-1.097634	0.2771
GDP volatility	-0.792131	0.442379	-1.790616	0.0788
Foreign exchange flexibility	-1.383482	0.228746	-6.048120	**0.0000
Debt service ratio	-0.004384	0.003503	-1.251445	0.2160
Population growth	-1.80E-06	8.22E-07	-2.189357	**0.0328
Crisis dummy	0.044742	0.025873	1.729288	0.0893
R-squared	0.354787	Mean dependent var		0.002297
Adjusted R-squared	0.262614	S.D. dependent var		0.070911
S.E. of regression	0.060892	Akaike info criterion		-2.631547
Sum squared resid	0.207638	Schwarz criterion		-2.330478
Log likelihood	94.52529	Hannan-Quinn criter.		-2.512756
F-statistic	3.849130	Durbin-Watson stat		2.272220
Prob(F-statistic)	0.001143			

**Indicate significance at the 5 % level

7.4 Preliminary Results

According to the model, the targeted level of reserves-GDP is 8.9 perecent as illustrated by the constant of 0.08869. It was observed that foreign exchange flexibility, GDP volatility and population growth significantly impact the targeted level of reserve holdings. The crisis dummy was also reported to be significant, indicating that structural changes such as structural reforms in the economy and economic shocks impact reserve holdings. In line with previous literature we find that exchange rate flexibility is negatively related to reserve demand. Conflictingly, however, we observed a negative coefficient in the relationship between GDP volatility and reserve demand. Trade openness was also seen to significantly impact reserve demand. This was also contrary to previous studies as we found a negative rather than a positive relationship between openness and reserve holdings.

In calibrating the optimal level of reserve holdings, we employ the model proposed by Jeanne and Rancière (2006) in their examination of international reserve optimality in emerging markets. The model starts by first presenting some stylized facts on the behaviour of domestic absorption and reserves in sudden stops. Jeanne and Rancière (2006) posit that in an open economy, real domestic absorption can be written as the difference between real output and the trade balance:

$$A_t = Y_t - TB_t \tag{7.3}$$

Recall from the balance of payment equation that the change in reserves is equal to the sum of the capital and financial account:

$$CA_t + KA_t = \Delta R_t \tag{7.4}$$

Where CA_t represents the current account, KA_t is the capital/financial account and ΔR_t is the change in reserves ($\Delta R_t = R_t - R_{t\text{-}1}$).

The current account can be expressed as a sum of the income and transfers from abroad (IT_t) and the trade balance (TB_t):

$$CA_t = TB_t + IT_t \tag{7.5}$$

Substituting equation (7.5) into equation (7.4) we get:

$$TB_t + IT_t + KA_t = \Delta R_t \tag{7.6}$$

We can transpose equation (7.4) to derive the balance of trade function:

$$TB_t + \Delta R_t - IT_t - KA_t \tag{7.7}$$

Substituting equation (7.5) into equation (7.1) we can write domestic absorption as:

$$A_t = Y_t + KA_t + IT_t - \Delta R_t \tag{7.8}$$

Jeanne and Rancière (2006) define a sudden stop as an abrupt fall in the capital account, which ceteris paribus will reduce the domestic absorption. This can be amplified by an associated fall in domestic output or reversed by a reduction in reserves.

7.4.1 *Assumptions*

The model assumes the following:

1. The economy is assumed to be a small open economy in discrete time ($t = 1, 2, \ldots$) with one single good consumed domestically and abroad.
2. The model assumes that the economy follows a deterministic path that may be disturbed by sudden shocks. The only source of uncertainty in the model is the risk of a sudden stop.

7.4.1.1 The Consumer

Jeanne and Rancière (2006) distinguish the domestic economy into the private sector and the government, modeling the private sector (consumers) illustrated below, subject to a budget constraint:

$$C_t = Y_t + L_t - (1 + r) L_{t-1} + Z_t \tag{7.9}$$

Here L_t is the foreign debt of the representative consumer, Z_t is a transfer from the government and r is a constant rate of interest. It is assumed that the consumer does not default on the external debt. Output (Y_t) and external debt both grow at the same rate g until a sudden stop occurs. The sudden stop is modeled as a debt rollover crisis associated with a fall in output. When the sudden stop occurs, the representative consumer is unable to roll over her external debt, and output falls by a fraction γ below its long-run growth path.

The model assumes that the consumer's external debt is short-term, implying that L falls to zero in a sudden stop. This is a matter of normalization. The private external debt that is rolled over does not contribute to the sudden stop hence not playing a significant role in the model. After the sudden stop, private external debt remains equal to zero and output goes back to its long-run growth path.

Jeanne and Rancière (2006) assume that the sudden stop occurs with probability π in each period. After the sudden stop, all the uncertainty is resolved and the economy grows at rate $g < r$.

$$Y_t^b = Y_t^a = (1 + g)^t Y_0, Y_t^d = (1 - \tilde{a})(1 + g)^t Y_0, \tag{7.10}$$

$$L_t^b = \ddot{e}(1 + g)^t Y_0, L_t^d = L_t^a = 0, \tag{7.11}$$

The superscripts represent before (b), during (d) and after (a) the sudden stop and λ is the level of private external debt as a share of output in the pre-sudden-stop period.

7.4.1.2 The Government

Unlike the private sector, the government can issue a long-term security that does not have to be repaid in a sudden stop.[6] The security stops yielding any income after the sudden stop. This assumption, which could be interpreted as a contingent default, simplifies the government's problem by making it independent of the history of sudden stops. The government security has a long maturity in the sense that its life expectancy, $1/\pi$, is large if π is small.

Jeanne and Rancière (2006) posit that the pre-sudden-stop price of the security is equal to the present discounted value of the one unit of good it pays in the next period (with certainty) plus the expected market value of the security,

$$P = \frac{1}{1 + r + \ddot{a}}[1 + (1 - \eth) \times P] \qquad (7.12)$$

Implying that,

$$P = \frac{1}{r + \ddot{a} + \eth} \qquad (7.13)$$

The model works on the premise that the price of the long-term security is constant before the sudden stop and falls to zero when the sudden stop occurs. In addition, it assumed that the interest rate used to compute the present value of the long-term security is higher than the short-term interest rate r. The difference δ can be interpreted as a term premium. It does not include the default risk premium, which is already counted in π.

The government issues the long-term security to finance a stock of reserves,

$$R_t = PN_t \qquad (7.14)$$

Here N_t is the number of securities issued by the government in period t. The reserves must be accumulated before the sudden stop because the government cannot issue any long-term security during the sudden stop. The government's budget constraint is expressed as:

$$Z_t + R_t + N_{t-1} = P(N_t - N_{t-1}) + (1 + r)R_{t-1} \tag{7.15}$$

Solving for N_t in equation (7.14) and substituting this into equation (7.15), we can derive an expression for the transfer before the sudden stop:

$$Z_t^b = -\left(\frac{1}{P} - r\right)R_{t-1} = -(ä + ð)R_{t-1} \tag{7.16}$$

According to Jeanne and Rancière (2006) the transfer is negative. The government taxes the representative consumer so as to pay for the cost of carrying the reserves, which is proportional to the term premium plus the probability of a sudden stop. In the event that the sudden stop occurs, the government transfers the reserves (net of the last payment on the long-term security) to help the representative consumer repay the external debt that is not rolled over,

$$Z_t^d = (1 - ä - ð)R_{t-1} \tag{7.17}$$

The model assumes that $\delta + \pi < 1$ to ensure that this transfer is positive. After the sudden stop the government becomes inactive:R_t, N_t and Z_t are all equal to zero.

Using equations (7.14) and (7.16) to substitute for Zt in equation (7.9) gives expressions for the level of domestic consumption respectively before, during and after the sudden stop,

$$C_t^b = Y_t^b + L_t^b - (1 + r)L_{t-1}^b - (ä + ð)R_{t-1}, \tag{7.18}$$

$$C_t^d = (1 - ã)Y_t^b - (1 + r)L_{t-1}^b + (1 - ä - ð)R_{t-1}, \tag{7.19}$$

$$C_t^a = Y_t^a. \tag{7.20}$$

Equations (7.18) and (7.19) illustrate the tradeoff of the optimal level of reserves. Jeanne and Rancière (2006) posit that increasing R_{t-1} raises period t consumption if there is a sudden stop at the cost of lowering it if there is no sudden stop. Accumulating reserves, in other terms, is equivalent to an insurance that transfers purchasing power from the non-sudden-stop state to the sudden-stop state.

Finally the model proposed by Jeanne and Rancière (2006) specifies the government's objective function assuming that the government maximizes the welfare of the representative consumer,

$$U_t = \sum_{s=0}^{\infty} (1+r)^{-s} u(C_{t+s}), \tag{7.21}$$

Where the flow utility function has a constant relative risk aversion σ,

$$u(C) = \frac{C^{1-ó} - 1}{1 - ó} \tag{7.22}$$

The government's issue is to determine the level of reserves R_t that maximizes U_t in each period before the sudden stop occurs.

In concluding, Jeanne and Rancière (2006) state that:

Increasing reserves is equivalent, in the model, to lengthening the maturity of the country's consolidated external debt.

Aggregating the budget constraints of the representative consumer and of the government, equations (7.9) and (7.15), gives:

$$\begin{aligned} C_t = Y_t + (L_t - PN_t) - (1+r)(L_{t-1} - PN_t) \\ +PN_t - (1 + r + ä + ð)PN_{t-1} \end{aligned} \tag{7.23}$$

7.4.2 *Optimal Reserve Formula*

According to Jeanne and Rancière (2006), the government chooses the level of reserves R_t so as to maximize U_t in each period before the sudden stop. The optimal level of reserves in period t maximizes the expected utility of period t +1 consumption, since R_t matters only for the level of consumption in t +1:

$$R_t = argmax(1 - ð)u(C_{t+1}^b) + ðu(C_{t+1}^d), \tag{7.24}$$

here C^b_{t+1} and C^b_{t+1} are given by equation (7.14) and (7.15). The first-order condition is

$$ð(1 - ä - ð)u'\left(C^d_{t+1}\right) = (1 - ð)(ä + ð)u'\left(C^b_{t+1}\right) \tag{7.25}$$

The left-hand side is the probability of a sudden stop times the marginal utility of reserves conditional on a sudden stop. The right-hand side is the probability of no sudden stop times the marginal cost of reserves conditional on no sudden stop. This can be manipulated to obtain a closed-form expression for the optimal level of reserves:

$$p_t = \frac{u'\left(C^d_t\right)}{u'\left(C^b_t\right)} \tag{7.26}$$

Here p_t is the marginal rate of substitution between consumption in the sudden-stop state and consumption in the non-sudden-stop state. Jeanne and Rancière (2006) state that p_t can be interpreted as the relative price of a 'sudden-stop dollar' in terms of a 'non-sudden-stop dollar'. This, they state, is a measure of the liquidity premium generated by a sudden stop.

The first-order condition in equation (7.18) illustrates that when reserves are set optimally, this price should be constant and equal to the following:

$$p \equiv \frac{1 - ð}{ð} \frac{ä + ð}{1 - ä - ð} = 1 + \frac{ä}{ð(1 - ä - ð)} \tag{7.27}$$

According to Jeanne and Rancière (2006), if the term premium δ is equal to zero, then p is equal to 1, which implies that domestic consumption is perfectly insured against the risk of a sudden stop:

$$C^d_t = C^b_t \tag{7.28}$$

However, they posit that if the term premium is strictly positive, then p is larger than 1, implying that domestic consumption is lower in a sudden stop:

$$C^d_t < C^b_t \tag{7.29}$$

The optimal level of reserves in normal times is a fixed fraction of the level of output:

$$R_t = \tilde{n}Y^b_{t+1} \tag{7.30}$$

Where the optimal reserve to output ratio > is given by the following, which is the formula for the optimal level of reserves:

$$\tilde{n} = \ddot{e} + \tilde{a} - \frac{p^{1/\acute{o}} - 1}{1 + (p^{1/\acute{o}} - 1)(1 - \ddot{a} - \eth)}\left(1 - \frac{r - g}{1 + g}\ddot{e} - (\ddot{a} + \eth)(\ddot{e} + \tilde{a})\right) \tag{7.31}$$

Jeanne and Rancière (2006) state that a good approximation to the exact formula, in the range of parameter values that we will consider in the calibration, can be obtained by setting $\delta + \pi = r - g = 0$ in the last term of equation (7.31):

$$\tilde{n} \approx \ddot{e} + \tilde{a} - \left(1 - p^{1/\acute{o}}\right)$$

The approximate formula shows that the optimal level of reserves is increasing one for one with the amount of short-term debt and the output cost of a sudden stop. (Jeanne and Rancière 2006). If the term premium δ is equal to zero, then p is equal to 1, and reserves should be set to the level that perfectly smoothes the impact of the sudden stop on domestic consumption, $\rho = \lambda + \gamma$. The optimal level of reserves falls with an increase in p, which in turn could be caused by a decrease in the probability of a sudden stop, π, or an increase in the term premium, δ. An increase in the risk aversion parameter σ decreases $p^{1/\sigma}$ and raises the optimal level of reserves.

7.4.3 Guidotti–Greenspan Rule of Thumb

The Guidotti–Greenspan rule states that a country's reserves (gross international reserves) should equal short-term external debt (one year or less maturity), implying a ratio of reserves to short-term debt. The rationale is that countries should have enough reserves to resist a massive withdrawal of short term foreign capital. This is illustrated as follows:

$$\tilde{n} = \ddot{e}$$

This rule perfectly smoothes consumption in a sudden stop if there is no output cost (Jeanne and Rancière 2006). Based on the Guidotti–Greenspan rule we calculate the optimal reserve ratio to be 7.4 percent of GDP over the period spanning 2005–2013. This is lower than the 70 percent ratio of gross international reserves to GDP calculated for the same period.

7.5 Adequacy of Reserves

Large increases in international reserves in recent times have created discussions around reserve adequacy and the optimal level of reserves for developing and emerging market countries. One view for holding reserves is as an insurance against capital flows volatility (Aizenman and Marion 2003; Stiglitz 2006). Others (Durdu et al. 2009) account for the increase as being influenced by financial globalization. Jeanne and Rancière (2006) posit that reserves have been accumulated to absorb against the risk of BOP shocks/sudden stops. Dooley et al (2003) proposed that countries that practice export-led growth strategy will exhibit increased accumulation of reserves over time. Cheung and Qian (2009) believe that this phenomenon occurs when economies imitate each other's behavior.

Ben-Bassat and Gottlieb (1992) proposed that in preventing output reduction in the case of a BOP deficit, countries will seek to hold increased levels of reserves. It is against this backdrop that we will analyze the reserve adequacy for Jamaica. Though there is not a universally precise and unique measure of the level of optimal reserves, there are a number of different ratios attempting to define a specific benchmark for reserve adequacy. Here, a simple ratio proposed by Heller (1966) is used to analyze the effects of adjustments to an external disequilibrium. This measure tries to condense several different factors that are expected to influence the amount of international reserve that a country should hold into a single index. This index is not to be considered as the one to solve all problems, but it is useful in providing a measure to be used to assess a country's external liquidity position.

7.5.1 The Model

In employing the model proposed by Heller (1966) to analyze the effects of an adjustment to an external disequilibrium, two major assumptions must hold. First, the country being examined must be so small that it does not have any influence on world prices of traded goods. The second assumption is that there are no foreign repercussions due to any actions of the domestic country. These two assumptions hold perfectly well in the case of Jamaica, where the size of the domestic economy is too small to impact the global marketplace.

Heller (1966) states that there are two different types of policies in which a country can use to remedy external imbalances.

1. The first is expenditure-switching, which involves a change in relative prices between domestic and foreign-traded goods (usually through the use of tariffs or import quotas to switch spending from imported to home-produced goods).
2. The second is expenditure-changing, which is intended to change total expenditure through fiscal policy or monetary policy. Due to the difficulties with quantifying the cost associated with the welfare gained from changes in terms of trade and the cost of reallocating capital resources, the focus will be placed on expenditure-changing policies.

In assessing the issue of reserve adequacy, we examine an economy in equilibrium in terms of full employment as well as in balance as it relates to balance of payments. In the economy, relative prices are on the highest possible indifference curve and the economy produces home goods for consumption and trade, in addition to consuming foreign goods. If there is a decline in the foreign demand for this country's export, this creates a balance of payment deficit. This deficit has to be offset to bring the balance of payment to equilibrium. The amount that is necessary to bring the balance of payment to equilibrium is dependent mainly on the propensity to import (Heller 1966). The total cost of adjustment of an imbalance is inversely proportional to the propensity to import.

It is more favourable to avoid the cost of adjustment and this is accomplished by using the resources available at the monetary authority, more specifically liquid international reserves. Liquid international reserves are assets of a country that could have been invested to gain interest and as such, an opportunity cost[7] is associated with holding reserves. Reviewing the demand for money, we recall that liquidity is demanded for transactionary, speculative or precautionary purposes. Heller (1966) points out that while transactional purposes are important for individual economic units, it plays no role in the decision of the central bank in deriving their optimal portfolio composition. He also stated that central banks will not be primarily involved in speculative activities.

Heller (1966) proposes that precautionary motives are of dominant influence on the decisions of central banks to hold certain stocks of liquid international reserves. If there was certainty that there would be no imbalance in a country's international account then there would be no reserve holdings. In Jamaica, the reserves are divided into three tranches: (1) There is a working tranche, which is the highly liquid portion that is made up of investments between one week and 30 days; (2) there is a liquid tranche that entails instruments less than one year and; (3) there is an investment tranche that is made up of instruments between one year to those over five years. With the precautionary motive the underlying reason for holding reserves, some key parameters must be examined. These include the cost of adjusting to an external imbalance, the cost of holding liquid international reserves and the probability that there will be a need for the reserves of a given magnitude (Heller 1966).

We can manipulate the total cost of adjusting to an external imbalance to get the marginal cost of adjusting national income expenditure to correct for external imbalances by taking the first difference of equation (7.32):

$$TC_a = \frac{\Delta B}{m} \tag{7.32}$$

Here, TC_a is the total cost of adjusting to an external imbalance, ΔB is the external imbalance and m is the propensity to import.

This gives us:

$$MC_a = \frac{1}{m}$$

7.5.2 *Opportunity Cost of Holding Reserves*

The government of a country is charged with maximizing the welfare of its citizens. In maximizing welfare, the cost of adjusting to an imbalance in the international accounts and the costs of financing have to be compared to choosing the least costly way of addressing international disequilibrium. The calculation of opportunity cost, which is actually the opportunity cost of holding reserves is challenging. We develop a proxy that accounts for the spread between the return on reserve holdings and the returns made in investing in short-term domestic debt:

$$r = \left| r_{holding\ reserves} - r_{holding\ debt} \right| \tag{7.34}$$

This proxy replaces the marginal cost of holding one additional dollar of reserves. Heller (1966) proposes that the optimal reserve is then given by the amount that minimizes the total cost of adjusting and/or financing an external imbalance. At this point, Heller (1966) posits that marginal cost of adjusting has to be equal to the marginal cost of financing. While there is a certain cost to hold additional reserves, the cost of adjusting is incurred only in the case that a cumulative balance-of-payment deficit of a certain magnitude occurs. This probability of a deficit is represented by $\eth_i$.

$$r = \eth_i \frac{1}{m} = MC_a \tag{7.35}$$

Both r and m are known parameters. Simplification gives:

$$\eth_i = r \times m \tag{7.36}$$

7.5.3 *Reserve Imbalances*

It is important to ascertain the amount of reserves that should be held if there must be an adjustment with probability $\eth_i$ to an external disequilibrium. Heller (1966) claims that the typical amount of reserve imbalance is determined by the absolute change in the international reserves of a country. If there is an initial amount of reserves and a country experiences a year-to-year change of size h in the reserve, then the stock of reserves at the end of the year is $(R_0 \pm h)$. In the event that there is no structural disequilibrium in the international accounts then the probability of an increase or decrease are equal.

7.5.3.1 Probability of Balance-of-Payment Surplus/Deficit

Heller (1966) defines a phenomenon called a 'cycle' as a consecutive series of balance-of-payment deficits followed by a consecutive series of balance-of-payments surplus. The probability that a country will actually use an amount of reserves R_i, is given by the probability of the occurrence of *I* consecutive deficits of *h*. With the probability of a deficit being 0.5, the probability of a decrease of size R_i, necessitation the use of the R_i^{th} reserve dollar is given by (Heller 1966):

$$P_r(R_i) = (0.5)^i \text{ } where \text{ } h = 1 \tag{7.37}$$

The probability of a running out of reserves matches that of the probability of having to adjust as a country running out of reserves will have to adjust. Combining equations (7.36) and (7.37) produces:

$$r \times m = \eth_i = P_r(R_i) = (0.5)^i \tag{7.38}$$

Which simplifies to:

$$r \times m = (0.5)^i \tag{7.39}$$

We can solve for *i*, which is associated with the amount of reserves that will be used up with the relevant probability in the case where *h* is one:

$$i = \frac{\log(r \times m)}{log(0.5)} \tag{7.40}$$

If *h* is not equal to one then we have to multiply the amount of reserves *Ri* by *h* in order to obtain the amount of reserves associated with a given probability. This gives the optimal level of reserves as:

$$R_{opt} = h\frac{\log(r \times m)}{\log(0.5)} \tag{7.41}$$

This simplified method of calculating the optimal international reserves that a country should hold links the following three parameters: (1) the opportunity cost of holding international reserves (r); (2) the propensity to import (*m*) and; (3) the stability of a country's international account reflected by historic imbalances (*h*), given a probability π_i of adjustment as well as financing.

7.6 Data and Analysis

In calculating the optimal reserve of Jamaica, data was collected from the Bank of Jamaica for the period Q1 1996 to Q4 2013. Recall the measure accounts for three parameters. The change in gross international reserves to GDP is used to account for imbalances in the country's stock of international reserves. The opportunity cost of holding reserves is determined by finding the absolute value of the difference between the rate of return on holding short-term domestic debt and the rate of return on holding reserves. As this measure tends towards zero, the imbalance between using debt or the reserves disappears adjusts. An increase in the propensity to import or the opportunity cost of holding reserves will decrease the level of the optimal reserves, while an increase in the imbalance in the country's stock of international reserves will cause the optimal level of reserves to increase. Summary statistics are given in Table 7.2.

7.7 Results

The gross international reserves accounts for the actual level of international reserves held by a country. With Jamaica's high debt-to-GDP ratio, a significant amount of reserve activities are focused on debt servicing. An adjustment lag of two quarters is practiced by the monetary authorities in addressing debt servicing (this was also determined using prescribed test and criterion for appropriate lag length – Bayesian Schwarz information criterion). External debt to GDP is lagged twice by two quarters to compare the amount of debt to the reserve holdings in an effort to ascertain whether an increased accumulation of external debt is the primary factor for increased reserve holdings. Figure 7.3 compares Jamaica's gross international reserve holding to its external debt to GDP ratio from 1995 to 2013.

The data shows that changes in international reserve holdings tend to be consistent with the ratio of external debt to GDP. The level of optimal reserves derived for Jamaica over the period 1996 to 2013 is compared to actual levels of international reserve holdings and illustrated in the graph shown in Fig. 7.4.

Over the period, it was observed that actual reserve holdings were consistently higher than the optimal level derived. There was some level of convergence in the first quarter of 2000. The optimal level was observed to be higher than the actual holdings in the first quarter of 2010. It should be noted that this was a period of bust in the business cycle, which would require more reserves to buffer increased probability of imbalances.

Table 7.2 Summary statistics

	Optimal reserve (JMD millions)	*Actual reserve (JMD millions)*	*Excess reserve (JMD millions)*	*External debt to GDP(JMD)*	*Foreign exchange rate(JMD)*	*Gross international reserve(JMD millions)*
Mean	27,565.421	117,744.709	90,179.288	346,676.467	63.366	118,794.752
Standard Deviation	37,900.177	74,742.364	68,782.820	77,780.338	20.975	74,747.077
Kurtosis	32.281	−0.844	0.431	−0.567	−1.157	−0.883
Skewness	4.846	0.372	0.004	0.049	0.242	0.338
Range	288567.213	271664.274	368458.755	310639.406	71.348	271664.274
Minimum	393.581	22,854.728	-131,995.033	190,500.155	35.030	22,854.728
Maximum	288,960.793	294,519.001	236,463.722	501,139.561	106.378	294,519.001
N	71	71	71	71	71	71

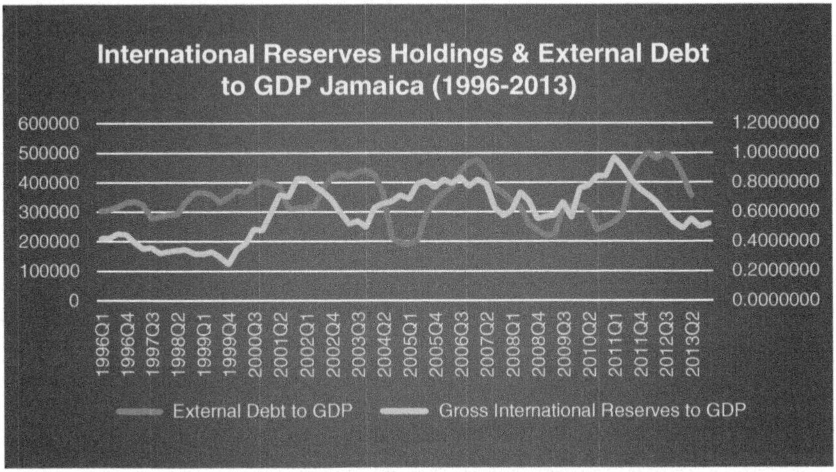

Fig. 7.3 Comparison of international reserve holding to external debt to GDP

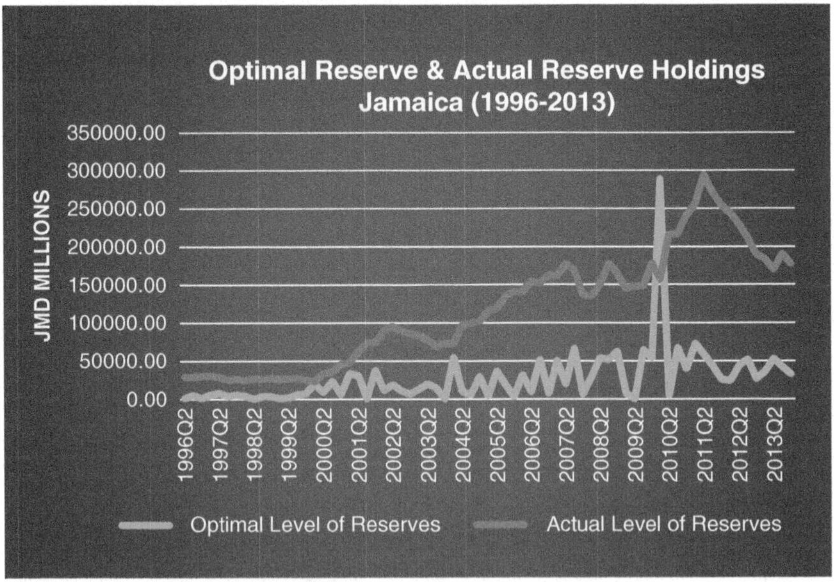

Fig. 7.4 Comparison of actual reserve holding to optimal reserves

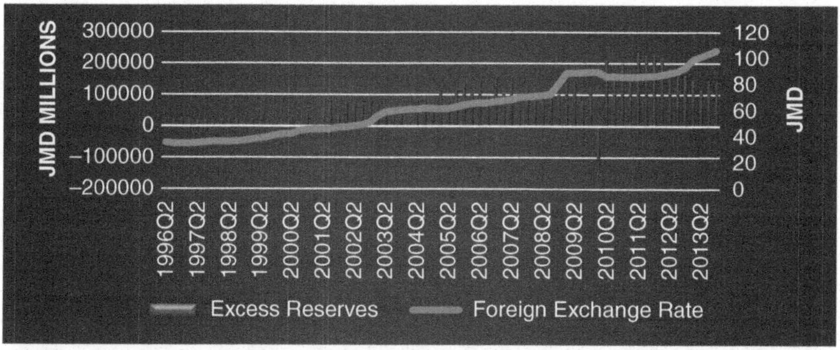

Fig. 7.5 Comparison of excess reserves to foreign exchange rate

Of importance is the consistent divergence of the actual reserve holding from the optimal level of reserves. This is consistent with a rapid depreciation in the domestic currency. A further examination of this phenomenon was conducted, assessing the trends in excess reserve holdings based on the difference between the actual reserve holdings and the optimal level derived and the behavior of the domestic currency.

The results show that excess reserves tend to be moving consistently with the accumulation of excess reserve.

7.7.1 Rate

Further correlation analysis determined a strong positive relationship between excess reserve holdings and the depreciation of the domestic currency of 0.715. Figures 7.5 and 7.6 illustrate the relationship between actual reserve and the foreign exchange rate.

7.7.2 Sensitivity Analysis

VAR estimation was used to generate a 10-year forecast of actual and optimal reserve holdings. The VAR model captures the linear interdependencies among multiple time series. For the actual reserve holdings, the external debt to GDP and the foreign exchange rate were used as exogenous variables while the opportunity cost of holding reserves, historic international account imbalances and the propensity to import were used for the optimal reserves.

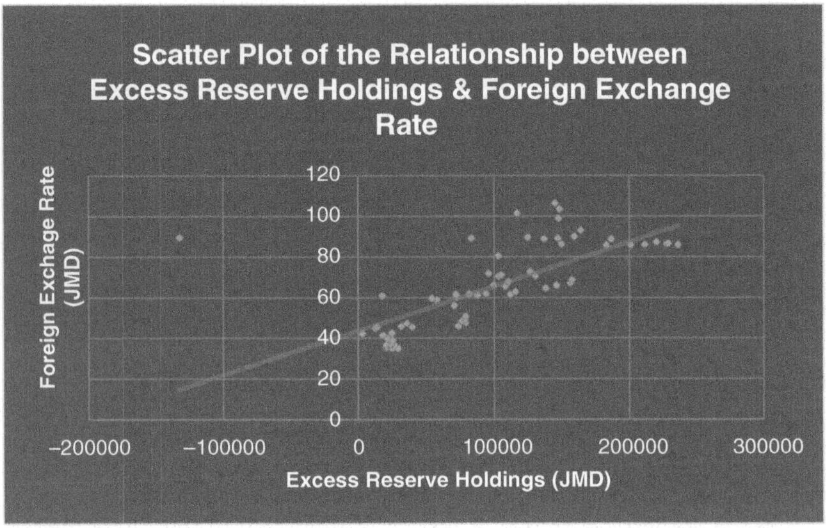

Fig. 7.6 Relationship between excess reserve and foreign exchange rate

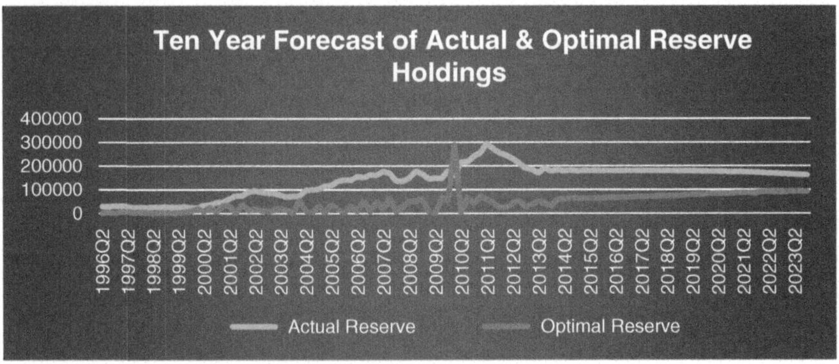

Fig. 7.7 Forecast of actual & optimal reserve holdings

The analysis shows that the actual reserve holdings are expected to trend downwards in the future while the optimal reserve is expected to gradually increase as both converge (see Fig. 7.7). The upward trend in the optimal reserve hints to the fact that higher levels of reserve holdings are expected in

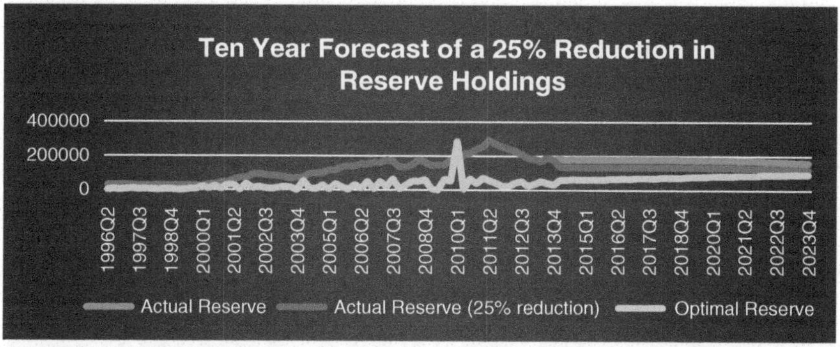

Fig. 7.8 Sensitivity analysis of a year on year reduction in actual reserves of 25 percent

the future based on the expected increases in the country's propensity to import, debt servicing requirements and the impact of foreign exchange depreciation. With the notion that reserves are held in excess, future reserves were adjusted and compared to the optimal levels previously forecast.

A year-on-year reduction of the actual reserves of 25 percent narrows the gap between the actual and optimal level of reserves (see Fig. 7.8). Reduction in the actual reserve sees a faster convergence between the actual and optimal level, however, there still exists an average difference between the actual and optimal level of approximately JMD \$55 billion. This 25 percent reduction amounts in total to approximately JMD \$1.758 trillion worth of liberalized funds.

An annual reduction of the actual reserves of 50 percent narrows the gap between the actual and optimal level of reserves and leads to convergence (see Fig. 7.9). It is, however, forecast that a year-on-year reduction of 50 percent will lead to the actual reserve being less than optimal after the fourth quarter in 2021. The average difference between the actual and optimal level to this point is approximately JMD \$15.939 billion. This 50 percent reduction amounts in total to approximately JMD \$2.852 trillion worth of liberalized funds.

Reducing the actual reserve by 75 percent yearly brings the actual reserve below the optimal level, indicating that such a reduction will not be sustainable in the event of BOP imbalances (see Fig. 7.10).

With debt servicing and imports dependent on the nominal exchange rate it is important to assess the impact of depreciation on the level of reserve holdings. The nominal exchange rate is forecast using a compound

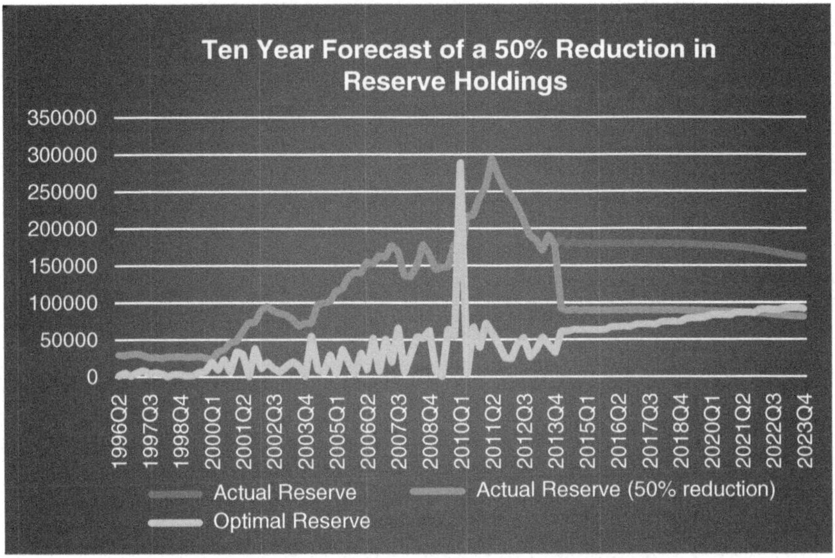

Fig. 7.9 Sensitivity analysis of a year on year reduction in actual reserves of 50 percent

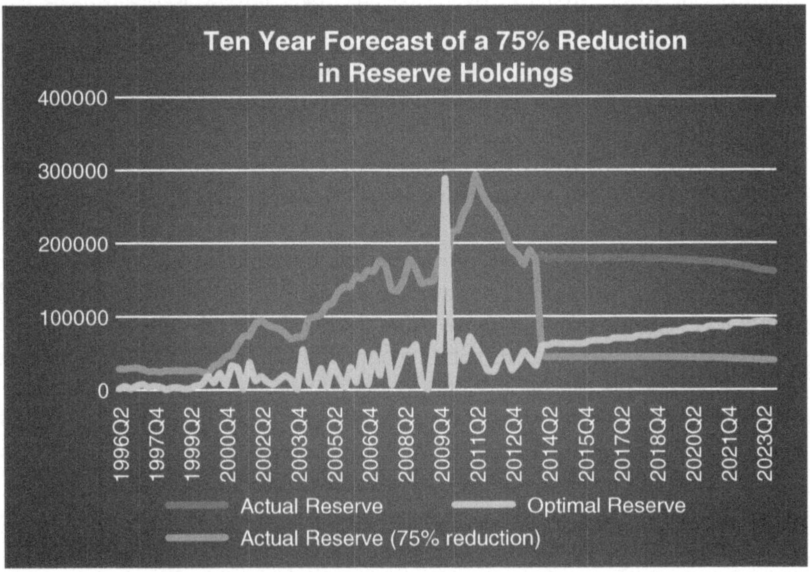

Fig. 7.10 Sensitivity analysis of a year on year reduction in actual reserves of 50 percent

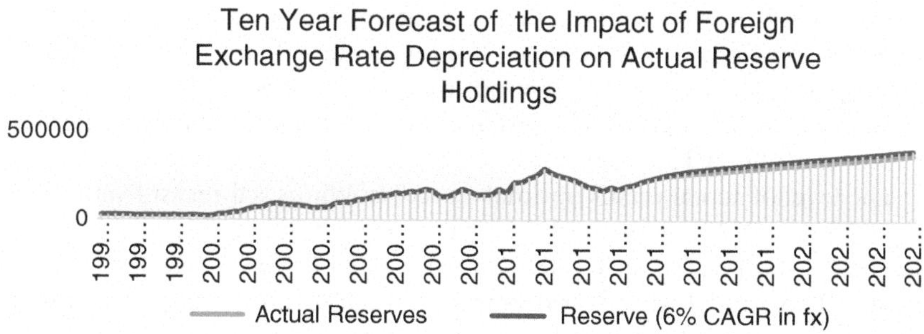

Fig. 7.11 Sensitivity analysis of the effects of foreign exchange rate depreciation on the actual level of reserves

annual growth rate (CAGR)[8] over the sample period (see Fig. 7.11). This was calculated to be 6 percent. The nominal exchange rate forecast from this depreciation was then used in the VAR forecast estimation of the actual reserves.

An annual depreciation of 6 percent is forecast to increase the actual level of reserves to enable the country to correct BOP imbalances.

7.8 Conclusion

Adequacy of reserves and the optimal level of reserves in Jamaica are analyzed in Chapter 7. In calibrating the optimal level of reserve holdings, a model proposed by Jeanne and Rancière (2006) and corroborated by a simple model proposed by Heller (1966) is employed. According to the model the targeted level of reserves-GDP is 8.9 percent or an average of US $1.226 billion per annum over the last five years. It was observed that foreign exchange flexibility, GDP volatility and population growth significantly impacted the targeted level of reserve holdings. The crisis dummy was also reported to be significant indicating that structural changes such as structural reforms in the economy and economic shocks impact reserve holdings. In line with previous literature we find that exchange rate flexibility is negatively related to reserve demand, however, we found conflicting results in terms of the relationship between GDP volatility and reserve demand, observing a negative coefficient. Trade openness was also seen to significantly impact reserve demand. This was also contrary to previous studies as we found a negative rather than a positive relationship between openness and reserve holdings. Based on the Guidotti–Greenspan rule, we calculate the optimal reserve ratio to be 7.4 percent of GDP or an average of US $979 million per annum over the period spanning 2005–2013.

The level of actual versus optimal reserve holdings is forecast from 2015 to 2025 in a VAR framework. Actual reserve holdings include moneys necessary to service external debt and accounts for exchange rate movements. The model also incorporates the opportunity cost of holding reserves, historic international account imbalances and the propensity to import, which are used to measure optimal reserves. The analysis shows that the actual reserve holdings are expected to trend downwards in the future while the optimal reserve is expected to increase, both converging gradually over time.

A sensitivity analysis is conducted to verify the resilience of the country's foreign currency flow to changes in the country's actual reserve position. This is important since the country borrows to support its reserve holding; the breaking point where foreign currency inflows become insufficient to offset outflows must be determined. The results suggest that a year-on-year reduction in Jamaica's actual reserve holdings by 25 percent narrows the gap between the actual and optimal level of reserves. Here there is a faster rate of convergence between the actual and optimal level. However, the actual reserves remain higher than the optimal by approximately JMD $55 billion on average. This 25 percent reduction, when aggregated over the 10-year period, amounts to approximately JMD $1.758 trillion worth of liberalized funds.

The situation is different if actual reserve holdings fall further. An annual reduction of the actual reserves by 50 percent eliminates the gap between the actual and optimal level of reserves and leads to even more convergence. It is forecast that a year-on-year reduction of 50 percent will lead to the actual reserve being below the optimal level after the fourth quarter in 2021. The average difference between the actual and optimal level to this point is approximately JMD $15.939 billion. This 50 percent reduction amounts in total to approximately JMD $2.852 trillion worth of liberalized funds. The results suggest that for Jamaica to maintain a steady flow of foreign currency where the inflows are just enough to offset outflows, reserve holdings cannot fall below 45 percent of their 10-year forecast value.

Notes

1. Normally weeks of imports are calculated on the Gross International Reserves, but the NIR is more suitable in this case.
2. Central Bank of Costa Rica.
3. Gross international reserves represent the official holdings of foreign assets, by the Central Bank and the Central Government.
4. Outline how it is calculated.
5. Outline calculation.
6. The long-term security issued by the government is a bond that yields one unit of good in every period until the sudden stop occurs.
7. According to Heller (1966), the differential between the social yield on capital invested and the yield on international reserves is the appropriate concept of the opportunity cost of holding liquid international reserves.
8. $CAGR = \left(\frac{T_n}{T_0}\right)^{\left(\frac{1}{n}\right)} - 1$

CHAPTER 8

Foreign Direct Investment, Savings, Investment and GDP Growth

8.1 Introduction: FDI and Real GDP

Foreign Direct Investment (FDI) is normally welcomed by host countries as a means to help their economies grow. According to the Economic Survey of Europe,[1] FDI through Transnational Corporations (TNCs) can improve productive output in host countries in four ways: (1) through increased competitiveness by introducing new products or adopting new management styles to remain competitive; (2) through corporations to improve efficiency in forward and backward linkages; (3) through the transfer of human capital; education and skills training via employment transfers and; (4) by imitating good practices of foreign firms.

Considering this, Jamaica has been able to attract increasing amounts of FDI[2] but has failed to materialize growth beyond 0.7 percent on average per annum. What role has FDI played thus far in helping Jamaica attain its growth objectives? Dunning (1994) outlines the cost and benefits of FDI and highlights some host country features that, if present, enhance the benefits of FDI. He suggests that FDI inflows can enhance the competitiveness of the host country by: (1) providing additional resources and capabilities; capital, technology, management skills and access to markets; (2) injecting new entrepreneurship, management styles, work culture and more dynamic competitive practices; and (3) helping to allocate resources more efficiently, FDI brings a competitive stimulus and spillover effects on suppliers and consumers. FDI can help to upgrade domestic resources and

A. Haughton, *Developing Sustainable Balance of Payments in Small Countries*, DOI 10.1007/978-3-319-53031-4_8

capabilities and increase the productivity of domestic firms and enhance the cluster of related activities to the benefit of these firms.

FDI from TNCs are, however, driven by a global agenda to increase operation efficiency and profits and reduce costs. These motives will dictate when, how and which country they choose to engage with international business. TNCs will only transfer benefits by integrated marketing and production activities to the extent that it enhances their global corporate pursuits. Dunning (1994) argues that sometimes TNCs can hamper growth in host countries by reducing competition, limiting their affiliates access to certain markets, limiting the type of technology they can adopt and the type of research and development they pursue. Some of these TNCs also limit the amount of taxes paid through market domination and transfer pricing. The disadvantages of FDI include: (1) it might provide too few or the wrong type of resources and assets. It can restrict access to foreign markets compared with those serviced by domestic firms, and can fail to adjust to localized capabilities and needs; (2) sometimes foreign entrepreneurship, management styles and working practices are unable to accommodate changes in the local business culture in certain instances; (3) it can limit the upgrade of indigenous resources by restricting domestic production processes to mainly primary or low value added production and importing a large proportion of other intermediate goods. Dunning (1994) believes these disadvantages will restrict the growth of GDP in host country economies.

A more open, stable economy with a highly educated and skilled labour force is equipped to accommodate and make good use of FDI than economies with more unskilled and uneducated labour. The aim of the government of a country therefore should be to find the right balance between national growth and developmental objectives and the cost-cutting, profit-maximizing objectives of the TNCs, which makes the research relevant. There are instances where a nation attracts increasing amounts of FDI but fails to grow consistently year after year. Dunning (1994) outlines the following conditions as necessary for FDI to have a positive impact on a nation's output: (1) local resources must be available at low real cost, especially those that are complementary to foreign firms' operations.

There must be minimal structural distortions or institutional impediments to the upgrading of domestic resources and assets. The country must advance development strategies that help to promote dynamic comparative advantage; (2) the policies designed to promote entrepreneurship should be customer driven and efficiency must be endorsed in domestic capital markets; (3) the form and efficiency of the macro-organizational policies and administrative regime is also important. The benefits of FDI will depend on the governments legal and commercial facilities and their ability to assign priority to policies that help upgrade human and technological capabilities and encourage regional clusters of related activities.

Technological advancement, regional integration and the realignment of economic policies have altered the perception of host governments as to how FDI can contribute to their economic and social goals. Dunning (1994) argues that it is difficult for governments to formulate and implement policies that affect the cost and benefit of inbound FDI because they either do not have knowledge of, or are uncertain about the true nature of these cost and benefits. Due to the fact that decisions regarding the operation of these TNCs in domestic economies are made by head offices in parent countries based on information only privy to them. The aim of government therefore is to find the balance between their national objectives and the profit-maximizing objective of the FDI, TNC or otherwise.

The inflow of FDI to Jamaica from 1962 to 1989 was low and stable below US $100 million per annum, with the exception of 1968, 1969 and 1970 when it increased to little less than US $200 million per annum before reverting to stability (see Fig. 8.1). This stability of less than US $100 million per annum continued up until 1989 after which it increased

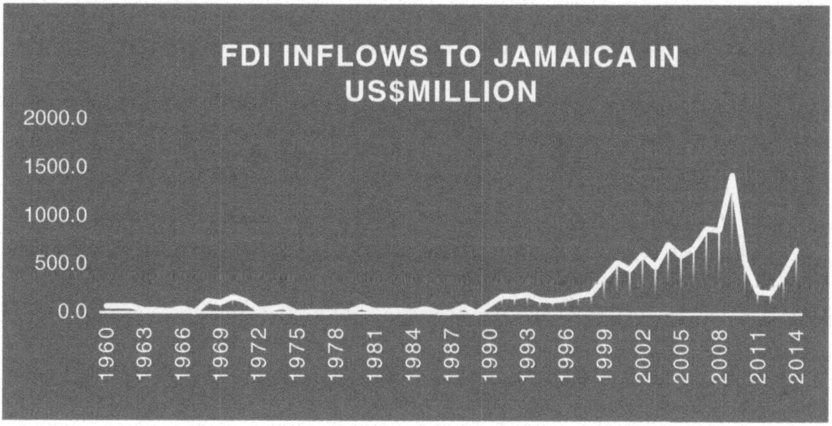

Fig. 8.1 Foreign direct investment inflow

to little less than US $200 million per annum once more up to 1993 when it fell for a year. From 1994 onwards FDI inflows gradually increased to about US $523 million in the year 2000. Afterwards it continued along the same path, increasing to approximately US $880 million in 2007 before rapidly increasing to its highest point of US $1.4 billion in 2008. After the global financial crisis in 2008, FDI flows fell sharply to little more than 1992 levels; they have been gradually improving but have failed to reach pre-crisis heights (see Fig. 8.1).

Notwithstanding low flow of FDI into the country, Jamaica experienced high and positive economic growth during the 1960s and early 1970s; averaging more than 5 percent per annum up to 1973. The economy was adversely affected by the oil price shocks in 1974, which were accompanied by a slowdown in international demand for Jamaica's bauxite. Borrowed funds were redirected from capital expansion and infrastructural development to social safety net programmes. The economy, however, reverted to a steady growth path between 1980 and 1984 with the decline of the socialist movement resulting from a change in leadership after the 1980 election.

Real GDP growth was positive for 10 years in a row, between 1985 and 1995. Real growth was particularly highest in 1987, 1989 and 1990 (see Fig. 8.2). The trajectory shifted once more and real GDP encountered negative growth three years in a row in 1996, 1997 and 1998. Total output in the country improved in 1999 and grew steadily reaching highs of 4 and 3 percent in 2003 and 2006, respectively. After 2007, growth in output was mainly negative or very low. Jamaica entered its third economic crisis aligned with the

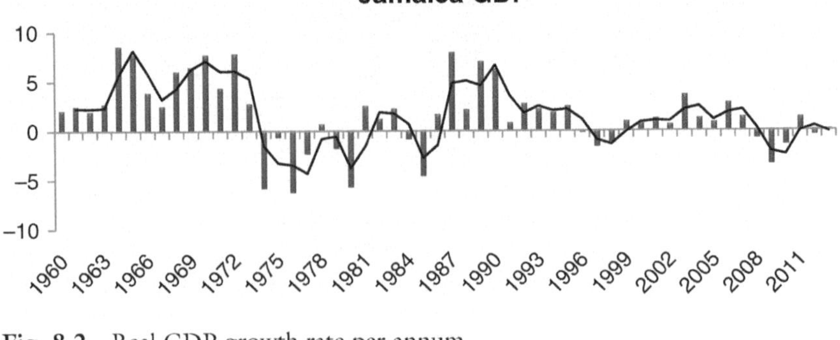

Fig. 8.2 Real GDP growth rate per annum

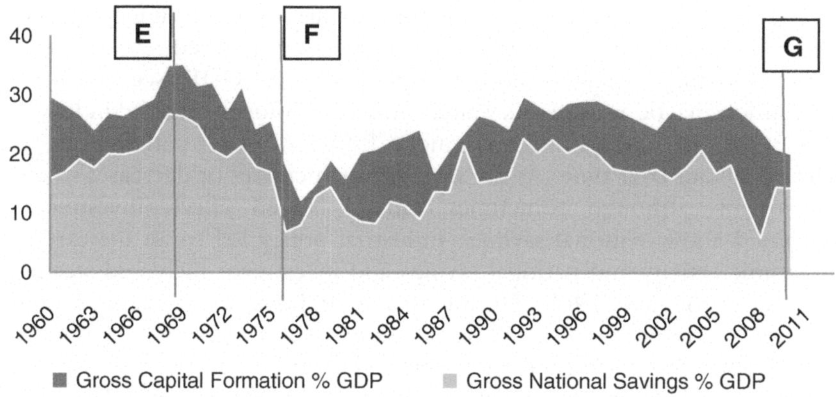

Fig. 8.3 Gross capital formation and gross national savings

global financial crisis of 2008. Policies explored to boost economic growth and increase the inflow of foreign currency during this period were futile and Jamaica reverted to the International Monetary Fund (IMF) once more for assistance.

Household expenditure as a percent of GDP has consistently been more than 60 percent, increasing to an average of 75 percent of GDP over the last eight years. If Jamaica wants to increase economic growth it must increase national savings and reduce domestic household consumption expenditure. The inflow of FDI can help to increase domestic savings needed for more local investment and should be able to fill an investment gap where savings fall short.

8.1.1 Saving,Investment and GDP

In any economy, domestic investments above the rate of domestic savings are subsidized by foreign borrowings. In Jamaica, domestic investments are consistently greater than domestic savings (see Fig. 8.3). The difference, therefore, has been borrowed from the rest of the world. By doing so, Jamaica and other countries that accumulate current account deficits should grow faster due to a higher inflow of foreign capital, according to economic theory. However a lack of empirical evidence to support this suggests that less developed financial systems in these countries like Jamaica cause inefficient allocation of foreign capital inflow (Ghosh and Ramakrishnan 2006). As a result, these countries fail to grow consistently.

Between 1960 and 1962, just before Jamaica received independence, domestic investment or Gross Capital Formation declined, even though national savings increased, both as a percentage of GDP (see Fig. 8.3). Precaution maybe as investors waited. After the country received independence, national savings and investment displayed similar patterns of parallel behaviour over time. As the savings rate increases or decreases so did investment, although sometimes with a lagged effect, investments remained above national savings. Industrial policy led to an increase in economic activity and national savings and investment increased steadily between 1962 and 1969. During this time Jamaica experienced high positive economic growth averaging more than 7 percent per annum. The country was on a good economic trajectory and many governments from other developing countries around the world admired Jamaica's approach to economic planning and emulated Jamaica's growth model.[3] National savings peaked to roughly 27 percent of GDP between 1968 and 1969 and investment increased to 35 percent of GDP in a time when GDP growth was more than 8 percent per annum (see point **E** on Fig. 8.3).

Economic conditions changed for the worse during the 1970s. Global economic crises resulting from rising world oil prices in 1973 and 1978 led to economic depression, not just in Jamaica but the world. Jamaica's savings rate plummeted to its lowest point of 7 percent in 1976 (see point **F** on Fig. 8.3). As a result, investment fell to its lowest point of 12 percent of GDP the following year in 1977. A lower savings rate and low levels of domestic investment had a negative impact on growth of the nation's output. The times of great prosperity came to an end and economic depression ensued between 1975 and 1977 and 1979 and 1980. A change in economic thought, ideas and practical implementation was necessary if the country was to escape the crisis. This was not to occur, and the longevity of the economic prosperity Jamaica experienced during the 1960s and early 1970s was in jeopardy. Political tension in the late 1970s and early 1980s redirected focus from core economic activities in a time when foreign currency inflows to the island began to increase.[4]

From 1976 to 1978, investment and national savings increased steadily before falling in 1979. Even though national savings continued to decline up to 1982, investment increased from 1980 to 1985. Savings and investment both increased gradually between 1986 and 1989 encouraged by a gradually fall in household expenditure (see Fig. 8.4). As a result, real GDP increased and remained positive in the forthcoming years. Real GDP inched above 5 percent in 1987, 1989 and 1990. Jamaica's GDP was also positive in 1988

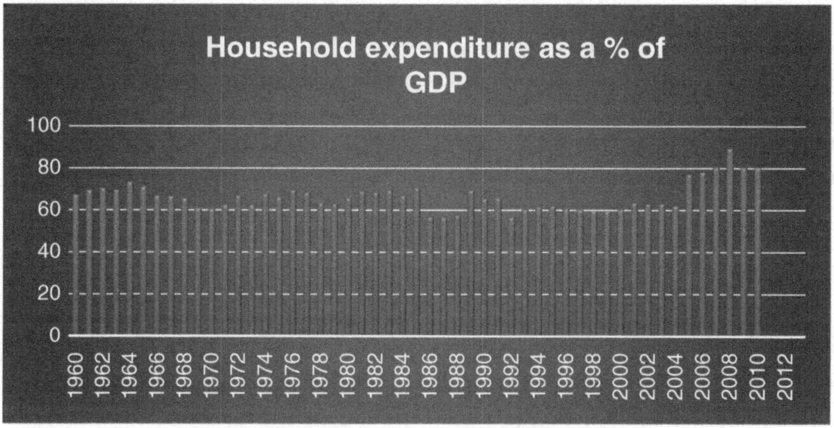

Fig. 8.4 Household expenditure

when the country experienced one of its worse external shocks from Hurricane Gilbert. From 1990 to 1996, investment and national savings maintained a steady pace, but declined gradually from 1996 to 2001 during the time of domestic financial crisis, turmoil in the domestic financial sector following financial liberalization. Afterwards, both savings and investment increased once more before declining sharply with the global financial crisis of 2008 (see point G on Fig. 8.3). They maintained a slow pace from 2008 to present, but have failed to reach the heights of the late 1960s and early 1970s.

Since the IMF's endorsement of the latest Extended Fund Facility (EFF) and Jamaica's improved ranking on the World Bank's Doing Business 2015 index, the flow of FDI to the island is expected to increase. Can this lead to an increase in GDP? The next section is an empirical analysis of the relationship between the real GDP growth, gross national formation, national savings and foreign direct investment.

8.2 Empirical Analysis

Data on real GDP, nominal US dollar exchange rate, FDI inflows, Gross Capital Formation and the Consumer Price Index from 1960 to 2010 were collected from the World Bank, the IMF International Financial Statistics (IFS) and the Edward Seaga Database Collection. Logged FDI flows are employed and Gross Capital Formation and national savings are expressed as a percentage of GDP. Before data analysis, the stationarity properties of the variables are examined using the augmented Dickey–Fuller and the Phillips Perron unit root tests. All variables are first difference stationary except percentage change in real GDP, which is stationary in levels. Strong correlation between gross national savings and Gross Capital Formation would introduce multicollinearity if both variables are employed as regressors in the same model. As such only gross capital formation is employed in this case.

The following econometric model is analyzed:

$$rgdp_t = \propto_0 + \acute{a}_1\Delta GCF_t + \acute{a}_2\Delta FDI_t + \acute{a}_3\Delta CPI_t + \acute{a}_4\Delta FX_t + \acute{a}_t rgdp_{t-1} + \mathring{a}_t$$

Where $rgdp_t$ is real GDP and the regressors, GCF_t is gross capital formation, $FDI_t$is foreign direct investment, CPI_t is the consumer price index and FX_t is the real exchange rate. One lag of the dependent variable is introduced as recommended to remove serial correlation from the model. All non-stationary variables enter the regression with a lag (Δ). The model is examined using ordinary least squares; descriptive statistics are given in Table 8.1 while Table 8.2 provides the results.

8.3 Results of FDI Flows on GDP Growth

The results can be expressed in equation form as follows:

$$\begin{aligned} rgdp_t = {} & 1.12 + 0.35\Delta GCF_t - 0.836\Delta FDI_t - 0.221\Delta CPI_t \\ & +0.113\Delta FX_t + 0.519 rgdp_{t-1} + \mathring{a}_t \end{aligned}$$

Table 8.1 Descriptive statistics for growth analysis

	RGDP	*FX*	*GNS*	*INF*	*FDIIN*	*GCF*
Mean	1.696	21.763	16.805	15.189	213.439	25.407
Median	1.870	5.510	17.100	11.131	64.900	26.512
Maximum	8.578	88.500	26.750	60.035	1436.554	35.156
Minimum	−6.264	0.670	5.970	−4.905	1.900	12.226
Std. Dev.	3.584	27.537	4.923	12.321	299.073	4.7609
Skewness	−0.110	1.080	−0.301	1.336	2.032	−0.571
Kurtosis	2.920	2.897	2.642	5.102	7.255	3.402
Jarque-Bera	0.117	9.941	1.045	24.582	73.589	3.121
Probability	0.942	0.007	0.592	0.005	0.000	0.209
Observations	51	51	51	51	51	51

Table 8.2 Results from the regression analysis; ** represents significance at the 5% level

Variables	*Coefficient*	*Std Error*	*p-value*
ΔGCF	0.345	0.133	**0.013
ΔFDI-inflow	-0.836	0.361	**0.025
ΔCPI	-0.221	0.155	0.161
ΔFX	0.113	0.149	0.449
LRGDP	0.519	0.124	**0.000
Constant	1.12	0.544	2.064
F-test	**7.08		**0.000
R-squared	0.44		
Durbin-Watson	1.88		

The F-test indicates that null hypothesis of no joint significance of the regressors must be rejected. All the variables employed in the model are jointly significant and 44 percent of the variation in real GDP is explained by the model as shown by an R-squared of 0.44. Gross Capital Formation, FDI and lagged real GDP are all significant at the 5 percent level as indicated by the (**) beside the figures in Table 8.2. For the most part, the results of the regression support a priori assumptions. There exists a positive relationship between gross capital formation and growth in real GDP. A 1 percent growth in gross capital formation as a percentage of GDP will result in a 34.5 percentage point growth in real GDP. There is strong evidence to support the claim that that growth fuels growth.

Surprisingly, the model indicates that there is a significant negative relationship between FDI inflows and real GDP in Jamaica. A 1 percent increase in FDI flow result in 0.81 percent or 81 basis points fall in real GDP growth. In this case, it appears the cost of FDI inflow outweighs the benefits as it relates to GDP growth. TNCs can hamper growth in Jamaica by reducing competition, limiting their affiliates access to certain markets, limiting the type of technology that the country can adopt and the type of research and development they pursue. Some of these TNC also limit the amount of taxes paid through market domination and transfer pricing. The disadvantages of FDI include: (1) it might provide too few or the wrong type of resources and assets. It can restrict access to foreign markets compared with those serviced by domestic firms, and can fail to adjust to localized capabilities and needs; (2) sometimes foreign entrepreneurship, management styles and working practices are unable to accommodate changes in the local business culture in certain instances; (3) it can limit the upgrade of indigenous resources by restricting domestic production processes to mainly primary or low value added production and importing a large proportion of other intermediate goods.. These disadvantages have restricted growth and development in the Jamaican economy.

The results also indicate that a 1 percent increase in CPI triggers a 0.22 percent decline in real GDP growth. Changes in the CPI though not statistically significant, indicate some economic importance. The results indicate a negative relationship between changes in the CPI and real GDP growth. In this case, a 1 percent increase in the CPI contributes a 0.22 percent decline in real GDP growth. Policies aimed at reducing inflation are essential to increase growth in a sustainable manner.

Average real GDP growth over the 50-year period is about 0.7 percent per annum despite the increasing inflow of FDI. The negative relationship between the two materializing from the econometric analysis should force Jamaica to rethink its growth and development strategy. Attempts to increase FDI and the praises expressed when it increases might not be warranted. The results here indicate that real GDP growth can be better fuelled through policies targeting local indigenous investments. Jamaica is better off by expanding gross capital formation, which can be achieved by policies geared towards increasing national savings rather than policies aimed at increasing FDI inflows.

Weak GDP growth reduces the amount of goods and services available for a country to export, which does not help the country's current account position. The next section explores the dynamics of the current account and components to get a better understanding of its response to various policy options.

8.4 Conclusion

FDI should promote economic growth in any host country through a variety of avenues including the expansion and advancement of resources, equipment, infrastructure and technology. An investigation of the relationship between FDI flows, gross capital formation (gross investment), national savings and GDP growth is conducted. Jamaica is a unique case as the findings suggest that there is a negative relationship between real GDP growth and FDI, contrary to the preposition of the existing literature. Jamaica operates a small open economy with a highly educated and skilled labour force to some extent, but is unable to manifest growth from the accommodation FDI. Less developed financial systems and high inefficiency in the domestic economy results in misallocation of foreign capital in some instances. Cyclical instability in the nation's economy is also a disadvantage. As outlined earlier, the aim of the Jamaican government should be to find the right balance between national growth and developmental objectives and the cost-cutting, profit-maximizing objectives of the foreign direct investors. Dunning (1994) outlines that if a government is able to implement the following conditions, FDI can have a positive impact on a nation's output: (1) Provide local resources at low real cost, especially those that are complementary to foreign firms operations. There must be minimal structural distortions or institutional impediments to the upgrading of domestic resources and assets. The country must advance development strategies that help to promote dynamic comparative advantage; (2) Policies designed to promote entrepreneurship should be customer driven and efficiency must be endorsed in domestic capital markets. (3) The form and efficiency of the macro-organizational policies and administrative regime is also important. The benefits of FDI will depend on the government's legal and commercial facilities and its ability to assign priority to policies that help upgrade human and technological capabilities and encourage regional clusters of related activities. Jamaica has been making strides in the right direction since the beginning of the latest EFF but still has a far way to go.

The results of the analysis indicate that an increase in national savings lead to an increase in domestic generated capital investment. Less is borrowed from abroad thereby setting a platform to increase GDP intrinsically. Investment and savings are important drivers for real GDP growth in the country. The results also suggest that GDP growth is more likely to occur in period t +1 if investment occurred in time t. The results insinuate that government policy should target local indigenous production and capital expansion instead of focusing on attracting FDI. Efforts to increase national savings can also help capital formation, which is necessary for GDP growth.

Notes

1. See Chapter 5 on Economic Growth and Foreign Direct investment in transition Economies.
2. See Fig. 69.
3. See "From Third World to First" by Lee Kuan Yew (2000).
4. Further details are provided in Chapters 1 and 2.

CHAPTER 9

Commercial Banks and the Monetary Transmission Mechanism

9.1 Introduction

The Bank of Jamaica (BOJ) reduced interest rates by more than 100 basis points or 1 percent since the start of 2015 in an attempt to stimulate economic activity and boost growth in output in the Jamaican economy. This increase in the supply of money to the domestic economy is only effective as far as commercial banks absorb the changes in the BOJ's policy rate in their retail deposit and lending rates. In response to the depressing effect of the 2008 global financial crisis, most economies worldwide, both developed and developing, have implemented some form of expansionary monetary policy and/or other type of stabilization policy. This policy action was particularly necessary in Jamaica, given that the country's budget is tied up with debt repayment and salaries and wages little room is left for capital expansion and otherwise necessary to boost economic growth. Under these circumstances, fiscal policy is ineffective such that monetary policy must intervene to balance this shortfall.

These policies, however, are only effective if the mediums through which they enter the real economy are operating efficiently. More specifically, the central bank can influence the economy via interest rates only if the government policy rate is successfully transferred to the retail lending and deposit rates. If the central bank, for example, increases or decreases its policy interest rate, commercial banks should respond accordingly by transferring any costs associated with the change in the central bank's rate to the retail lending and deposit rates. This process of interest rate

A. Haughton, *Developing Sustainable Balance of Payments in Small Countries*, DOI 10.1007/978-3-319-53031-4_9

pass-through ultimately determines the effectiveness of monetary policy since it is the retail rate that truly influences the market demand and supply of loans and deposits, therefore it has the real impact on economic activity such as inflation, investment and overall growth in GDP.

If the central bank can transfer all the cost associated with an increase in its policy rate to the retail rates then this is considered to be complete pass-through. This situation is rare since according to recent research by Wang and Lee (2009) only the US economy has achieved complete pass-through in its deposit rate, while according to Haughton and Iglesias (2013) only Trinidad and Tobago and St. Lucia have accomplished full pass-through in their lending rate. If the central bank can transfer a part of the cost to the retail rates then this is considered to be incomplete pass-through, and if they transfer more than the cost then it is considered to be over pass-through. Kwapil and Scharler (2010) show that if interest rate pass-through is incomplete there is no guaranteed equilibrium under the standard Taylor rule.

Cottarelli and Kourelis (1994) believe that profit-maximizing institutions such as commercial banks will only change the lending rate or borrowing rate if the cost of doing so is less than the adjustment cost associated with the change. If it is cheaper to keep the current interest rates fixed even when the money market rate has changed then this is the action that will be taken. Whether pass-through is incomplete, complete or more than complete, monetary policy is only effective if there is a long-run relationship between the central bank's interest rates and the retail interest rates. If the adjustment towards the long-run equilibrium is the same between increases and decreases in the interest rate then the pass-through is symmetric. However, if there are different adjustment patterns for increases and decreases towards the long-run equilibrium the adjustment process is asymmetric.

The transition of Jamaica's retail lending rate, retail deposit rate and 3 month Treasury bill rate are illustrated in Figs. 9.1 and 9.2. Stability tests confirm that monetary policy instruments display two different variances from 1990 to present. The first episode of variation arises just before and after the liberalization of the Jamaican financial market in 1992. During this time, Jamaica operated a high interest rate regime with high volatility. Between 1990 and 1997, the government of Jamaica's Treasury bill rate fluctuated between a low of 15 percent and a high of 52 percent. The retail lending and deposit rates followed suit, fluctuating within a similar broad band. The lending rate during this time was marginally higher than the

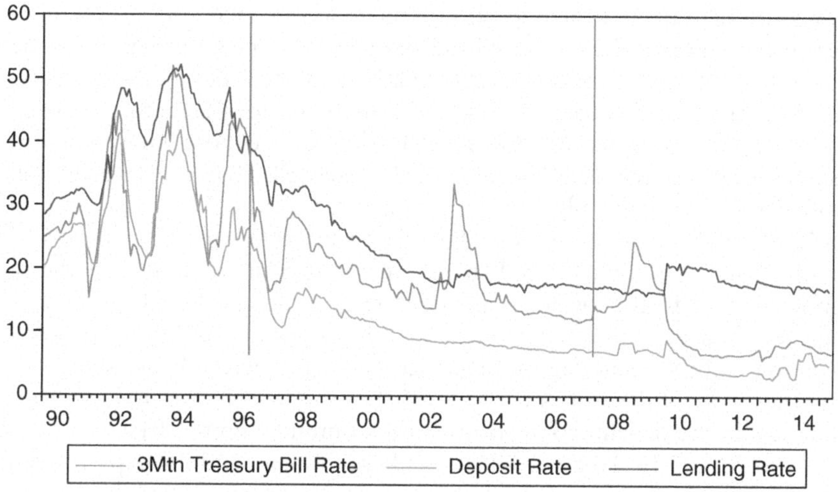

Fig. 9.1 Treasury bill, retail lending and retail deposit rates from 1990 to present

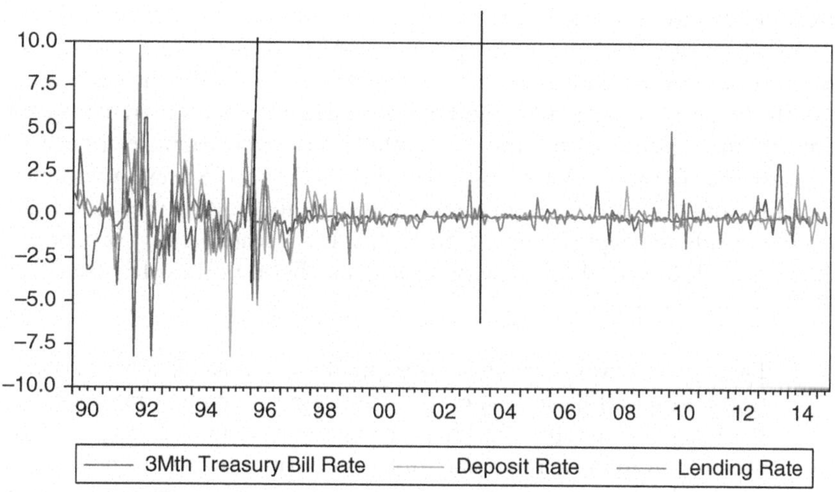

Fig. 9.2 Change in the Treasury bill, retail lending and retail deposit rates from 1990 to present

Treasury bill rate and the deposit rate much lower. Here, due to the high Treasury bill rate, which reduced the amount of leverage remaining for the commercial to capitalize on; here the mark-up on the lending rate is small.

After the local financial crisis in 1997, the volatility of Jamaica's Treasury bill rate, and by extension the retail lending and deposit rates, reduced significantly and the absolute value of the rates fell. Here the Treasury bill rate descended from a high of 29 percent to little more than 15 percent up to 2008 with just one deviating fluctuation in 2003 when it increased to more than 30 percent but fell sharply to the regular trend in a couple of months. Due to the lower Treasury bill rate, commercial banks had more leverage and as a result the gap between the policy rate and both the retail lending and the retail deposit expanded. The commercial banks started to transfer more of the cost associated with Treasury bill changes to borrowers and less of the benefits to depositors; this continued up to 2010.

After 2010, the Treasury bill rate fell even further and the gap between the Treasury bill rate and the retail deposit rate narrowed, while the gap between the Treasury bill rate and the retail lending rate expanded. The widening gap between the lending rate and the Treasury bill rate is signalling that commercial banks during this time, though they might be increasing the level of pass-through, are doing so at a huge mark-up to the disadvantage of local investors who were hoping to benefit from a lower BOJ policy rate (see Fig. 9.1).

Results from Haughton and Iglesias (2013) showed that due to the high initial interest rate position coming from the 1990s into the mid-2000s, Jamaica's retail lending and deposit rates both demonstrate upward adjustment rigidity. Wang and Lee (2009), however, found evidence to suggest that for some Asian countries and the United States the interest rate adjustment process is rigid on the downside for lending rates and rigid on the upside for deposit rates. Although some research shows otherwise, Lowe and Rolling (1992) provide four main theoretical explanations for interest rate stickiness:

1. Diverse selection via agency costs. Banks face possible adverse selection and moral hazard when they increase the lending rate because the less risky investors find higher interest rates unattractive, and an increase in interest rates may not necessarily lead to an increase in the bank's net receipts because there is a higher probability that borrowers will default. As a result, banks may be unwilling to increase lending rates resulting in upward stickiness.

2. Switching costs. The higher the switching cost the less attractive is a reduction in the lending rate to potential customers because of the high administrative fees associated with switching from one bank to the next. This means that banks will more or likely be less willing to reduce their interest rate because it will not attract more customers anyway given the high cost of switching banka.
3. Risk sharing. This arises if the borrowers are risk averse, which means they are more comfortable with a steady rate of interest. With this in mind commercial banks may be unwilling to constantly change their interest rates, which may potentially cause them to lose customers.
4. Consumer irrationality. Lowering interest rates will again attract the more risk-averse borrowers via a process of reverse adverse selection. According to Ausubel (1991), addressing the issue of credit card interest rate stickiness, the theory implies that it is disadvantageous for the bank to compete by reducing credit card rates because they are more likely to attract those who 'fully intend to borrow', i.e., high-risk credit card holders. Hannan and Berger (1991) found that deposit rates demonstrate upward rigidity and the more compact financial markets with smaller firms have more deposit rate rigidity (asymmetric adjustments). According to Wang and Lee (2009), the linear model used by most researchers to test for interest rate pass-through is biased towards rejecting the existence of interest rate pass-through given that it does not account for asymmetries in the adjustment process and other asymmetries.

Considering this, we wish to investigate interest rate pass-through and the monetary transmission mechanism in Jamaica using an updated dataset from January 1990 to May 2015 using the ARDL Bounds Test procedure. The speed of adjustment mechanism is examined using the error correction model. At first sight our data shows almost a parallel movement between the lending and deposit rates in Jamaica, especially over the last four years. It is expected that the level of pass-through has updated since Haughton and Iglesias (2013).

9.2 Interest Rate Pass-through

A clear understanding of the interest rate pass-through process and the speed of adjustment of the monetary transmission mechanism is necessary to determine how changes in monetary policy affect the economy of developing countries. In most of these countries the financial systems function less efficiently due to deficiencies in the market organization for equities and securities as well as by capital controls and ceilings on bank lending and borrowing rates. Most empirical papers thus far discuss the interest rate channel and the credit channel. The interest rate channel consists of two assets: money and other assets. A fall in the level of reserves will cause reduction in deposits. Likewise, as capital market borrowing becomes more expensive investment spending will decrease. This presumed inefficiency of the money channel resulted in the creation of the credit channel.

The credit channel is comprised of a broad channel and the bank lending channel. The broad lending channel assumes that information asymmetries and moral hazard restrict the ability of firms to obtain external finance. In recent years, commercial banks' lending channels have been said to be more relevant to developing countries based on the premise that investments are mostly financed by banks where changes in monetary policy affect the supply of loans directly.

According to Ramey (1993), there are two key conditions that must be satisfied before a lending channel can be made operational. First, banks must not be able to shield their loan portfolio from changes in monetary policy and second, borrowers must not be able to fully insulate their real spending from changes in the availability of bank credit. In light of this, Gambacorta (2001) also highlighted the implication of this mechanism on the real economy by drawing attention to the fact that monetary tightening will cause overall investment and thus productivity and consumption to decline.

A study by Urquhart (2006) examined the bank lending channel to the conduct of monetary policy in Jamaica and how individual bank lending characteristics affect the efficacy of this channel. Monthly bank balance sheet data panel were used along with macroeconomic data spanning January 2000 to December 2005. The Arellano and Bond (1991) Generalized Method of Movements (GMM) approach was used to estimate a model of the banking lending channel of monetary transmission. The hypotheses examined in this study were: (1) smaller banks are most affected by changes in monetary policy; (2) less liquid banks are impacted more greatly by monetary shocks; and (3) less capitalized banks experience greater changes in the amount of loans that they offer given a change in monetary policy. The findings illustrated that the bank lending channel exists as tightening monetary policy lead to a reduction in the loan portfolio. In addition, the results also inferred that the characteristic size, liquidity and capitalization played a major role in the efficacy of the transmission process.

A prior study by Hulsewig et al (2004) in Germany had a similar finding. Using monthly time series data for over 16 periods, it was found that the flow of bank lending channel began with a tightening in monetary policy, which led to a decline in deposits as a result of an increase in the interest rates, which caused loan-to-deposit ratio to decline significantly. This deferred from the view of Kashyap and Stein (1995) who stated that changes in the bank lending channel were not due to a shift in loan supply but a reduction in the demand for loans. This is on the basis that a contractionary monetary policy is aimed at reducing credit demand.

Leith (2006) examined the effects of monetary policy on private money market rates in Jamaica. This was done using the generalized autoregressive conditional heteroskedasticity (GARCH) model to estimate the volatility of the relationship between monetary policies and/or the money market. The data used in the study included daily money market data, BOJ open market operations and announcement of interest rate changes between the period June 2005 to May 2009. The results showed that volatility is at its highest in the 30-day segment of the private money market with the lowest in the interbank segment. The findings showed that BOJ open market research had no impact on the overnight money markets. Further, with respect to the US federal funds market, Cassola and Morana (2006a, 2006b) estimate the underlying factors accounting for the volatility of the euro overnight interest rate and its transmission along the euro area money market yield curve. The estimates show repetitive intra-day, daily and monthly patterns that can be explained by the microstructure of the money market. Likewise, Ghosh and Bhattacharyya (2009) in their study on India's transmission mechanism approximate conditional volatility on the money market. Using the GARCH model they found that the extent of the money market is positively related to conditional volatility. The empirical results suggested that monetary policy expansion led to a reduction in the spreads and call rates.

In contrast to previous empirical research, Ramlogan (2004) seeks to establish the strengths of the various channels through which monetary policy are transmitted and close the gap on how money shocks are transmitted in the developing countries. In his study, he analyzed the transmission mechanism in four Caribbean countries: Jamaica, Trinidad and Tobago, Barbados and Guyana. His study estimated the Vector Autoregression

(VAR) for the four countries using the OLS where quarterly data was used. The sample period used for Jamaica and Barbados was Q1 1970 to Q4 1999, for Trinidad and Tobago Q1 1970 to Q2 2000, while for Guyana the data extended from Q1 1972 to Q4 1998. The results yielded that the credit and exchange rate channel were more important than the money channel in the spread of impulses from the financial sector to the real sector. Further analysis of his findings supported prior expectations that in the developing countries where money markets are emergent the money market will not be the main conduit to monetary policy shocks. These findings supported the findings of Bernanke (1986, 1993), Bernanke and Blinder (1992) and Gertler and Gilchrist (1994), which stated that the credit channel is important in explaining the variability in economic activities.

The empirical evidence points to numerous factors that influence the monetary transmission mechanism. One highlight is that in developing countries, the money market being undeveloped contributes to the composition of finance affecting investments. Further empirical research by Robinson on the transmission mechanism of monetary policy in the Caribbean, particularly Jamaica, attempted to assess the channels through which monetary policy transmission is transmitted. Using the VAR model, the investigation pointed to a process where monetary policy impulses are transmitted by both the money and credit channels via portfolio substitution process. His findings captured the idea of both Keynesian and Monetarist.

Adding to his research, Robinson and Allen (2004) sought to further investigate monetary policy rules and the transmission mechanism in Jamaica using a macroeconomic model. This model was used to stimulate the impact of certain shocks on variables within the model such as inflation and output. In light of this model, which captures the transmission mechanism of monetary policy as well as the dynamics of the economy, the results showed that monetary policy had a major impact on inflation. The results also revealed that the stabilization of inflation is mainly achieved through the exchange rate. Output gap had a minor impact on inflation and is affected by monetary policy through both the credit and the real exchange rate channel.

All in all, the debate on the effectiveness of the monetary transmission mechanism has been ongoing – since before the global financial crisis – and has continued as central bankers and academics look for evidence of its existence in different countries across the world. The global crisis in the

2000s, which had a devastating impact on prices, output and the stability of the financial system, also highlighted the shortcomings of the micro-prudential framework. Taking into consideration the aforementioned, Betty (2011) examined the conduct of monetary policy in Jamaica by giving alternative monetary policies in the case of dysfunctional mechanism transmission. Her study examined substitutes to supplement the traditional interest rate tool with the perspective of enhancing the transmission of lower interest rates to the private sector. The findings assert that there is some advantage in using macroprudential policy tools and quantitative easing and a mixture of monetary and administrative measures to augment the traditional interest rate tool. Macro-prudential policies seem to focus on financial stability or containing systemic risks, rather than risks to individual financial institutions (Moreno 2011).

Shirakawa (2009) argues that the current regulatory framework does not have the effective mechanisms and tools necessary to control innate procyclicality of the financial system. He further argued that measures against procyclicality need to address the build-up of financial imbalance in the upsurge and their loosening in downturns from a system-wide perspective. This is all in an effort to achieve stability against shock in a sense, serving as a shock absorber instead of a transmission of risk to the economy and thus functioning as an automatic stabilizer in periods where there are booms and bust cycles. The next section discusses the current literature on pass-through and provides an idea of the important global findings surrounding the issue.

9.3 Literature Review

The literature on interest rate pass-through is extensive for a variety of countries and groups of countries using various techniques and procedures. We follow the recent methodology of Wang and Lee (2009) who examine the interest rate pass-through mechanism between the money market rate and the retail rates in the United States and nine Asian countries: Hong Kong, Indonesia, Japan, Korea, Malaysia, Philippines, Singapore, Thailand and Taiwan using the Threshold Autoregressive (TAR) and Momentum Threshold Autoregressive (MTAR) models. They also examined the impact of interest rate volatility on interest rates using an Error-Correction (EC)-EGARCH(1, 1)-M model. The TAR and MTAR models account for asymmetric adjustments and the EC-EGARCH(1, 1) deals with the problem of heteroskedasticity in the cointegrating errors and volatility in the model.

The results from the TAR model showed an asymmetric cointegrating relationship in the deposit rate for four of the countries: Hong Kong, Indonesia, Malaysia and the United States and the lending rate for Hong Kong. The MTAR model showed asymmetry in the deposit rate for Hong Kong, Malaysia, Philippines, Singapore and Taiwan and the lending rate model for Hong Kong, Philippines and Taiwan. The countries displaying asymmetry in the MTAR framework are used in the EC-EGARCH-M (1, 1). The results show that adjustment rigidity exists in some countries Hong Kong, Philippines and Taiwan lending rates displayed downward adjustment rigidity and at the same time Hong Kong, Malaysia, Philippines, Singapore and Taiwan deposit rates display upward rigidity. Interest rate volatility has a positive effect on Hong Kong, Japan and Malaysia lending rates and Philippines and US deposit rates and a negative effect on Korea, Malaysia and Taiwan deposit rates and Philippines, Singapore and Thailand lending rates.

The conditional variance equation shows positive asymmetry for the deposit rates of Hong Kong, Japan, Korea, Taiwan, Thailand and the United States and the lending rates of Hong Kong and Singapore. The leverage effect (negative asymmetry in the conditional variance) exists for Korea and Thailand lending rates. Overall the results found complete pass-through only for the US deposit rate; there is incomplete pass-through for the US lending rate and both deposit and lending rate for the remainder of the countries. The results also show that in the cases where interest rate pass-through is incomplete, commercial banks mark up the retail interest rates to cover the cost associated with an increase in the money market rate and mark down the retail rate if the money market rate decreases. These results reiterate the importance of asymmetric cointegration models.

There are also many researchers who examined the issue before Wang and Lee (2009). Many of whom examined interest rate pass-through in various ways for the European Monetary Union (EMU). Toolsema et al. (2002) use monthly data to analyze the similarities between interest rate pass-through of six[1] EMU countries over time. First they use the model developed by Cottarelli and Kourelis (1994) to establish a linear relationship between the government money market rate and the respective retail interest rates given the impact multiplier. Second, they use the fully modified OLS estimator proposed by Phillips and Hansen (1990) to account for any cointegration among the variables. The Hansen (1990) parameter instability test indicates an unstable relationship between the money market rate and the lending rate over time for all six countries.

Therefore, any long-run stability between the variables assumed under the cointegration will be rejected given that the data in itself is unstable. The results for the full sample indicate no cointegration. However, the results from the rolling regression indicate cointegration and stable impact multipliers among subsamples of the data. An error-correction mechanism comprising rolling regression techniques is used to estimate the short-run dynamics of the sample periods that are cointegrated. Their results show little convergence among the different pass-through rates for the different countries in the study. Their model is limited since is does not account for asymmetric adjustments or heteroskedastic errors, which are important when dealing with interest rate models. Angeloni and Ehrmann (2003) examine the interest rate pass-through in Europe before and after the inception of the EMU. They split the data set into two subgroups; group one consists of data before the EMU and group two consists of data after the countries join the union. They employ OLS along with specific VARs to examine if monetary policy has converged between countries given the introduction of the union. The results of their paper confirm the premise, however, that there is little evidence to suggest that the speed of adjustment parameter has increased since the countries joined the union.

Sander and Kleimeier (2002) also investigated the interest rate pass-through in EMU countries finding that short-run and long-run pass-through are different depending on the sample period. Sander and Kleimeier (2006) analyzed the interest rate pass-through in four[2] countries from the Southern African Customs union (SACU). They made an effort to correct for the asymmetry in the EMU found in Toolsema et al. (2002), by modelling interest rate pass-through by using TAR, MTAR and BTAR (Band Threshold Autoregression) cointegration models and an error-correction mechanism. They employed an automatic model selection procedure to establish which model best suit the data. The results suggest that the central bank's lending rate had long-run impact of the respective money market rate. There was complete pass-through in South Africa, which occurred more swiftly than usual, while to the other extreme Namibia illustrated more interest stickiness and asymmetric convergence, which they believe is due to market imperfections. Their methodology, like Toolsema et al. (2002), does not treat heteroskedasticity in the cointegrating errors.

Egert, Crespo-Cuaresma and Reininger (2007) also investigated the interest rate pass-through in five European countries.[3] Instead of the standard cointegration and error-correction model, they use a cointegrated VAR model and error-correction procedure. The results show that short- to long-term deposit rate has a significantly higher pass-through than the overnight deposit rate. Additionally, the money market rate pass-through more to the corporate lending rates than the deposit or household lending rates. The pass-through for these countries are also declining over time, which Egert et. al (2007) believe will continue to decline in the future. This is contrary to modern developments where the interest rate pass-through should increase as financial markets get more developed in these countries. The pass-through for these countries appears to be greater than some EMU members, for example in Austria and Germany there was insufficient evidence to support pass-through to the long-term market rates; this is because the yield curve tends to get less stable at longer ends of the maturity spectrum. The research also found asymmetries in the monthly money market rate, and among the short-run and long-run dynamics.

The most recent research on interest rate pass-through in the EMU is by Karagiannis, Panagopoulos and Vlamis (2010) who examine interest rate pass-through in Europe and the United States as it relates to the recent global financial crisis. They use a disaggregated general-to-specific (GETS) model to analyze the short-run and long-run interest rate elasticities and also the effectiveness of the interest rate pass-through mechanism in the euro area and the United States. The findings indicate varying results for the transmission of interest rate pass-through and the completeness of the pass-through in the United States and the euro area. For the euro area there is evidence to suggest that the money market rate is more influential than the central bank's rate as it is transmitted to both the lending and deposit rate while the central bank's rate is transmitted to the lending rate only. Both upward and downward movements in the money market rate are transmitted to the retail lending rate, confirmed as both parameters are statistically significant.

There is complete pass-through from the money market rate to the deposit rate and incomplete pass-through from the money market rate to the lending rate. For the United States, the interest rate pass-through from the central bank rate to the both the deposit rate and the lending rate are both significant, both upward and downward movements are significant although the magnitude of the speed of adjustment parameter for upward adjustment is ten times greater in absolute terms which may indicate asymmetry. The results also suggest that there is complete pass-through from the central bank rate to both the deposit and lending rate in the

United States. There exists no pass-through from the money market rate to either retail rates in the United States, indicating that the central bank rate is more effective. For the EU there is negative asymmetry relates to the deposit rate; banks pass only negative movements to the depositors. On the contrary, as it relates to the loan rate there is higher positive asymmetry, banks are more likely to pass on the increases in money market rate to the lender than the decreases. This is not surprising considering they are profit maximizing entities. For the United States, the asymmetry is the same as the EU for deposit rates, but in this case there is negative asymmetry for the lending rate.

Other single-country studies such as Burgsteller (2003) analyze the level and the speed of pass-through from the central bank rate to the lending rate in Australia. They employ a structural VAR and regular time series cointegration tests. The results suggest that in the short term the Australian lending rate is relatively inflexible to changes in the central bank's rate. There is also incomplete and asymmetric pass-through as the level of pass-through was significantly different for negative as opposed to positive adjustments. Lending rates tend to adjust quicker to decreases in policy rate than increases. Atesoglu (2003) investigates the interest rate pass-through transmission from the federal funds rate to the prime interest rate. He split the data set into two sub-periods that capture the effects of both. He employed OLS and standard time series cointegration tests in the analysis. The results showed cointegration in both sub-samples indicating that the federal funds rate is being transmitted to the prime rate. There were, however, no tests for asymmetries or incomplete pass-through between both variables. Although there was an increase in the level and the speed of transmission after joining the EMU, interest rate pass-through between the policy rate and the lending and deposit rate is not complete.

Chionis and Leon (2006) examined interest rate transmission from the policy rate to the lending and deposit rate in Greece. They employed a standard cointegration test and error-correction mechanism accounting for a structural break after Greece entered the EMU in 2001. The results show that the pass-through transmission increase for both the lending rate and the deposit rate after Greece joined the EMU also the speed of transmission increase because of the stability gained from joining the EMU. Scholnick (1996) examined asymmetric interest rate pass-through in Singapore and Malaysia. Using an asymmetric error-correction model, he showed that deposit rate adjustment was more rigid when it is above its equilibrium path than when it is below in both countries. There is downward rigidity in the deposit lending rate in both countries, which suggests that banks reduce deposit rates quicker than they are willing to increase them. As already stated, we follow the recent methodology of Wang and Lee (2009) since they allow for the most important characteristics to take into account when modelling the interest rate pass-through. The next section outlines the data sources, the TAR, MTAR and EC-EGARCH (1,1).

For the countries with asymmetric cointegration, the literature shows that the lending rate displays downward rigidity or sticky on the downside while the deposit rate displays upward rigidity or sticky on the upside (see Wang and Lee 2009). De Bondt (2005) claims that if there is asymmetric information in the market mechanism, the borrower has less incentive to repay their debt; in this situation the banks loses more as interest rates increases. Wang and Lee (2009) suggest that in this case, the bank has to increase its lending rate to cover losses that may occur due to borrower's default. This is why the lending rate in some countries will not fall in response to a decline in the Treasury bill rate; they are rigid downwards. Jamaica does not display this characteristic since its lending rate is rigid on the upside. Our results show that the lending rate is associated with a mark-up for all countries. Commercial banks mark up the lending rate regardless if there is pass-through or not. The aim of the bank is to cover the cost or any losses they may incur due to an increase in the Treasury bill rate.

You will find that the retail interest rates in each country in our sample move together. If the deposit rate for a particular country is rigid downwards then the lending rate is also rigid downwards and vice versa. The nature of the banking system does not allow each interest rate to move independent of the other.

9.4 Data and Methodology

Data on the average lending rate, average deposit rate and the government Treasury bill rate are collected from the Bank of Jamaica and the IMF International Financial Statistics from January 1990 to May 2015. Before analysing the concept of pass-through, the stationarity properties of the variables on question must be ascertained. The augmented Dickey–Fuller unit root test is employed to examine the stationarity properties of the variables used in the analysis. The results from the unit root tests confirm that the variables of interest are integrated of different orders over time.

The model is specified in VAR terms as follows:

$$z_t = \grave{a} + \grave{u}t + \sum_{i=1}^{p} \tilde{a}_i z_{t-i} + \mathring{a}_t, t = 1, 2 \ldots, T \tag{9.1}$$

where $\grave{a}$ represents a $(k+1)$ vector of intercepts/drifts and $\grave{u}$ is a vector of $(k+1)$ trend coefficients. Given this, Pesaran et al (2001) derived the following Vector Error-Correction Model (VECM) corresponding to equation (9.1):

$$z_t = \grave{a} + \grave{u}t + Đz_{t-1} + \sum_{i=1}^{p} \grave{e}_i \Delta z_{t-i} + \mathring{a}_t, t = 1, 2 \ldots, T \tag{9.2}$$

Here the $(k+1) \times (k+1)$ matrices $Đ = I_{K+1} + \sum_{i=1}^{p} \grave{i}_j$ and $\grave{e}_i = -\sum_{i=1}^{p} \grave{i}_j i = 1, 2 \ldots, p-1$, as outlined by Lin (2012), contain the long-run multipliers and the short-run dynamic coefficients of the VECM and z_t is the vector of dependent variables y_t and regressors x_t

After regressing the ARDL model, the Bounds Test procedure requires conducting an F-test on the joint significance of lagged levels of the variables in the model. The null hypothesis is that the lagged levels of the variables are insignificant, i.e., $Đ = 0$ against the alternative that they are jointly significant, i.e., $Đ \neq 0$. Under the ARDL model, the F-statistic can no longer be compared to the critical values of the F-tables. Instead, the Bounds Test provides two asymptotic critical values for which to compare the calculated F-statistic. It provides a lower bound critical value assuming the variables are I(0) and an upper bound critical value assuming the variables are I(1). If the F-statistic is greater than the critical value for the upper bound, the null of no cointegrating relationship can be rejected. If the F-statistic falls between the upper and lower bound then the test is inconclusive and if the F-statistic is lower than the critical value for the lower bound then the null of no cointegrating cannot be rejected. The results are shown in the section that follows.

9.5 Results

The initial analysis employs an ARDL model to examine the precipitation of lags in an attempt to see how long it takes for the government policy rate to impact the retail lending and deposit rate and to what magnitude. The analysis takes different lags of the dependent variable (LR/DR), with a maximum lag of three months. We assume inefficiency after three months. Based on previous literature, for example, Haughton and Iglesias (2013) and Urquhart (2006), it assumed that no instantaneous relationship between the policy rate and the lending/deposit rates.

Long-run relationships (cointegration) are used to evaluate the presence and the extent of pass-through. The results indicate that there is insufficient pass-through in both the lending and the deposit rate in response to the government's Treasury bill rate (see Tables 9.1 and 9.3). For the lending rate, the results suggest that roughly 66 percent of the changes in the deposit rate are passed through to the retail lending rate within a three-month period. The speed of adjust slows after three months and disappears after a short while. For the lending rate, the interest pass-through is more than that of the deposit rate, 86 percent of the changes in the government policy rate is pass-through to the commercial lending rate after three months. The effect disappears after and the remainder never to be transferred. These results are supported by the results of Haughton and Iglesias (2013) who also found evidence to suggest that the retail deposit rate and the retail lending rate are characterized by insufficient pass-through, from Haughton and Iglesias (2013).

Here the speeds of adjustment parameter for both the retail lending and retail deposit rate are estimated to be negative (see Tables 9.2 and 9.4). Such that these retail rates do not vary a great deal with the long run equilibrium error which is required for stable, effective monetary policy. This result is an improvement on the results of Haughton and Iglesias (2013) where the speed of adjustment parameters is estimated to be positive, and as a result, the deposit rate changes to a great extent over time with the long run equilibrium error.

In Haughton and Iglesias (2013), there is a leverage effect in the conditional variance, and as a result, the retail lending rate fluctuates considerably with the long run equilibrium error. This indicates that the collusive price arrangement is supported for the deposit and lending rate see Wang and Lee (2009).

Wang and Lee (2009) outline that under the classical assumption of the Bertrand model, if information in the banking system is symmetric and the market is perfectly competitive, the marginal price must equal to marginal cost. Therefore, any changes in marginal cost should offset a unit elastic change in marginal prices. The one to one ratio indicates that under such market mechanism the pass-through is complete. This only exists in the lending rate for Trinidad and Tobago, St. Lucia and by extension the rest of the Organisation of Eastern Caribbean States (OECS) but not in the other countries in Caribbean Single Market and economy (CSME). This is good news for Trinidad and Tobago and the OECS since the retail lending rate stimulate investment and the supply of loanable funds which is a key avenue for expansionary monetary policy.

The results here and the results from Haughton and Iglesias (2013) indicated that where pass-through does not exist in countries like Jamaica because their markets are too small to be perfectly competitive and changes in the marginal cost are not fully transferred to marginal prices. This results in incomplete pass-through due to asymmetric information in the banking system. Fundamentally, there is incomplete pass-through in Jamaica because interest rates are not determined by the market but by other external factors, see Wang and Lee (2009). For example, the government might want to stimulate the economy by artificially inducing commercial banks to reduce the retail lending rate. This new loan rate is different from the real equilibrium rate that would have been determined by the market mechanism. The pass-through coefficient in this case does not reflect a true change which contributes to incomplete pass-through in the long run. This is a disadvantage to central banks because they fail to achieve the objective they tried to achieve in the first instance and monetary policy is less effective.

9.6 Conclusion

The central banks' attempt to influence economic activity through monetary policy relies on the effectiveness of the monetary transmission mechanism and the speed of adjustment, after the policy decision is made. This chapter analyzes the monetary transmission mechanism and the speed of adjustment in Jamaica from 1990 to present using monthly data on the retail deposit and lending rates and the Bank of Jamaica's Treasury bill rate. Stability tests confirm that monetary policy instruments display two different variances from 1990 to present. The first episode of high interest rate and high volatility occurred from 1990 to 1997 during the initial stages of liberalization of the financial sector. The lending rate during this time was marginally higher than the Treasury bill rate and the deposit rate much lower. Here, due to the high central bank's Treasury bill rate, little leverage remained for the commercial banks to explore; here the mark-up on the lending rate is small. The second episode of falling rates and mild volatility occurred from 1997 to 2010. Due to the lower Treasury bill rate, commercial banks had more leverage and as a result, the gap between the policy rate and both the retail lending and the retail deposit expanded. The commercial banks started to transfer more of the cost associated with Treasury bill changes to borrowers and less of the benefits to depositors. After 2010, the Treasury bill rate fell even further and the gap between the Treasury bill rate and the retail deposit rate narrowed, while the gap between the Treasury bill rate and the retail lending rate expanded. The widening gap between the lending rate and the Treasury bill rate is signalling that commercial banks during this time might be increasing the level of interest rate pass-through, but is doing so at a huge mark up to the disadvantage of local investors, who were hoping to benefit from a lower BOJ policy rate. Updated interest rate pass-through and the speed of adjustment for the deposit and lending rates are analyzed in an ARDL Bounds Test framework with error-correction mechanism. The results indicate that both pass-through for the lending and deposit rates are incomplete in Jamaica. For the lending rate, up to 65 percent is passed through to the retail deposit and 85 percent is passed through to the retail lending rate within three months of the government's policy action. The remaining effect, however, depreciates after and no significant additional pass-through occurs.

Appendix

Unit root Tests

Variables were evaluated without intercept and trends.

Table 9.1 Results from the Bounds Test for the Deposit Rate

Bounds Test				
Test statistic	*Value*	*K*		
F-statistic	24.16724	2		
Critical value bounds				
Significance	*I0 Bound*	*I1 Bound*		
10%	3.17	4.14		
5%	3.79	4.85		
2.5%	4.41	5.52		
1%	5.15	6.36		
Dependent Variable: D(D_DR(-3))				
Variable	*Coefficient*	*Std. Error*	*t-Statistic*	*Prob.*
D(D_DR(-4))	-0.228737	0.073876	-3.096226	0.0022
D(D_DR(-5))	-0.087553	0.056584	-1.547302	0.1229
D(D_TBILL)	0.018589	0.060028	0.309665	0.7570
D(D_TBILL(-1))	-0.470601	0.091039	-5.169244	0.0000
D(D_TBILL(-2))	-0.190979	0.077695	-2.458066	0.0146
D(D_TBILL(-3))	-0.104443	0.061215	-1.706170	0.0891
D(LIB)	4.311743	1.196804	3.602713	0.0004
C	0.518820	0.197042	2.633044	0.0089
D_TBILL(-1)	0.528902	0.127104	4.161184	0.0000
LIB(-1)	-0.556592	0.207230	-2.685863	0.0077
D_DR(-4)	-0.655984	0.079844	-8.215800	0.0000
R-squared	0.500288	Mean dependent var		-0.004266
Adjusted R-squared	0.482313	S.D. dependent var		1.603763
S.E. of regression	1.153915	Akaike info criterion		3.161518
Sum squared resid	370.1628	Schwarz criterion		3.301070
Log likelihood	-445.8393	Hannan-Quinn criter.		3.217436
F-statistic	27.83205	Durbin-Watson stat		1.998956
Prob(F-statistic)	0.000000			

Table 9.2 Error Correction Model for the Deposit rate

Speed of Adjustment (ECM)

ARDL Cointegrating And Long Run Form
Dependent Variable: D_DR(-3)
Selected Model: ARDL(3, 4, 1)
Date: 09/11/15 Time: 05:40
Sample: 1990M01 2015M05
Included observations: 289

Cointegrating Form

Variable	*Coefficient*	*Std. Error*	*t-Statistic*	*Prob.*
D(D_DR(-4))	-0.228737	0.073876	-3.096226	0.0022
D(D_DR(-5))	-0.087553	0.056584	-1.547302	0.1229
D(D_TBILL)	0.018589	0.060028	0.309665	0.7570
D(D_TBILL(-1))	-0.279622	0.059860	-4.671241	0.0000
D(D_TBILL(-2))	-0.086537	0.061590	-1.405049	0.1611
D(D_TBILL(-3))	-0.104443	0.061215	-1.706170	0.0891
D(LIB)	4.311743	1.196804	3.602713	0.0004
CointEq(-1)	-0.655984	0.079844	-8.215800	0.0000

Cointeq = D_DR(-3) - (0.8063*D_TBILL -0.8485*LIB + 0.7909)

Long Run Coefficients

Variable	*Coefficient*	*Std. Error*	*t-Statistic*	*Prob.*
D_TBILL	0.806271	0.194724	4.140595	0.0000
LIB	-0.848483	0.310200	-2.735275	0.0066
C	0.790904	0.296787	2.664882	0.0082

Table 9.3 Results from the Bounds Test for the Lending Rate

Bounds Test

ARDL Bounds Test
Date: 09/11/15 Time: 05:58
Sample: 1990M07 2014M08
Included observations: 290
Null Hypothesis: No long-run relationships exist

Test Statistic	*Value*	*k*
F-statistic	39.54368	2

Critical Value Bounds

Significance	*I0 Bound*	*I1 Bound*
10%	3.17	4.14
5%	3.79	4.85
2.5%	4.41	5.52
1%	5.15	6.36

Test Equation:
Dependent Variable: D(D_LR(-3))
Method: Least Squares
Date: 09/11/15 Time: 05:58
Sample: 1990M07 2014M08
Included observations: 290

Variable	*Coefficient*	*Std. Error*	*t-Statistic*	*Prob.*
D(D_LR(-4))	-0.214394	0.056571	-3.789853	0.0002
D(D_TBILL)	0.054419	0.056387	0.965099	0.3353
D(D_TBILL(-1))	-0.248940	0.081708	-3.046700	0.0025
D(D_TBILL(-2))	-0.240545	0.068244	-3.524802	0.0005
D(D_TBILL(-3))	-0.186636	0.055009	-3.392834	0.0008
C	0.701200	0.184172	3.807315	0.0002
D_TBILL(-1)	0.498006	0.115914	4.296326	0.0000
LIB(-1)	-0.764045	0.195311	-3.911940	0.0001
D_LR(-4)	-0.864243	0.083022	-10.40979	0.0000
R-squared	0.588206	Mean dependent var		-0.002201
Adjusted R-squared	0.576482	S.D. dependent var		1.677689
S.E. of regression	1.091810	Akaike info criterion		3.044094
Sum squared resid	334.9661	Schwarz criterion		3.157987
Log likelihood	-432.3937	Hannan-Quinn criter.		3.089726
F-statistic	50.17245	Durbin-Watson stat		1.974453
Prob(F-statistic)	0.000000			

Table 9.4 Error Correction Model for the Lending rate

Speed of Adjustment (ECM)

ARDL Cointegrating And Long Run Form
Dependent Variable: D_LR(-3)
Selected Model: ARDL(2, 4, 0)
Date: 09/11/15 Time: 05:59
Sample: 1990M01 2015M05
Included observations: 290

Cointegrating Form

Variable	*Coefficient*	*Std. Error*	*t-Statistic*	*Prob.*
D(D_LR(-4))	-0.218510	0.056353	-3.877497	0.0001
D(D_TBILL)	0.054374	0.056357	0.964805	0.3355
D(D_TBILL(-1))	-0.003237	0.056605	-0.057181	0.9544
D(D_TBILL(-2))	-0.054860	0.056838	-0.965214	0.3353
D(D_TBILL(-3))	-0.184581	0.054895	-3.362426	0.0009
D(LIB)	-0.769388	0.195398	-3.937535	0.0001
CointEq(-1)	-0.858460	0.082558	-10.398318	0.0000

Cointeq = D_LR(-3) - (0.5746*D_TBILL -0.8962*LIB + 0.8244)

Long Run Coefficients

Variable	*Coefficient*	*Std. Error*	*t-Statistic*	*Prob.*
D_TBILL	0.574632	0.140251	4.097179	0.0001
LIB	-0.896242	0.221287	-4.050132	0.0001
C	0.824395	0.211521	3.897458	0.0001

Notes

1. Belgium, France, Germany, Italy, the Netherlands and Spain
2. South Africa, Lesotho, Namibia and Swaziland
3. Czech Republic, Hungary, Poland Slovakia and Slovenia

CHAPTER 10

Concluding Remarks and Policy Recommendation

This book reviews and analyzes the foreign currency liquidity management strategies that Jamaica has pursued to achieve specific objectives of the government, households and the private sector, taking the local and global economic environment into account. The results of all nine preceding chapters show that the Jamaican economy has found itself in a deadlock in trying to unearth macroeconomic stability, growth in output and increased productivity necessary for sustained economic development. Although it appears to be in a deadlock, Jamaica has made significant strides in the right direction under the supervision of the IMF, the World Bank, the IDB and other multilateral lenders since 2013. The debt-to-GDP ratio is trending downwards.

The government achieved a balanced budget in the 2014–2016 fiscal years. Highway expansion and slow but improving infrastructural development should help to progress travel and commerce across the island, which should contribute positively to GDP growth. Jamaica is ahead of its Caribbean counterparts in many regards and was ranked by Forbes Magazine in November 2015 as the best Caribbean country in which to do business. However, the country has a far way to go to fulfill the potential of its resources. Mismanagement of the economy over the last 50 years has been a major setback.

The process through which a country improves its economic well-being and transforms itself from a developing 'Third World' country to a developed 'First World' country has not been properly understood by the

A. Haughton, *Developing Sustainable Balance of Payments in Small Countries*, DOI 10.1007/978-3-319-53031-4_10

Jamaican government, economists, practitioners and technocrats. Due to country-specific differences (heterogeneity), there is no step-by-step list of procedures or actions that, if followed carefully, can lead a nation from developing to developed status. Jamaica is trying to move along that path through a development programme called Vision 2030. It aims to make Jamaica the place of choice to live, work, raise families and do business. A strategic plan was established in 2009. The government is ahead in some areas, based on its markers, but behind in others. At the time of writing this conclusion, the Planning Institute of Jamaica (PIOJ), which has oversight for the plan, has launched an upgraded Vision 2030 Development Plan with an e-dashboard. This is to allow members of the public to track the progress of the plan online.

Jamaica's aim to achieve stability, growth and development from now onwards should be guided by clear plans of action, linking short-run stability and growth tactics to long-run developmental strategic objectives. It has to be reiterated, **'the solution is strategy'.** Jamaica cannot continue on the path of four-year cycles geared at winning elections. These are calculated and manipulated to gain votes, rather than to support the nation's long-run strategic objectives. The country's leaders must relieve themselves of this mentality and find a balance between narrow partisan objectives and the objective of building a nation.

The Jamaican economy has not been easy to manage because some aspects of conventional economic theory suited for more defined and symmetric markets do not hold true in Jamaica, at least in the short run. Lack of understanding of the difference between economic theory and economic applications has led to the belief that the approach to economic application in developed countries should work seamlessly in developing countries. Supporters of conflicting schools of thought within the discipline use time and energy to debate the differences among themselves without strategizing how to move the country forward collectively. As a result, underproduction and underdevelopment have not only been characteristic of the country's physical output but have also characterized the country's economic thoughts and ideas.

Recommendations by Sir Arthur Lewis (1954) were misinterpreted by Jamaica; instead of increasing output using mainly domestic inputs, the country gradually replaced those with imported inputs. The wage rate has been kept low to ensure cheap supply of labour, but there has been no measure put in place to ensure that a portion of the profits earned by the companies who receive government subsidies are reinvested into the domestic economy. China has done a better job at implementing Lewis' recommendations. That country has since grown at an average rate of 7 percent over the period 1990 to 2015, which amounts to an aggregate of 175 percent expansion of its economy. In contrast, Jamaica has grown at an average rate of 0.7 percent over the 50 years since its independence in 1962, amounting to just an aggregate 35 percent growth.

What accounts for the varying difference in economic growth rates in these two countries? One might argue that China is more developed than Jamaica or that China has a larger supply of labour, and as a result China can grow faster. However, recall Jamaica had high growth rates in the 1960s, but these were not sustained.

An exploration of the impact of Jamaica's exchange rate policies on the progression of the nation's economy since independence reveals that there is trade-off between foreign consumption and nominal currency changes. The currency board arrangement under colonialism, initially replaced by a crawling peg after the establishment of the Bank of Jamaica in 1962, served the country well. When Jamaica was the leading exporter of sugar and bauxite from the region and a major competitor in the market for these commodities globally, GDP grew at annual average of more than 5 percent. The dual exchange rate system, which was introduced to curtail foreign consumption spending in some areas, had to be scrapped in favour of an auction and allocation system with tight exchange rate controls and import restrictions. Even so, the country accumulated negative reserves. The floating exchange rate system that followed should have been supported by controls when the financial sector was liberalized. This was, however, not advised by the Washington Consensus.

Results from analyzing the sustainability of Jamaica's foreign currency debt show that Jamaica's current foreign debt is unsustainable. However, the debt is trending down, which should improve how it is managed. Debt servicing remains an issue though as exchange rate depreciations increase Jamaica's foreign debt obligations when it is converted to local currency. Jamaica's debt servicing requirements increase by US $56 million on average per annum; US $33 million in principal payment and US $23 million in interest as a result of currency depreciation.

This is an important consideration for future foreign currency liquidity management strategies as there appears to be a trade-off between the gains of devaluation and the losses from paying higher foreign currency debt. Foreign currency debt is less sustainable if the country imports more and/or if there is an increase in real interest rates. Growth in real GDP improves

Jamaica's ability to sustain its foreign currency debt obligations, while a larger foreign currency debt stock is more difficult to sustain. An increase in domestic prices can reduce the value of foreign debt servicing though it would not be considered the preferred strategy.

From exploring this foreign debt position, it is clear that Jamaica has a dependent relationship with multilateral and bilateral creditors including the IMF, IDB and the PetroCaribe arrangement with Venezuela.

The country has also borrowed to pay for imports, but that is unsustainable. Ways must be found to ensure that these imports are used to create value-added products and re-exported to generate the foreign currency needed to service the debt. Chapter 4 on the composition of Jamaica's current account highlights that Jamaica's goods balance is in a constant negative. The outflow of foreign currency this causes will continue to result in more current account problems. Overall, an increase in production is required. The IMF policy of promoting a depreciation of the currency to reduce imports is counterintuitive if not supported by a strong push towards import substitution. A new economic strategy is needed.

Jamaica's unsustainable current account deficit must be rectified (Rochester 2009). An analysis of the economic, financial and political factors that influence the long-run level of Jamaica's current account balance shows that there are long-run relationships between the current account-to-GDP ratio and changes in the Real Effective Exchange Rate (REER), political stability, openness and trade, investment, external debt stock, corruption control and changes in foreign reserves.

On average, there is a positive co-movement between the growth of the Real Exchange Rate (RER) and imported consumer goods, which is not congruent with a priori expectations using the elasticities approach. Heavy reliance on imported goods partially explains why the growth rate of the RER and the importation of consumer goods appear to be positively correlated. An analysis of the country's main exports shows that services generate the most income for the island, while the export of primary products generates considerably less revenue than the export of goods with added value. Little relationship exists between each item of export and the RER. From a goods point of view, bauxite generates the most foreign currency inflow of all Jamaica's exports. Foreign currency revenues from the island's export of agricultural products including bananas, sugar and coffee do not increase irrespective of depreciations in the RER.

Oil still accounts for a significant portion of the country's import bill. The cost of energy has been a major hindrance to economic progress, especially the expansion of the nation's manufacturing sector. Efforts to find and provide cheaper energy have progressed at a slow pace. Drought conditions have affected agricultural output from 2012 to 2015. As this book goes to press in 2017, the IMF has relaxed the primary surplus target[1] for Jamaica over two of the last four years of the Extended Fund Facility (EFF). The government has already identified improved irrigation for agriculture as one area in which the money freed up (some JMD $13 billion over two years) by the reduced target will be spent.

The Jamaican economy is fragile. Policies to depreciate the domestic currency to improve the current account in the short run may lead to further worsening of the current account in the long run if people do not adjust their consumption habits. Also, consumers and producers can make better decisions if they are better able to predict expected inflation and exchange rate movements; policies geared towards such are welcomed. Measures to vertically diversify the country's offering of exports should be put in place; moving goods from primary production to other stages if the country intends to increase the value added of its exports where it can fetch higher prices abroad. This should be supported by policies that encourage increasing the domestic share of inputs in the production process. Policies should also create disincentives for the use of imported inputs in domestic production where that can happen. Labour productivity continues to be an issue; policies geared towards improving such are also welcomed. Other than bauxite and its byproduct alumina, Jamaica's main exports have been basic agricultural items, which have maintained the same flow of foreign currency to the island over the past 25 years.

Alejandro (1963), Krugman and Taylor (1978), Van Wijnbergen (1986) and Saibene and Sicouri (2012) found evidence to suggest that there might be channels through which currency devaluations might lead to losses in GDP growth. For example, through distributional channels; if the country uses a high proportion of imported inputs or through fiscal effects. Chapter 5 analyzes the impact of exchange rate depreciation on output growth in the island. The results from this chapter show that a 1 percent depreciation of the domestic currency in one year leads to a potential loss of 0.3 percent to real GDP growth in the year that follows. As a result, Jamaica has potentially lost more than US $4 billion or JMD $480 billion in GDP output due to currency depreciation. The findings suggest that pursuing policies to reduce the uncertainty in exchange rate determination can lead to favourable growth in GDP. Currency depreciations make it difficult to predict real exchange rate movements, which also lead to unpredictable input prices. The result is output volatility. Jamaica has lost a potential 2.96 percent of GDP growth on average per annum over the 25-year period from 1990 to 2015 because of currency depreciation.

Jamaica's Balance of Payments (BOP) as a whole is becoming more sustainable as current account deficits are sustained by capital account surpluses and reserves. The capital account is important for maintaining the optimal foreign currency flow for Jamaica in the liquidity management strategy. Openness and domestic credit to GDP prove to be the most significant drivers of capital account inflow. The results show that positive shocks to openness and domestic credit lead to increases in the optimal capital requirements needed to sustain economic activity. There is a trade-off between allowing the currency to depreciate and accumulating reserves. If the country doesn't borrow reserves to supply foreign currency in the domestic market, the exchange rate will depreciate out of control.

An analysis of Net International Reserves (NIR) adequacy and optimality in Jamaica shows that the targeted level of reserves-GDP should be 8.9 percent or an average of US $1.226 billion per annum. Based on the Guidotti–Greenspan rule, we calculate the optimal reserve ratio to be 7.4 percent of GDP or an average of US $979 million over the period spanning 2005–2013. The level of actual versus optimal reserve holdings is forecast from 2015 to 2025. The analysis shows that the actual reserve holdings are expected to trend downwards while the optimal reserve is expected to increase, both converging gradually.

Jamaica has been increasing its reserves position, which was more than US $2.4 billion at the end of October 2015. This is sufficient for the short term but not in the long run when debt repayment comes due. The current level of the nation's NIR is enough but remains susceptible to external shocks. Observed is that foreign exchange flexibility, GDP volatility and population growth significantly impact the targeted level of reserves. The results suggest that structural reforms in the economy and economic shocks impact reserve holdings. In line with the literature on the topic, exchange rate flexibility in Jamaica is negatively related to reserve demand. Conflictingly, there is a negative coefficient in the relationship between GDP volatility and reserve demand. Trade openness significantly impacts reserve demand. This is contrary to previous studies. This study finds a negative rather than a positive relationship between openness and reserve holdings. It appears the more open Jamaica becomes, the quicker its reserves deplete.

The results highlight that Jamaica's foreign currency flows might encounter long-term liquidity problems in light of the country's adverse economic growth, stability and development challenges. From an understanding of the underlying factors that influence the level of foreign currency flows across time, proper liquidity management is needed to determine the conditions necessary for the stream of inflows to offset the stream of outflows sustainably in the long run. Liquidity management deals with how to manage the risk associated by being able to satisfy payment obligations or can satisfy these obligations at minimal cost. A liquidity risk management framework is important for Jamaica to identify, measure and manage its liquidity position. The central bank requires a liquidity risk strategy, which will derive from recommendations made by a capital and risk committee. Like companies, the central bank must develop a liquidity score card. Liquidity risk control is concerned with a tactical approach in dealing with access to secure and unsecured funding sources. The nation's liquidity management strategy should involve short-run and long-run stress testing and scenario analysis to see how the country performs under different circumstances. Liquidity must be managed properly, balancing foreign current debt servicing with reserve accumulation of exchange rate depreciation policies. Jamaica's foreign currency flows can become sustainable if the country can generate foreign revenue without borrowing and increasing output to the extent where it can export more and import less.

Chapter 8 investigates the relationship between Foreign Direct Investment (FDI) flows, gross capital formation (gross investment), national savings and GDP growth. The findings suggest that there is a negative relationship between real GDP growth and FDI, contrary to the preposition of the existing literature. Jamaica operates a small open economy with a highly educated and skilled labour force to some extent, but is unable to manifest growth from the accommodating FDI. Less developed financial systems and high inefficiency in the domestic economy results in misallocation of foreign capital in some instances. Cyclical instability in the nation's economy is also a disadvantage. The benefits of FDI will depend on the governments' legal and commercial facilities and their ability to assign priority to policies that help upgrade human and technological capabilities and encourage regional clusters of related activities. Jamaica has been making strides in the right direction since the beginning of the latest EFF but still has a far way to go.

The results of the analysis indicate that an increase in national savings lead to an increase in domestic generated capital investment. Less is borrowed from abroad thereby setting a platform to increase GDP intrinsically. Investment and savings are important drivers for real GDP growth in the country. The results also suggest that GDP growth is more likely to occur in period t +1 if investment occurred in time t. The results insinuate that government policy should target local indigenous production and capital expansion instead of focusing on attracting FDI. Efforts to increase national savings can also help capital formation, which is necessary for GDP growth.

Chapter 9 analyzes the monetary transmission mechanism and the speed of adjustment in Jamaica from 1990 to present. The results show that both pass-through for the lending and deposit rate are incomplete in Jamaica. Stability tests confirm that monetary policy instruments display two different variances from 1990 to present. The first episode of high interest rate and high volatility occurred from 1990 to 1997 during the initial stages of liberalization of the financial sector. The second episode of falling rates and mild volatility occurred from 1997 to 2014. An episode of lower rates but increased leverage by commercial banks has been occurring from 2010 to present. After 2010, the gap between the Treasury bill rate and the retail deposit rate narrowed, while the gap between the Treasury bill rate and the retail lending rate expanded. The widening gap between the lending rate and the Treasury bill rate is signalling that commercial banks, though increasing the level of pass-through, are doing so at a huge mark-up to the disadvantage of local investors, who were hoping to enjoy a lower BOJ policy rate. A lack of fiscal space puts pressure on monetary policy. At the same time, commercial banks demonstrate a collusive strategy in interest rate determination such that borrowers find it difficult to access credit to invest in the local economy.

This has been one of the greatest obstacles to growth in productive output in the country over the last 25 years. Firms find it difficult to access investment capital even if monetary policy is expansionary. Albeit, interest rates have been trending downwards over the last years but more needs to be done. If the situation does not improve such that credit is offered to investors on all levels at a cheaper rate, then production on a whole might not increase and Jamaica is bound to remain on the same anemic growth trajectory for the next 40 years, just as it has been doing for the last 40 years. Change must come.

The solution in this case rests on the establishment of social enterprises and social entrepreneurship, which helps people to understand how to survive on their own. These social enterprises should be geared towards supplying domestic demand first to reduce the nation's import content. The remainder can be done in the form of niche goods and services for export. These, if developed properly, will be able to sustain themselves to become solid foreign exchange earners for the country. There are several avenues that can be explored but are out of the scope of this book, however. The Internet opens a global marketplace; internet entrepreneurship has become prevalent. The key questions here are: How to identify a niche? How to market the right goods and/or the right services? How to source funding? If there is lack of start-up capital, then individuals can barter services in the short run and pool capital together in a Grameen Bank–style model or partnership. There is a market for everything; develop a product to complement a product. Ideas can be sold; copyrights and patents are becoming very important. It is essential to learn as much from other businesses and use this knowledge to enhance your own business. Without these essential changes in how institutions operate, Jamaica will not escape the deadlock.

Note

1. The IMF reduced Jamaica's primary fiscal balance from 7.5 to 7.25 percent of GDP as of November 2015.

References

Adedeji, O.S. (2001). The size and sustainability of the Nigerian current account deficits. International Monetary Fund, Working Paper WP/01/87.

Adedeji, O.S., & Handa, J. (2008). The size and sustainability of the Nigerian current account deficits. *The Journal of Developing Areas*, *41*(2), 1–25.

Ahn, B. (2008). Capital flows and effects on financial markets in Korea: Developments and policy responses. *Financial Globalization and Emerging Market Capital Flows*, 305–320.

Aizenman, J., & Marion, N. (2003). The High Demand for International Reserves in the Far East: What is Going On?. *Journal of the Japanese and International Economies*, *17*, 370–400.

Aizenman J. & Noy I. (2009). Endogenous Financial and Trade Openness. *Review of Development Economics*, *13*(2), 175–189.

Aizenman, J., & Pasricha, G.K. (2013). Why do emerging markets liberalize capital outflow controls? Fiscal versus net capital flow concerns. *Journal of International Money and Finance*, *39*, 28–64.

Alejandro, D.C.F. (1963). A note on the impact of devaluation and the redistributive effect. *Journal of Political Economy*, *71*(6), 571–580.

Allen, C., & Robinson, W. (2004). Monetary policy rules and the transmission mechanism in Jamaica. Bank of Jamaica Working Paper.

Angeloni, I., Ehrmann, M., Grauwe, P., & Miles, D. (2003). Monetary transmission in the Euro area: Early evidence. *Journal of Economic Policy*, *18*(37), 469–501.

Arellano, M., & Bond, S. (1991). Some tests of specification for panel data: Monte Carlo Evidence and an application to employment equations. *The Review of Economic Studies*, *58*, 277–297.

A. Haughton, *Developing Sustainable Balance of Payments in Small Countries*, DOI 10.1007/978-3-319-53031-4

Atesoglu, H.S., (2003). Monetary transmission-federal funds rate and prime rate. *Journal of Post Keynesian Economics, 26*(2) 357–362.

Ausubel, L.M. (1991). The failure of Competition in the Credit Card Market. *American Economic Review, 81*, 50–81.

Baharumshah, A.Z., & Ismail, H.B. (2012). The present value model and Thailand's current account balance. *Journal of Economic Studies, 39*(3), 337–355.

Barnichon, R. (2008). International reserves and self-insurance against external shocks. IMF Working Paper WP/08/149.

Ben-Bassat, A., & Gottlieb, D. (1992). On the effect of opportunity cost on international reserve holdings. *Review of Economics and Statistics, 74*, 329–338.

Bernanke, B.S. (1986). Alternative Explanations of the Money-Income Correlation. *Carnegie-Rochester Conference Series on Public Policy, 25*, 49–99.

Bernanke, B., (1993). How Important is the Credit Channel in the Transmission of Monetary Policy? A Comment. *Carnegie-Rochester Conference Series Public Policy*, December, 39, 47–52.

Bernanke, B., & Blinder, A. (1992). The Federal Funds Rate and the Channels of Monetary Transmission. *American Economic Review*, September, *82*, 901–921.

Brissimis, S., Hondroyiannis, G., Papazoglou, C., Tsaveas, N., & Vasardani, M. (2013). The determinants of current account imbalances in the Euro area. *Economic Change and Restriction, 46*(3), 299–319.

Burgsteller, L. (2003). Interest rate Transmission to commercial rates in Austria. Johannes Kelper University of Linz Working Paper 0306.

Cassola, N., & Morana, C. (2006a). Volatility of interest rates in the Euro area: Evidence from high frequency data. *The European Journal of Finance.*

Cassola, N., & Morana, C. (2006b). Comovements in volatility in the Euro money market. ECB Working Paper No. 703.

Cheung, Y.W., & Qian, X., (2009). Empirics of China's Outward Direct Investment. *Pacific Economic Review, 14*(3), 312–341.

Chinn, M. & Ito, H. (2006). What Matters for Financial Development? Capital Controls, Institutions, and Interactions. *Journal of Development Economics, 81*, 163–192.

Chinn, M.D. & Prasad E.S. (2003). Medium-term determinants of current accounts in industrial and developing countries: an empirical exploration. *Journal of International Economics, 59*, 47–76.

Chionis, D. P., & Leon, C. A. (2006). Interest rate transmission in Greece: did EMU cause a structural break?. *Journal of Policy Modeling, 28*, 453–466.

Cottarelli, C., & Kourelis, A. (1994). Financial structure, bank lending rates, and the transmission mechanism of monetary policy. *IMF Staff Papers*, Vol. 41, No. 4.

De Bondt, G. (2005). Interest rate pass-through: empirical results for the Euro area. *German Economic Review*, *6*(1), 37–78.

Dooley, M P., Folkerts-Landau, D., & Garber, P. M. (2003). An Essay on the Revived Bretton Woods System. National Bureau of Economic Research (Cambridge, MA), Working Paper No. 9971.

Dunning, J. (1994). Re-evaluating the benefits of foreign direct investment. *Transnational Corporations*, *3*(1), 23–51.

Durdu, C. B., Mendoza, E. G., & Terrones, M.E. (2009). Precautionary demand for foreign assets in Sudden Stop economies: An assessment of the New Mercantilism. *Journal of Development Economics*, *89*(2), 194–209.

Égert, B., Crespo-Cuaresma, J., & Reininger, T. (2007). Interest rate pass-through in central and Eastern Europe: Reborn from ashes merely to pass away? *Journal of Policy Modeling*, *29*(2), 209–225.

Engle, R. F., & Granger, C. W. J. (1987). Co-Integration and Error Correction: Representation, Estimation, and Testing. *Econometrica*, *55*(2), 251–276.

Fischer, S. (1997). Capital account liberalization and the role of the IMF. IMF Working Paper.

Fountas, S., & Wu, J.L. (1999). Are the US current account deficits very sustainable? *International Economic Journal*, *13*(3), 51–58.

Fratzscher M., Schneider D., & Van Robays, I. (2014). Oil prices, exchange rates and asset prices. European Central Bank working paper, no. 1689.

Gambacorta, L. (2001). Bank-specific characteristics and monetary policy transmission: The case of Italy. European Central Bank, Working Paper No.103.

Gertler, M., & Gilchrist, S. (1994). Monetary Policy, Business Cycles, and the Behavior of Small Manufacturing Firms. *The Quarterly Journal of Economics*, *109*(2), 309–340.

Ghosh, S., & Bhattacharyya, I. (2009). Spread, volatility and monetary policy: empirical evidences from the indian overnight money market. *Macroeconomics and Finance in Emerging Market Economies* 09/2009, *2*(2), 257–227.

Ghosh, A., & Ramakrishnan, U. (2006). Back to basics: Do current account deficits matter? *Finance and Development: A Quarterly Magazine of the IMF*, *43*(4). http://www.imf.org/external/pubs/ft/fandd/2006/12/basics.htm

Gonçalves, F. (2007). The Optimal Level of Foreign Reserves in Financially Dollarized Economies: The Case of Uruguay. IMF Working Paper 07/265.

Gould, D.M., & Ruffin R.J. (1996). Trade deficits causes and consequences. Federal Reserve Bank of Dallas Economic Review 10–20 fourth quarter.

Hannan, T.H., & Berger, A.N. (1991). The rigidity of prices: evidence from the banking Industry. *American Economic Review*, *81*, 938–945.

Hansen, B.E. (1990). Tests for Parameter Instability in Regressions with I(1) Processes. *Journal of Business & Economic Statistics*, *10*(3), 321–335.

Haughton, A.Y., & Iglesias, E.M. (2013). Interest rate volatility, asymmetric interest rate pass through and the monetary transmission mechanism in the Caribbean compared to US and Asia. *Economic Modelling*, *29*(6), 2071–2089.

Heller, R. (1966). Optimal international reserves. *Economic Journal*, *76*, 296–311.

Henry, C., & Longmore, R. (2003). Current account dynamics and the real effective exchange rate: The Jamaican Experience. Bank of Jamaica Working Paper.

Hulsewig, O., Mayer, E., & Wollmershauser, T. (2004). Bank loan supply and monetary policy transmission in Germany. CESifo Working Paper No. 1380.

Jeanne, O., & Ranciere, R. (2006). The optimal level of international reserves for emerging market countries: formulas and applications. IMF Working Paper Series WP/06/229

Jeanne, O., & Rancière R. (2011). The optimal level of international reserves in emerging market countries: A new formula and some applications. *The Economic Journal*, 121.

Johansen, S. (1988). Statistical Analysis of Cointegration Vectors. *Journal of Economic Dynamics and Control*, *12*(2–3), 231–254.

Johansen, S., & Juselius, K. (1990). Maximum Likelihood Estimation and Inference on Cointegration–with Applications to the Demand for Money. *Oxford Bulletin of Economics and Statistics*, *52*(2), 169–210.

Karunaratne, N.D. (2009), An Econometric Evaluation of the Sustainability of Australia's High Current Account Deficit. *International Journal of Apllied Economics & Econometrics, Bangalore, India*, *XVII*(4).

Karunaratne, N.D. (2010). The sustainability of Australia's current account deficits—A reappraisal after the global financial crisis. *Journal of Policy Modeling*, *32*(1), 81–97.

Karagiannis, S., Panagopoulos, Y., & Vlamis, P. (2010). Interest rate pass-through in Europe and the US: Monetary policy after the financial crisis. *Journal of Policy Modeling*, *32*(3), 323–338.

Kashyap, Anil K., & Stein C.J. (1995). The impact of monetary policy on bank balance sheets. NBER Working Paper No. 4821.

Konya, L. (2008). The Sustainability of the Current Account in the Czech Republic, Hungary and Slovenia. *Empirical Economics*, *36*(2), 367–384.

Krause, S., & Rioja, F. (2006). Financial development and monetary policy efficiency. Emory University Working Paper.

Krugman, P., & Taylor, L. (1978). Contractionary effects of devaluation. *Journal of International Economics*, *8*(3), 445–456.

Kwapil, C., & Scharler J. (2010). Interest rate pass through monetary policy rules and macroeconomic stability. *Journal of International Money and Finance*, *29*, 236–251.

Leith, D. (2006). The effect of monetary policy on private money market rates in Jamaica: An Empirical microstructure study. Bank of Jamaica Working Paper.

Lewis, A. (1954). Economic development with unlimited supply of labour. *The Manchester School*, *22*, 139–191.

Lin, C.H. (2012). The comovement between exchange rate and stock prices in Asian emerging markets. *International Review of Economics and Finance*, *22*, 161–172.

Lowe, P., & Rolling. T. (1992). Loan Rate Stickyness, Theory and Evidence. Reserve bank of Austrailia Discussion Paper 9206.

Mann, C.L. (2002). Perspective on the US account current account deficit and sustainability. *Journal of Economic Perspective*, *16*(3), 131–152.

Miller-Betty, S. (2011). Monetary policy alternatives in the face of a dysfunctional transmission mechanism. Bank of Jamaica Working Paper.

Moreno, R. (2011). Policy making from a "macroprudential" perspective in emerging market economies. BIS Working Paper No 336.

Nechi, S. (2010). Balance of payments sustainability and optimal international reserves. Retrieved from https://qspace.library.queensu.ca/bitstream/1974/2600/1/Nechi_Salem_200908_PhD.pdf

Pesaran, H., Shin, Y., & Smith, R. (2001). Bounds testing approaches to the analysis of level relationships. *Journal of Applied Econometrics*, *16*, 289–326.

Phillips, P.C.E., & Hansen, B.E. (1990). Statistical Inference in Instrumental Variables Regression with I(1) Processes. *Review of Economic Studies*, *57*(1): 99–125.

Ramey, V. (1993). How important is the credit channel in the transmission of monetary policy? *Carnegie-Rochester Conference Series on Public Policy*, *39*, 1–45.

Ramlogan, C. (2004). The transmission mechanism of monetary policy: Evidence from the Caribbean. *Journal of Economic Studies, 31*(5), 435–447.

Rochester, L., (2009). Revisiting current account sustainability measures for Jamaica an assessment. Bank of Jamaica Working Paper.

Rochester, L. (2013). Estimating Jamaica's fundamental equilibrium exchange rate. Bank of Jamaica Working Paper.

Rodriguez. C.S., & Funk, K. (2012). Estimation of international reserves for Costa Rica: A micro-founded approach. Research Document No. 01-212, Research Department, Central Bank of Costa Rica.

Saibene, G., & Sicouri, S. (2012). The effects of currency devaluation on economic growth in developing countries, the role of foreign currency denominated debt. *Atlantic Economic Journal*, *40*, 191–209.

Sander, H., & Kleimeier, S. (2002). Asymmetric adjustment of commercial bank interest rates in the euro area: an empirical investigation into interest rate pass-through. *Journal of Credit and Capital, 35*, 161–192.

Sander, H., & Kleimeier, S. (2006). *Interest rate pass-through in the common monetary area of the SACU countries.* Maastricht: METEOR, Maastricht research school of Economics of Technology and Organizations.

Sarwono, H.A. (2014). *Capital flows in Indonesia: Managing the benefits and risks.* Indonesian Banking Development Institute.

Schmidt, R.H., Hackethal, A., & Tyrell, M. (1997). Disintermediation and the role of banks in Europe: An international comparison. *Journal of Financial Intermediation.*

Scholnick, B. (1996). Asymmetric Adjustment of Commercial Bank Interest Rates: Evidence from Malaysia and Singapore. *Journal of International Money and Finance, 15*(3): 485–496.

Sheffrin, S., & Woo, W.T. (1990). Present value tests of an intertemporal model of the current account. *Journal of International Economics, 29*(3), 237–e253.

Shirakawa, M., (2009). Preventing the Next Crisis: The Nexus between Financial Markets, Financial Institutions and Central Banks. Speech at the London Stock Exchange, May 13, 2009.

Stiglitz, J. (2006). *Making Globalization Work.* New York: W. W. Norton.

Tai, P.N., Sek, S.K., & Har, W.M. (2012). Interest rate pass-through and monetary transmission in Asia. *International Journal of Economics and Finance, 4,* 163–174.

Tang, T.C. (2007). Sustainability of balancing item of balance of payments accounts: Fresh empirical evidence for G7 countries. *Applied Economic Letters, 14,* 251–254.

Toolsema, L.A., Sturm, J.E., & De, H.J. (2002). Convergence of pass-through from money market to lending rates in EMU countries: new evidence. CCSO Centre for Economic Research, Groningen, Working Paper 2002:6.

Urquhart, F.M. (2006). The reaction of bank lending to monetary policy: The Jamaican Case. Bank of Jamaica Working Paper.

Van Wijnbergen, S. (1986). Exchange rate management and stabilization policies in developing countries. In Sebastian, E., & Ahmed, L. (Eds.), *Economic adjustment and exchange rate in developing countries* (Chapter 2, pp. 17–42). Chicago: University of Chicago Press.

Wang, K.M., & Lee M. (2009). Market volatility and retail interest rate pass through. *Economic Modelling, 26,*1270–1282.

Wilson, S., & McLean, E. (2014). Understanding the impact of exchange rate adjustments on the trade balance of selected Caribbean Countries: An empirical analysis. Bank of Jamaica Working Paper.

Wu, J.L., Chen S., & Lee, H. (2001). Are current account deficits sustainable evidence from panel cointegration. *Economic Letters, 72*(2), 219–224.

Yan, H. D., & Yang, C.l. (2012). Are There Different Linkages of Foreign Capital Inflows and the Current Account Between Industrial Countries and Emerging Markets? *Empirical Economics, 43,* 25–54.

Index

A. Haughton, *Developing Sustainable Balance of Payments in Small Countries*, DOI 10.1007/978-3-319-53031-4

The manufacturer's authorised representative in the EU is Springer Nature Customer Service Centre GmbH, Europaplatz 3, 69115 Heidelberg, Germany. If you have any concerns regarding our products, please contact ProductSafety@springernature.com

Printed and bound by CPI Group (UK) Ltd, Croydon, CR0 4YY
25/09/2026
02222854-0002